The Evolution of Modern States
Sweden, Japan, and the United States

The Evolution of Modern States begins with a simple question: Why do rich capitalist democracies respond so differently to the common pressures they face in the early twenty-first century? Drawing on insights from evolutionary theory, Sven Steinmo challenges the common equilibrium view of politics and economics and argues that modern political economies are best understood as complex adaptive systems. The book examines the political, social, and economic history of three different nations – Sweden, Japan, and the United States – and explains how and why these countries have evolved along such different trajectories over the past century. Bringing together social and economic history, institutionalism, and evolutionary theory, Steinmo thus provides a comprehensive explanation for differing responses to globalization as well as a new way of analyzing institutional and social change.

Sven Steinmo holds the Chair in Public Policy and Political Economy at the European University Institute in Florence and is a professor of political science at the University of Colorado at Boulder. He is also an Honorary Professor at the University of Southern Denmark and the NordWel Professor of Comparative Politics at the Institute for Future Studies in Stockholm, Sweden.

Continued after the Index

The Evolution of Modern States

Sweden, Japan, and the United States

SVEN STEINMO

European University Institute

CAMBRIDGE
UNIVERSITY PRESS

CAMBRIDGE UNIVERSITY PRESS
Cambridge, New York, Melbourne, Madrid, Cape Town, Singapore,
São Paulo, Delhi, Dubai, Tokyo, Mexico City

Cambridge University Press
32 Avenue of the Americas, New York, NY 10013-2473, USA

www.cambridge.org
Information on this title: www.cambridge.org/9780521145466

First published 2010

Printed in the United States of America

A catalog record for this publication is available from the British Library.

Library of Congress Cataloging in Publication data

Steinmo, Sven.
The evolution of modern states : Sweden, Japan, and the United States / Sven Steinmo.
    p.   cm. – (Cambridge studies in comparative politics)
Includes bibliographical references and index.
ISBN 978-0-521-19670-3 – ISBN 978-0-521-14546-6 (pbk.)
1. State, The – History.   2. Sweden – Politics and government.   3. Japan – Politics and
government.   4. United States – Politics and government.   5. Comparative government.
I. Title.   II. Series.
JC131.S84   2010
320.1 – dc22   2010000985

ISBN 978-0-521-19670-3 Hardback
ISBN 978-0-521-14546-6 Paperback

For Kirsten Amundsen
Teacher, Scholar, Mother

Contents

List of Figures

List of Tables

Preface

Systems within Systems

I started the research for this book several years ago because I was curious about the effects of "globalization" on democratic welfare states. I was puzzled by the fact that, despite the enormous competitive pressures facing rich democracies, there was almost no evidence of the oft-predicted "race to the bottom." I began this study with an analysis of the politics of taxation in four countries (Sweden, Germany, the United States, and Japan). I had some expertise in the political economy of taxation and thought that tax policy ought to be a good test of the various globalization hypotheses. It was, after all, rather obvious that taxes should be more sensitive to international competition than any other policy arena.

The deeper I looked into the relationship between tax policy and international competition, however, the more I realized that a nation's tax policies are so deeply intertwined with the structure of the national political economy and welfare state that I could not answer my original puzzle by looking at taxes alone. In other words, to really understand how and why tax systems were changing, I needed to examine how they related to other policy systems. This is fine as a general proposition, of course, but analytically and practically it presented rather significant problems: Trying to understand how different parts of a tax system affect other parts of the tax system is difficult enough – trying to understand their relationship to the broader political economy can be mind-bogglingly complex.

The deeper I looked at each of these countries, the more I came to see each of them as remarkably different *systems*. In other words, the more I tried to understand how the various parts of each system fit together, the more patterns I saw in each of these political economies. I also came to see that changes in taxation had hugely different political and economic implications in each of these countries because their tax systems were only part of their social welfare systems and their political economies. In other words, if I *really* wanted to explain something as specific and narrow as corporation tax, I needed to pay attention to a whole complex of other factors. And as I looked at this complexity, the differences, rather than the similarities, came into sharper focus.

I believe it was the attempt to bring Japan into this analysis that pushed me down this road. In the very early stages of this project, my colleague and friend T. J. Pempel convinced me that I should include Japan in my study if I wanted to look at the effects of globalization on rich industrial democracies. Professor Pempel correctly argued that comparative political economists such as myself almost never took Japan seriously and, if we really wanted to test our arguments for their generalizability, then Japan would be a good test case. Too much of our theorizing about comparative political economy, he argued, was based on the experience of too few countries. Frankly, he told me, most political economists are "Euro-centric" – tending to see the whole world through an Anglo-European lens – and often unintentionally assume that all capitalist democracies are some version of the same basic political economic model.

I spent most of the next two years learning about, traveling to, and living in Japan. The more I learned about Japan, the more I realized that Pempel was right. To be sure, Japan has many of the same institutions as most other advanced capitalist democracies (regular elections, a capital market, free press, etc.). But as I looked closer, I came to see that how these institutions were constructed, how they function, and *how they fit together* is really quite different from in the United States, for example. As I turned this logic back on myself, I soon realized that the differences in how these institutions evolved and function in Sweden are equally huge.

I soon realized that I had expected rich democracies to react to the forces of globalization in similar ways because I assumed that all capitalist democracies are *essentially* the same. But, the closer I actually looked at these systems, the more I saw how different they were. Eventually (perhaps I am just slow) this realization helped me solve my original puzzle. The straightforward explanation for why different political systems are adapting to the pressures of globalization in different ways is obvious: *They are different systems.*

The book you hold in your hands is my attempt to make some sense of the enormous complexity and diversity in the countries I studied. Although the research was originally motivated by the desire to understand how these countries are adapting to "globalization," the eventual book takes a long historical view of this question. Similarly, whereas tax policy clearly gets special attention in the analysis, the scope has broadened significantly. For reasons of space and intellectual limitations, I have decided not to bring the German case into the analysis.

In the comparative historical analysis that follows I construct what I call "evolutionary narratives" that explore how each of these systems (Sweden, Japan, and the United States) has evolved over time. I show that these different systems have evolved from quite different starting points, or initial conditions, and that each has fit different niches in the global political economy over time. Instead of trying to explain away these differences because they make structured comparisons difficult, I emphasize them because they matter.

In the final analysis I have come to realize that I (like many political scientists) have tried so hard to find variables that are comparable that I sometimes forget some of the most obvious facts about the countries I study. In my case, my favored variables were institutions. I have emphasized their "structuring" role in politics and history in many publications over the years. In the attempt to show the importance of institutions, however, I have either implicitly or explicitly denied or ignored some pretty obvious things about the countries that I wished to compare, such as their size, their cultural homogeneity (or diversity), their geographic endowments, and even their political cultures (or norms, values, and beliefs). It was not that I truly believed that these things did not matter, but rather that I did not feel I could compare all these variables in a coherent scientific study. I worried that my analysis would be overdetermined. But as I got further into this project – and once again, specifically because I was trying to understand Japan in comparison to the other countries – I came to see that the differences between these countries *was* in fact overdetermined. The problem was not the world; it was how we were trying to understand it.

The book that follows, then, does not attempt to hold some variables independent from others. Worse yet, in each of the narratives I emphasize different factors when trying to explain how each system evolved. This is simply because different factors mattered in each of these cases. I try to tell as coherent a story as I can in each case, and I have tried very hard to include as much detail as necessary to make sense of each narrative without overwhelming the reader with these details. But the truth is that I have left out far more than I have included.

So many people have helped me through this process that I do not know where to begin in thanking them. No matter what I say, I cannot hope to reveal the true depth of my gratitude to them. I first must thank the more than 260 policy makers, academics, and journalists who lent me their time and expertise and tolerated my naïve questions for the often lengthy in-depth interviews they offered me. Next, deep gratitude goes to several former students and researchers at the University of Colorado who aided me at various stages of this project. Some of them might not even recognize this final manuscript. Special thanks go to Erin Anna, Alisun Chopel, Emma Lance, Lindsay Stone, Christopher Vockrodt, and Jason Jordan. As I have already suggested, understanding the Japanese case was the biggest challenge for me. But I received extraordinary assistance and support from several academics including: Mari Miura, Takeshi Hieda, Toshimitsu Shinkawa, Naohiko Jinno, and T. J. Pempel. I have to single out three colleagues who did far more than help me with my research in Japan; in rather profound ways they each took me as their student. Without Ide Eisaku, Taka Akaishi, and Andrew DeWit this book and my basic understanding of how capitalist democracies actually work would have been very different.

Several colleagues and students have read parts or all of this manuscript and offered their advice, consultation, and criticisms. Although sometimes I wish that they had been more gentle, in the end this book is far better after their interventions. Claes Belfrage, Mark Blyth, Johan Christensen, Gus diZeriga, Takeshi Hieda, Joseph Hien, Orion Lewis, Bo Rothstein, Stefan Svalforss, Sara Tescione, and Kathleen Thelen have given me invaluable help in improving and sharpening my arguments and in avoiding many a mistake. Any errors that remain are all my own. Jeppe Olesen and David McCourt are owed a special thanks for reviewing endless versions of this manuscript and helping me make it far more readable and presentable than it ever would have been without them.

A number of institutions supported this project. I am especially indebted to the Abe Foundation of Japan, the German Marshall Fund, and the Swedish STINT Foundation. I have been lucky also to have been able to conduct research in several outstanding academic institutions including the University of Tokyo, the University of Colorado, and the European University Institute in Florence, Italy.

I would like to add a very special thanks to Maureen Lechleitner. Grazie di cuore.

Evolutionary Narratives

A GLOBAL STANDARD?

March 1, 2002. I had just arrived in Tokyo. Jet lagged, but thinking I should get oriented as soon as possible, I decided to attend a lecture entitled "Globalization and Corporate Governance" presented by an American professor, Christina Ahmadjian, then teaching at a major private university in Japan (Ahmadjian 2002). In her lecture – which was attended by a large number of top corporate executives and academics – Professor Ahmadjian exhorted the Japanese to adjust to the new realities of globalized capitalism and adopt what she called the "Global Standard." The Global Standard, she proceeded to explain, was used by the most successful companies in the world and differed from the standard governance practices in effect in most Japanese firms. Whereas Japanese firms were typically run in a manner similar to large hierarchical families, the Global Standard demanded greater separation and competition between the constituent parts of the firm, larger independence between financial interests and manufacturing interests, more flexibility in the labor market, and most importantly, greater transparency in corporate governance decisions. Professor Ahmadjian's major point was that the traditional "Japanese Model" firms needed to become more like American firms if they were to survive in the modern globalized economy.

I had heard versions of this argument before. Many had criticized Japanese firms for their lack of transparency, rigid employment ladders, and cozy relationships between financial institutions and borrowers. What I had not heard before – or at least not heard emphasized – was the notion of a so-called "Global Standard." The clear and unmistakable implication of Professor Ahmadjian's lecture was that the new world economy demanded a particular structural response. In what appeared to be a strange reverse echo, I was now hearing the argument that Japan must copy America.

It is important to understand that Professor Ahmadjian was not a flag-waving American anxious to show up the once-arrogant Japanese. Nor did she represent herself as a free market zealot from the American Enterprise Institute with the aim of spreading their version of truth, justice and the "Road to Freedom." Quite the contrary, Professor Ahmadjian was an extraordinarily well-informed expert on the Japanese economy and business structure. This was not merely Japan bashing. Her argument was more compelling: Even if the Japanese Model had once been successful and highly productive, the key point was that it no longer fit the realities of modern capitalism and the new world economy. The globalization of capital and manufacturing *required* a specific response. The Global Standard was not better because it was American, she assured her audience, rather it was better because it fit the world in which we live today.

The more I thought about her point of view, the more I realized it was the same argument I had been hearing around the world over the past several years – with regard to tax policy, government regulation, public enterprise, social welfare policy, and a range of other institutions built up over the past century in most democracies. These policies and institutions *may* have worked at one time and may have contributed to the enormous social and economic successes from which capitalist democracies have benefited over the past decades. But, perhaps sadly, the world had changed and they no longer work today. "There is No Alternative,"[1] armies of economists, pundits and politicians assured us. If you don't roll back the state you will suffer dire consequences! Vito Tanzi, former director of fiscal affairs at the International Monetary Fund (IMF), stated the argument quite simply as follows:

[the] process of deep economic integration among countries will require a change in the role of the state in pursuing social protection. The end process would be a world where industrial countries will have to do less public spending, will reduce the use of tax expenditures for achieving particular social objectives, and will also have to reduce the role of specific socially-directed regulations. (Tanzi 2002: 127)

In early 2009 – after the collapse of the world's financial system, the massive increases in public spending and the apparent worldwide commitment to re-regulating not just the banking industry, but capitalism more

[1] The phrase "There is No Alternative" (or TINA) was of course first coined by Margaret Thatcher as justification for a wide range of market-liberal reforms her government introduced in the 1980s.

generally – these neoliberal arguments sound rather absurd. The *International Herald Tribune* reported from the *World Economic Forum* in Davos, Switzerland, "we are seeing a paradigm shift towards a more European, a more social state." Daniel Yergin, co-author of *The Commanding Heights* agreed, "We're moving back towards a mixed economy" (Bennhold 2009: 1). Klaus Schwab, the founder and head of the World Economic Forum summed up the sentiment of the most powerful economic and political leaders in the world quite simply when he said, "The pendulum has swung and power has moved back to governments" (Schwartz 2009).

Now the conventional wisdom appears to be that if governments don't play a strong hand in the regulation of capitalism, the entire world economy will suffer dire consequences!

One could get whiplash trying to keep up with the experts.

WHAT WENT WRONG?

I too was once convinced that the increased competition for capital, labor and knowledge in an ever more fluid and open world economy would have significant negative implications for many advanced welfare states. But by the end of the 1990s, it had become increasingly obvious that there was something wrong with the "end of the state" argument. For some reason democratic countries were not cooperating with our theories. Globalization was supposed to undermine the welfare state, but if you looked at the actual behavior of most advanced countries it was difficult to find the so-called "race to the bottom." Well before the current financial crisis it became obvious to those who bothered to look at how rich democracies actually behaved that big governments were changing and adapting within the emerging world economy, but they were not dying.

I do not mean to suggest that increased capital mobility, or the intense trade competition from industrializing countries, does not matter. In the early years of the twenty-first century, such an argument would clearly be equally absurd. But what we do *not* see is a singular pattern. Indeed, in many ways what is most interesting today is the diversity of responses to the apparently common economic pressures and threats. As Pierson summarized in his excellent volume, *"In short, there is not a single 'new politics' of the welfare state, but different politics in different configurations"* (Pierson 2001a: 455, emphasis in original).[2] Rather than seeing a common or single

---

[2] Castles argued similarly, "Diverse welfare states will face diverse dilemmas" (Castles 2004: 19).

response to what appear to be common pressures, students of advanced welfare states have observed a diversity of responses.

My aim is to explain *why* we see such diversity.

The book that follows tells three stories of three different nations – Sweden, Japan, and the United States. I explore how and why these individual countries are reacting or responding to the pressures they face at the beginning of the new millennium and why they are reacting in such different ways. I treat each individual case separately and through each historical analysis I also try to shed light on the evolution of modern capitalism. I believe that we can learn a great deal both about these individual countries and the context in which they each "grew up" through a careful comparison of their life histories. I call these analyses "evolutionary narratives."

I will show that each country has evolved within a broadly common macroeconomic context – but also, importantly, that context has itself evolved over time. I will also argue that each country has *always* fit into different niches within the world economy and that each has also always been quite different from the others. These narratives, then, emphasize the unique or particular features of each of these systems – its geography, its political and economic institutions as well as its social structure. I treat each case as an individual – rather than as member of a class – in order to better understand how and why each has evolved so differently.

Imagine you wished to compare how different specific people were responding or reacting to the current economic crisis (housing foreclosures, growing unemployment, etc.). There are at least two approaches one could pursue. One approach (let's call it "comparative statics") would be to try to predict how these people behave by placing them each in different categories and then examine how these categories are responding to these economic forces. From the behavior of the broad class or category you could likely infer the behavior of the individuals you are interested in. Another approach (we'll call this an "evolutionary narrative") would look at these individuals *as individuals* to try to understand how they are reacting to the current crisis. In this case we would try to explore each person's particular life history and then understand how this history has shaped this person as an individual.

Each of these two approaches might teach us different things about these individuals, about the effects of the economic crisis on citizens and about how certain types or classes of individual are generally different from other types of individuals. But if we are interested in understanding how person X is dealing with the current crisis and/or how person Y is reacting, then I submit that the second approach is particularly useful. In this case we would want to know about the individual *and* the context in which he or she grew up.

The book that follows, then, offers three evolutionary narratives of three quite different modern industrial democracies. I believe we can learn a great deal about these countries today through these narratives. I further believe we can learn much about the evolution of democratic capitalism generally through these comparative narratives.[3]

I call these evolutionary narratives because I believe we can best understand the patterns we observe in these countries if we consider them as *evolving systems*. There are two related points here: First, I believe that we gain substantial insights into these countries' patterns of development when we consider them as *systems*. Second, these systems *evolve*. Throughout this volume I draw insights from evolutionary theorists from a variety of disciplines and apply them in my exploration of these national systems. I also draw from contributions of a diverse set of *system theorists* who likewise come from a variety of disciplines including economics, biology, computer sciences, and even political science and explore the effects, implications and ontological assumptions of complexity and emergence.[4]

The remainder of this introductory chapter outlines the move to evolutionary narratives as an approach to the study of political systems. I first argue that the diversity of states in the global economy necessitates their

---

[3] The fact is that there are not enough cases of advanced industrial nations to do much meaningful comparative statistical analysis. Even if we were to assume that all rich OECD countries were alike (which they are clearly not), eighteen is an insufficient number of cases. If we want to examine countries as different as the United States and Japan this problem is exacerbated. If we had several hundred cases of new nations that expanded across a continent as millions of foreigners flocked to the most resource rich geographic area in the entire world, and which then dominated the world militarily, economically, and culturally for most of the twentieth century – then treating the United States as a case among many similar cases would make sense. But the obvious truth is that there is only one country in the world that is like the United States in terms of its geographic endowment, its population, and its position in the world economy. Perhaps one might argue that Australia, or for that matter Brazil, due to their geographic size, natural resource endowment and inflow of immigrants are similar to the United States. This would indeed be a very interesting comparison to make. Because this is still a very small number of cases, I would suggest that an evolutionary narrative approach would be a very useful way of exploring both what is different and what is similar about these countries and their developmental paths. I can make the same point about Japan that was transformed into a democratic capitalist nation at the end of World War II after having had two nuclear bombs dropped on its cities. I will examine some similarities and differences between the Japanese case and the German case in the conclusion of this book.

[4] (Axelrod and Cohen 2000; Beinhocker 2006; Hoffman and Riley 1999; Holland 1992; Jervis 1997; LaPorte 1975; Lustick 2005; Sawyer 2005; Wimmer 2006).

being considered as separate systems within a large global system. I then suggest that we can be helped in this by taking evolution seriously. Evolution is often implicitly invoked in political science, but rarely as a body of theory. However, I argue that this body of thought has a good deal to say about the changes of subsystems within larger systems and that we in comparative politics have a great deal to learn from it.[5] In fact, in the third part of the chapter I show that historical institutionalists have anticipated many of the moves I want to make in this book concerning evolution: By bringing in notions such as "path dependence" and by acknowledging that time matters, scholars have moved toward a more complex picture of the world, both in space and time, one that often has striking resemblances to an evolutionary system. This book takes the next step by showing how it has been evolution that historical institutionalists, including myself, have been anticipating. The next task is to turn to the cases. I offer a very general overview of each system before a short conclusion wraps up the chapter.

POLITICAL SCIENCE

I was equally disappointed by the traditional philosophy of science, which was all based on logic, mathematics, and the physical sciences, and had adopted Descartes' conclusion that an organism was nothing but a machine. This Cartesianism left me completely dissatisfied... Where else could I turn? (Ernst Mayr 2004: 5)

Perhaps, if you were not an economist or a political scientist, it would not surprise you that rich countries are adapting in different ways to the challenges they face in the early twenty-first century. But it did surprise me – and most of my colleagues as well. The question is: Why?

I believe that the answer to this question lies in the kind of scientific paradigm that political science has increasingly tried to model. In the effort to be more "scientific," political science has attempted to become more formal

---

[5] Perhaps the most influential evolutionary theorist for this analysis has been Ernst Mayr who was widely considered one of the great philosophers of evolutionary biology until his death in 2005. For an outstanding introduction to evolutionary theory see his marvelous book, *What Evolution Is* (Mayr 2001) but see also (Mayr 1982, 1988, 1991). The philosopher, Daniel Dennett has also been particularly influential in my thinking in this regard, see especially his *Darwin's Dangerous Idea* (Dennett 1995). Other "evolutionists" who have been especially influential for the following work include biologists, Steven J. Gould (Gould 1989, 2002) and Richard Lewontin (Lewontin 2000); zoologist/primate anthropologist Robin Dunbar (Dunbar 1996); psychologist Leda Cosmides (Cosmides and Tooby 1997); economists, Richard Nelson and Sidney Winter (Nelson and Winter 2002) as well as (Hodgson 2002) and the anthropologist team of Robert Boyd and Jeremy Richersson (Boyd and Richersson 2000; Richerson and Boyd 2005).

and structured: The desire for methodological sophistication has pushed scholars toward quantifying the units of the analysis, isolating these variables and then holding them constant in order that their independent effects can be measured. This desire for methodological and analytic sophistication has certainly produced a large number of useful findings. The problem is that as we have developed ever more sophisticated comparative statics we have inadvertently built scientific models that are out of sync with the way the world actually works. Politics is not chemistry or physics, but too often we treat political and economic systems as if they are made up of sets of chemical reactions or physical relationships. In the desire to become a *predictive* science we look for linear relationships between independent variables even when we know that these variables are interdependent and nonlinear, we invent equilibrium where none is to be found, and we assume things about human nature and motivation that no one really believes are true.[6]

Indeed, at the heart of many of the deepest and most difficult battles inside political science is a fundamental struggle over the meaning and methods of science. For many, "science" is the search for systematic regularities and generalizable laws. In this view, one studies the empirical world only because it offers the evidence that can be used to build and test theory. Particular cases or specific events may be interesting – just as a good novel is interesting – but the goal of political science is not to understand any particular event, it is instead to build theories that can be used to explain many (or even all) events. Morris Fiorina describes his scientific orientation in the following way, "[we are] not as interested in a comprehensive understanding of some real institution or historical phenomenon, so much as in a deeper understanding of some theoretical principle or logic ... [F]or most PPT (Positive Political Theory) scholars, breadth trumps depth; understanding 90 percent of the variance in one case is not as significant an achievement as understanding 10 percent of each of nine cases, especially if the cases vary across time and place" (Fiorina 1995: 111).

"[T]he role of comparative research in the process of theory-building and theory-testing" Przeworksi and Tuene advise us in their classic text, "consists

---

[6] In their very popular text, *Research Methods in Social Science*, Nachmias-Frankfort and Nachmias argue as follows: "The ultimate goal of the social sciences is to produce an accumulating body of reliable knowledge. Such knowledge would enable us to *explain, predict* and *understand* empirical phenomena that interest us." (Frankfort-Nachmias and Nachmias 2008: 5–7). Later in their introduction they tell us: "Deductive and probabilistic explanations are essential components of scientific knowledge. **Prediction** constitutes another. In fact," they exhort their readers, "the ability to make predictions is regarded as the outstanding characteristic of science" (emphasis in original, p. 9).

of replacing the proper names of social systems by the relevant variables" (Przeworski and Teune 1970: 30). Along similar lines Lijphardt instructs: "methods aim at scientific explanation, which consists of two basic elements: (1) the establishment of general empirical relationships among two or more variables, while (2) all other variables are controlled, that is, held constant. These two elements are inseparable: one cannot be sure that a relationship is a true one unless the influence of other variables is controlled. The *ceteris paribus* condition is vital to empirical generalizations" (Lijphart 1971: 683).

On this view there is "A" or "The" Scientific Method that all good scientists should follow. This method is based on a basic understanding of how the world works which, indirectly at least, is based on a kind of Newtonian physics. It assumes that even if the world is complex, it can be understood and explained by breaking this complexity into discrete causal units or variables and then examining the independent effects of one variable on others.

At first blush this logic appears to make perfect sense. After all, physical phenomena and chemical reactions are very complex. By following "The Scientific Method," chemists and physicists have made incredible discoveries and found predictive laws from which they have been able to create antibiotics and even send men to the moon. Surely, social and political life is complex, but if we follow the same scientific methods we may one day be able to discover the laws that underlie social and political life and then be able to uncover the Laws of Politics from which we can then cure social ills like poverty and injustice.

The problem with this interpretation of science, in my view at least, is that it assumes the social world works according to the same kind of laws and principles as the physical world. Frankly, I do not think that it does. I agree with Peter Hall when he argues "a substantial gap has opened up in mainstream comparative politics between the methodologies popular today and the ontologies the field is now embracing" (Hall 2003: 374). Quite simply, we increasingly have tried to understand the world as if it was made up of discrete, stable and independent units (or variables) when in reality we know that human history is the product of complex, dynamic, and interdependent processes. In other words, while most people (including political scientists away from the day jobs) see the world as enormously complex and understand history to be a series of contingent events, political science and economics increasingly "envision a world of linear relationships among variables, parity in the size of cause and effect, recurrent patterns over time, and the fundamental insignificance of chance happenings" (Zuckerman 1997: 285).

POLITICS AS EVOLUTION

> When asked whether or not the adaptationist program is a legitimate scientific approach, one must realize that the method of evolutionary biology is in some ways quite different from that of the physical sciences. Although evolutionary phenomena are subject to universal laws, as are most phenomena in the physical sciences, the explanation of a particular evolutionary phenomenon can be given only as a 'historical narrative.' Consequently, when one attempts to explain the features of something that is the product of evolution, one must attempt to reconstruct the evolutionary history of this feature. (Mayr 1988: 149)

Social scientists frequently use the term "evolution" when they talk about politics and history. But in most cases all that is really meant by this term is that history is a linked chain of events. I submit that we can be more explicit in our understanding of the ways in which human social institutions evolve and that we can draw lessons from those who have studied evolutionary processes in other disciplines as far ranging as anthropology, linguistics, psychology, economics, and even biology. *I do not mean to suggest that the mechanisms driving the evolution of human institutions are exactly the same as they are for biological or linguistic evolution.* But I do believe that several of the concepts and ideas learned in the study of evolutionary processes in different arenas can be helpful for us as we try to understand the evolution of social institutions.

Allow me to explore this argument by way of another metaphor from outside politics: Consider the implications of global warming on similar species in different continents. A rise in the earth's temperature of, let's say, three degrees, will have enormous implications for virtually all life on earth. But this does not suggest that all animals – or even all populations of a particular species – will adapt in the same way. For example, would we expect all mammals to lose their hair? Obviously not.

There are two reasons we would not expect biological convergence even in response to a change like global warming. First, even if the overall temperature of the world were to increase, it is perfectly clear to climatologists that the mean temperature will not increase to the same degree on all parts of the globe. In fact, it appears quite likely that warming will melt the polar ice caps, which will have a significant effect on the flow of the Gulf Stream along the northern European coastline. It is therefore quite likely that Europe will become much *colder* if global warming continues. Therefore, the creatures that live there (including humans) will not only have to adapt to rising sea levels, but will also have to adapt to longer and colder winters.

Second, even in geographical areas where the average temperature may increase in similar ways (say North America and Africa) this rising temperature would not necessarily force a common evolutionary adaptation from even similar subspecies. Let me demonstrate with a fanciful illustration: Squirrels are found in many parts of the world. These animals can often look very similar. But over the years these populations have evolved in somewhat different ways as they have adapted to their particular ecologies. Therefore, even if temperatures were to rise in equal measures in Africa and North America, the evolutionary responses of African Ground Squirrels and American Grey Squirrels are likely to be quite different. This is because each of these similar species has already adapted to their own particular ecologies in quite different ways – setting them on rather different evolutionary trajectories as they continue to adapt to their now warmer ecological context. In one case, this general ecological change could create opportunities for expansion of terrain and further evolutionary adaptation. In another case, global warming would likely invoke very different adaptive responses – potentially even mass extinction.

I submit that the huge changes we are witnessing in the world economy (a.k.a. globalization) may have effects on advanced welfare states much like the effects of global warming on similar biological species. There is no question that all countries are in the process of adapting to this new economic (ecological) context. But this does not suggest that all countries will – or can – adapt in the same ways, or that the consequences of these adaptations will be similar across the world.

Evolutionary theory adopts a different scientific ontology than that commonly found in physics or chemistry. At the root of evolutionary biology is the assumption that the objects of analysis – living organisms – are fundamentally different than inanimate matter. Thus, as Ernst Mayr points out, "this required a restructuring of the conceptual world of science that was far more fundamental than anyone had imagined at the time" (Mayr 2004: 26). I submit that social systems – the object of analysis in political science – are also fundamentally different from inanimate matter. Like living organisms, they change, adapt and evolve.

From an evolutionary perspective outcomes are rarely the product of discrete variables operating independently on one another in predictable and repeatable ways. This is first because evolutionary theory assumes *complex causation* and is the study of *complex adaptive systems* (Holland 1992).

This means more than simply things are complex. Instead it accepts that many outcomes are the result of *emergent* phenomena. What this means is that complex phenomena are often the result of a series of unguided inter-actions at the micro level and that the outcomes may be unique to the par-ticular interaction. Just as genes at the micro level interact to form a unique individual, individuals within a social system interact with one another within a population. The character of the whole population, then, is dis-tinct from a simple aggregation of the constituent units. Thus, interaction is the key aspect of an emergent system, which implies that isolating factors as "independent" variables may be an ontological fallacy.

A second key ontological implication of evolutionary theory is that dif-ferent factors will matter in different cases. A key problem for traditional Newtonian political science is that it wants to equalize all variables into comparable constants – to treat national variation as an error term. *An evolutionary theory allows us to accept the fact that different variables mat-ter in different contexts.* Evolutionary theory does not assume constancy of variables and therefore similar variables can have very different effects in different contexts. (Recall the analogy of global warming above.) In the fol-lowing pages for example, I will argue that the fact that Sweden had a small and homogenous population in the mid twentieth century mattered greatly in the construction of its particular form of welfare state. This does not imply that population size matters so much today, but at critical moments it did matter. At some level this seems rather obvious, but virtually all analysts of the Swedish welfare state either dismiss or ignore this factor because it mattered only in a particular time in Swedish history, or because not all sim-ilarly small homogeneous countries developed Swedish-style welfare states.[7]

---

[7] In my own earlier efforts to show the power of institutional variation for explaining the American and the Swedish cases, I undervalued – and even argued against – the point that Sweden is different because it is a small homogenous polity and/or that America was different because of its history of slavery and racism. See (Steinmo 1993, 1995). Of course the truth is that slavery and racism have mattered enormously in the American story, whereas the fact that most Swedes could feel that other Swedes were similar to themselves does matter for the Swedish story. But admitting this does not force me now to say, that institutions do not matter, or for that matter that the particular timing of industrialization does not matter for these countries particular developmental paths. The simple reality is that lots of things matter, and different things matter in different cases. Polities, in this sense, are a lot like human beings: the fact that you are reading this book suggests that you are probably well-educated, upper middle-class, and interested in comparative politics. That (hopefully) means that you are like a lot of other people. But does this suggest that you are exactly like all the other people reading this book? Or that the unique features of your own personal story do not really matter for an explanation of who you are, or what you brought to this book?

Another example of the role particular events or variables play in specific cases is the impact race and slavery has had on the development of the United States of America. The United States is the only rich modern democratic country that allowed for slavery *while* it called itself a democracy, and the only democratic country that intentionally discriminated against the voting rights of a particular racial group well into the latter half of the twentieth century. Whereas a comparative statistics analysis would have to discount or ignore these facts (because the United States was unique in these regards) an evolutionary narrative would have to integrate them into the analysis. Instead of trying to discount or remove race as a variable when trying to explain American public policy, an evolutionary analysis specifically will attempt to show how and why race does matter for the development of the unique American welfare state. Instead of trying to explain away these variables (or treat them as error terms to be ignored), we are able to acknowledge them and integrate the unique features of particular cases into the explanation for that case. As illustrated in the empirical chapters of this book the evolutionary narrative allows us to look at *both* the unique features of a particular case and simultaneously search for the common factors that have shaped development in different places.

Evolutionary scientists admit that really important events are impossible to predict. Predictions can only be proximate and probabilistic *not* because we lack the tools, models, data sets, or computing power, but rather because of contingency and the complex interaction of *inter*dependent variables over time. In history, variables themselves change, adapt and are affected by history itself. Prediction requires linear analysis of variables that react to one another in predictable ways. For many, if not most, political scientists, such analysis denies the realities of the world in which we live.[8] Again we see that the study of evolution is not, and cannot be, "like physics" because what we study and what we are interested in explaining are not inanimate objects to which absolute, invariant, and fixed laws apply.

Rather than predict the future, the goal of evolutionary scientists is to understand the forces and dynamics that have shaped the world as we know it. Specifically they are interested in understanding how and why populations adapt, prosper, and sometimes die out. In other words, why is there

---

[8] For example in basic statistical analysis it is common to tell students that they must watch for multicollinearity and that they must be careful to only examine questions in which the multiple variables in an equation can be separately identified. This is not because this is the way the real world works, but rather because unless one takes these precautions the statistical inferences drawn are methodologically invalid. The problem, of course, is that the method we use can too easily define the questions we ask.

variation across time and space? They do this inductively rather than deduc-
tively. Evolutionary biologists, for example, do not have the goal of being
able to predict future evolutionary adaptations, not because they do not
have enough data, nor because their computer models are not powerful
enough, but because evolutionary theory assumes that random variation
within complex systems can set development along totally new and unpredictable paths.[9] Moreover, some adaptations that work in one setting can
be disastrous in others. For example, one continent might have many mar-
supials, and another none. For these reasons, evolutionary scientists are
necessarily engaged in path analysis and process tracing. They are interested
in both explaining adaptations and understanding the consequences of those
adaptations.

This epistemological framework might raise a number of objections from
social scientists accustomed to standards of science derived from physics. For
example, if explanations are constructed post-hoc and cannot be falsified
via experimentation, then how can they be falsified? Although falsification
might be a worthy goal in some arenas, the simple fact is that some research
questions defy these standard models of scientific study. Once again, given a
macro-level emphasis on the interaction of complex systems, it is impossible
to reduce these events to basic covering laws.[10] This may explain why Popper
himself came to question the utility of reductionism arguing that "as a
philosophy, reductionism is a failure... we live in a universe of emergent
novelty; of a novelty which, as a rule, is not completely reducible to any of
the preceding stages."[11]

In sum, evolutionary theory thus offers a distinctive approach to the study
of politics and history. Instead of attempting to reduce complex phenomenon
into constituent units and examine these units as independent variables, it
takes a systems approach and argues that not all outcomes are reducible.
Second, evolutionary theory takes history seriously meaning that *when* and
where something occurs can fundamentally shape what occurs. Finally, evolutionary theory takes contingency seriously. Random, unforeseeable and
emergent events can have fundamentally important consequences (Gould
2002).

In contrast to a mechanical view, human history is better understood as
an evolutionary process of adaptation. Taking this view, however, implies

---

[9] There is a huge literature dealing with these puzzles. Some interesting examples include:
   (Hoffman and Riley 1999; Pierson 2000; Jervis 1997; Mayr 1988; Holland 1992; Kerr
   2002; Futuyma and Slatkin 1983; Zimmer 2001; Ridley 2003).
[10] Reductionism may be applied to functional biology that focuses on proximate causes.
[11] Quoted in, Mayer 2004: 79.

acknowledging that: 1) History is not a linear process; 2) chance, or contingency, matters; 3) outcomes are often the product of emergent processes and therefore cannot always be simply reduced to, and understood in terms of, their constituent parts; and 4) there are *inter*dependent and iterative relationships between important causal variables.

It seems to me that our explanations for politics and history that accept these realities are more likely to be useful than a science that assumes that history works like gravity.

EVOLUTIONARY THEORY AND HISTORICAL INSTITUTIONALISM

As implied above, this analysis fits squarely within the tradition of Historical Institutionalism. In my view, Historical Institutionalism and evolutionary analysis share many basic principles. First, both take history very seriously. We do not see history simply as a chain of events. Instead, what happens at time A can fundamentally shape what happens at time B. In other words, historical changes have important long-term *evolutionary* consequences. Second, we believe that in order to understand the specific structure or behavior of an organism or institution, one must explicitly examine it in the ecology or context in which it operates and/or lives. The objects of our interest are constantly adapting to the environment in which they survive and as that context changes they must adapt. In other words, history is not a series of equilibria that are periodically upset. Third, both evolutionary analysis and historical institutionalism are explicitly interested in the interactive effects of multiple causal variables. Indeed, both are skeptical of the very idea that important causal variables can be truly "independent" of the things they affect.

I strongly believe that institutionalist approaches have offered important insights that help us better understand politics and public policy. Historical institutionalists in particular have helped us answer very important questions such as: Why are labor unions stronger in some countries than others (Rothstein 1992)? Why do national health care systems vary in the ways they do (Immergut 1992b)? Why are social welfare systems so hard to reform (Pierson 2001b)? Why is America becoming a more divided society economically and socially (Hacker 2005)? And even, why do some economic ideas have such powerful influences over policy makers at particular moments in history (Blyth 2002; Hall 1989)? In each case the key insights are that institutions shape actor's strategic choices, and over time also affect their preferences. Because actors know that institutions structure politics, actors fight about the structure of institutions. They are thus both the products of political action and the context in which politics takes place.

As important as these insights are, institutionalism has struggled with three important lacunae: 1) Institutionalists have difficulty explaining political change (Campbell 2004; Thelen 1999, 2003); 2) institutional analyses emphasize structure over human preferences and agency (Katznelson and Weingast 2005; Hall 2008); and 3) institutional analyses tend to undervalue the ways in which institutions themselves are effected by the political or historical context in which they operate (Steinmo 2008). Many institutionalists have tried to break away from the equilibrium assumptions of standard institutionalist theory. The notions of "path dependence" and "increasing returns" provide good examples of this move. These concepts have been very helpful for helping us understand that history and institutions are not static and that contingency and initial conditions (along with institutions) are important for understanding recurrent patterns over time. But rather ironically, these theories offer us no way of understanding *why things change*. As Mahoney notes, "once contingent historical events take place, path-dependent sequences are marked by relatively deterministic causal patterns or what can be thought of as "inertia" – i.e., once processes are set into motion and begin tracking a particular outcome, these processes tend to stay in motion and continue to track this outcome" (Mahoney 2000: 511). The problem is that the path itself becomes a new kind of equilibrium – rather like riding a bicycle.

I believe that these lacunae can be addressed by pushing historical institutionalism in the direction of evolutionary theory and by treating human social institutions as complex adaptive systems.[12] *Evolutionary theory is a theory of change.* Instead of seeing history as lurching between different equilibrium, evolutionists see history as a continuous adaptive process. In other words, the natural world (and in this I include human societies) is always changing. Evolutionary theorists and historical institutionalists alike see adaptation as an interactive, interdependent, and ongoing process between the individual, the population, and the broader environment or ecology.

---

[12] Thelen and I argued in *Structuring Politics* that historical institutionalism is an *approach* to the study of politics and *not* a theory. Some might argue that we do not need grand theories (indeed, I've made this argument in the past myself), instead we should be satisfied with proximate explanations or "meso-level" analysis (Thelen and Steinmo 1992). See also Steinmo, 2008.

Evolutionary theories move beyond equilibrium theories because any given institutional arrangement is part of an adaptive process in which multiple agents operate within a dynamic context.[13] A fundamental argument of this book is that in order to understand how modern capitalist democracies have evolved, we must understand that capitalism itself has evolved. In short, each system we study here is continually adapting within a dynamic context. The related point, of course, is that the changes in these countries' political economies may simultaneously shape the evolution of capitalism itself. The recent crisis of global capitalism is only the current iteration of this dynamic. In sum, from an evolutionary perspective, change is the normal state – not something that is punctuated occasionally. As Deeg argues: "it is not necessarily the case that an exogenous force must disturb an equilibrium before a path change can occur. As a given institutional path evolves its very own mechanisms of reproduction can undermine itself" (Deeg 2005: 195). In this way evolutionary theory builds context into the theory itself. Moreover, as all historical institutionalists understand implicitly, history itself is a context that shapes the current world. This is why you cannot go back down the evolutionary tree – at least not along the same branch that you came up.

Second, given the complexity of natural and social systems there is inevitably friction within the system. In this view, historical outcomes cannot be seen as the result of efficient equilibrium, but are instead phases in an ongoing process of adaptation and change.[14] Indeed, it is relatively rare to find an optimal or efficient fit in the relations between the subsystems within a large complex system or between that system (whether a phenotype, population, or institution) and the broader ecology or context in which it lives or operates.

Third, evolutionary theory explicitly and directly acknowledges the fact that historical outcomes are the products of multiple causal variables which often interact with each other and produce emergent outcomes. Political scientists have long accepted multi-variable causality. But *emergence* implies

---

[13] Of course, Steven J. Gould was famous for the phrase punctuated equilibrium and created a major battle among evolutionary theorists by arguing that adaptation is not the most important source of evolutionary change – random external shocks are. Gould's own position moderated on this later in his life and today most acknowledge that both environmental disruption and endogenous adaptation and/or mutation are the keys to evolutionary change (see Dawkins 2006; Gould 2002; Sterelny 2001).

[14] Historical institutionalists are by no means the only political scientists who have come to see the problems with classical equilibrium analysis and/or moved toward evolutionary theory as solutions to these problems. (See for example Axelrod and Cohen 2000; Axelrod 1984; Gintis 2000; Greif and Laitin 2004; Knight and Sened 1995; Maynard Smith 1982; Young 1998.)

something quite different. Emergence occurs when variables or processes combine in unique ways to produce unique outcomes. Emergence is fundamental in a variety of fields from biology to quantum mechanics. But it can be difficult for "normal" science because it undermines falsifiability.[15] The basic point is not hard to understand: When two or more things come together they can create something wholly new. The problem for "normal" science – especially when we consider the implications of emergence for complex adaptive systems – is that we find indeterminacy and *contingency throughout the system*. In other words, instead of simply having change as the product of an occasional exogenous punctuation, change is now endogenous to the system itself. This is the reality of the world in which we live, but it makes it difficult to model.[16]

In sum, taking an evolutionary approach to the study of human social institutions places change at the center of the analysis. In recent years a number of thoughtful works within the historical institutionalist tradition have moved in this direction. The contributions in Kathy Thelen and Wolfgang Streeck's excellent volume, *Beyond Continuity*, Paul Pierson's, *Politics in Time*, and Kathy Thelen's, *How Institutions Evolve*, are obvious cases in point. It is especially interesting to note that many of the concepts that these authors have rightly been lauded for bringing to political science – such as path dependency, increasing returns, drift, punctuated equilibrium, and endogenous adaptation – were originally developed by evolutionary scientists in other disciplines. [17] I seek to pursue this agenda further.

In each chapter that follows we will see many examples of evolutionary patterns that are commonly understood in a variety of domains. Many political scientists will be familiar with these ideas, if not necessarily the terms. For example this book suggests that the merging of different institutional

---

[15] This is why Popper recanted on many of his earlier ideas about the scientific method later in his life. See his *The Open Universe: An Argument for Indeterminism* (Popper and Bartley 1982).

[16] Randomized contingency is an exceptionally difficult problem for evolutionary game theorists. This may be why many are turning to Agent-Based Modeling which is less an attempt to map real behavior than an interesting effort to play out multiple plausible scenarios (Axelrod 1997; Holland 1992).

[17] Wolfgang Streeck specifically suggests that his and Thelen's ideas on adaptation developed in *Beyond Continuity* were drawn from evolutionary theory. "Basically what we did was introduce into historical institutionalism a model of *imperfect reproduction*, similar to received models of change in evolutionary biology" (Streeck 2009: 238, emphasis in original). Pierson similarly acknowledges Brian Arthur's work on increasing returns. (See Arthur 1994.) Steinmo and Thelen and Krasner also cite Gould when invoking Punctuated Equilibrium (Gould 2002). (See also Boyd and Richersson 2000; Dawkins 1976; Holland 1992; Lewontin 2000; Pierson 2004; Streeck and Thelen 2005; Thelen 2004.)

forms together is a kind of *symbiogenisis* – a pattern well understood in the world of viral and microbial evolution.[18] The analysis of the Swedish political history is a good example – where capital, labor unions, and ultimately the State, form a symbiotic and mutually beneficial set of relations and each evolve in this context. Similarly we will see many examples of what Kathy Thelen and Wolfgang Streeck have called institutional layering (where institutions adapt to new circumstances to take on new functions). In evolutionary theory this is the well-known process of *exaptation*.[19] Following several students of Japanese post-World War II history I describe Japan as a type of *hybrid* in which traditional social institutions were merged with more western political institutions in a process that created a new kind polity. Alternatively, I see the remarkable development of the early American polity as it spread across the massive North American continent as a type of *allopatric* evolution. Allopatry can occur when a population or species enters a new environment, which offers it highly advantageous ecological conditions for expansion and growth. In this process, both the host environment and the invading population can be fundamentally altered. We certainly see that what eventually becomes the United States of America is as much shaped by the remarkably open and rich geography of North America as it was by its initial founding ideas and institutions. Finally, I repeatedly emphasize the *co-evolution* of social, economic, and political institutions. In systems there are often processes of co-evolution ongoing precisely because the various subsystems are interconnected and inter-related. This helps explain why both institutional and biological change is sometimes quite slow in some contexts and quite rapid in others.

It is obvious that many of these specific insights and arguments about institutional change, humans as social creatures, the role of ideas, and the importance of environmental context have been made by other scholars – particularly historical institutionalists. I am not trying to reinvent the wheel here. But few have attempted to pull these insights into an integrated whole. Doing so, I argue, moves us toward an evolutionary theory of institutional change.

As I make the final revisions of this book before it goes to the publisher (November, 2009), a colleague sends me the epilogue to the forthcoming

---

[18] Symbiogenesis is one of the major forms of speciation in the world, but is not often discussed in evolutionary theory – even if it is widely understood to be the most common mechanism of evolutionary change in the microbial and submicrobial world. Sapp, following Margolis, argues that symbiogenisis is certainly as important a source of variation of life as classical Darwinian "descent with modification" (Sapp 2003).

[19] See (Ehrlich 2000) and (Gould 2002).

Oxford *Handbook of Comparative Institutional Analysis*, by Wolfgang Streeck. In his essay Streeck makes very similar arguments as those presented here. He too, apparently believes that social scientists should take evolution more seriously:

[Evolutionary theory] may serve as a model for a theory of institutional change in several ways. It provides an example of a non-teleological but nevertheless intelligible account of history in which the future is not predetermined, leaving space for human agency. It identifies imperfect reproduction as a source of continuous gradual change, and thereby defines a place where a (micro-) theory of action might be inserted into a dynamic (macro-) theory of social order. It elaborates a processual view of the natural world which seems eminently transferable to the social world; it introduces time as a central variable in a theory of nature, by implication suggesting its inclusion in theories of society as well; it demonstrates how path dependency may be accommodated in a non-teleological theory of change recognizing the causal significance of past events for present and future ones; and when read correctly, it is fundamentally subversive of an efficiency-theoretical construction of historical structures and processes, making space for explicit recognition of the role of non-efficient or non-rational forces in the evolution of social order. (Streeck 2010a) [in press, no page numbers, yet]

A NOTE ON COMMON MISPERCEPTIONS

Its main theme [general evolutionary theory] is not the unity of history as an evolution from beginning up until the present day. It is concerned, far more specifically, with the conditions for possible unplanned changes of structure and with the explanation of diversification or the increase in complexity. (Niklas Luhmann 2004: 231)

There have been many important scholars in the past who have explicitly examined history as an evolutionary process[20] but attempts to apply evolutionary theory to the study of human social institutions has largely fallen out of favor in recent years. The reticence to take evolution seriously in the social sciences stems from two sources: First, evolutionary theories have been misunderstood and sometimes used to justify malicious and racist ideas. Second, some scholars are troubled by the notion that history is itself the result of the interaction of millions of unplanned and uncontrolled factors.

Sociologist Herbert Spencer's term "survival of the fittest," after all, has been used to justify some of the most heinous acts of social/biological engineering from the Nazi ethnic cleansing to the eugenics policies in Sweden and America (King 2000). It is important to understand, however, that

---

[20] Some important examples include Thorsten Veblen, Schumpeter, Fredrik von Hayek, Herbert Spenser, Kenneth Boulding (Boulding 1981; Spencer and Peel 1972; Veblen 1898; Hayek and Shenfield 1983; Popper and Bartley 1982). See also DiZeriga 1989.

these interpretations of Darwinian theories were the products of significant *mis*understandings of evolutionary thought.[21] Neither Darwin nor any serious student of evolution today believes that evolution is progressive in any normative sense. One can think of evolution as progressive only in the sense that one thing evolves out of its antecedents, but no normative implications should be drawn from this, nor can one predict that any particular evolutionary development will necessarily lead to an adaptive advantage in the future. For example, it is common for evolutionary changes to lead to increased complexity, but it is also possible that increased complexity carries with it its own competitive disadvantages. Both biological and human history is littered with evolutionary adaptations that proved to be dead ends.

This is an extremely important point. *Evolution and evolutionary narratives are not teleological.* Ever since Darwin first published his famous, *On the Origin of Species*, many have incorrectly assumed that he understood evolution in teleological terms. But once again, this was a fundamental misunderstanding of evolutionary theory. As Mayr points out:

Perhaps such an interpretation was not altogether unreasonable in the framework of the Lamarckian transformational paradigm. It is no longer a reasonable view when one fully appreciates the variational nature of Darwinian evolution, which has no ultimate goal and which, so to speak starts anew in every generation . . . considering how often natural selection leads to fatal ends and considering how often during evolution its premium changes, resulting in an irregular zig zag movement of the evolutionary change, it would seem singularly inappropriate to use the designation teleological. To be sure natural selection is an optimizing process, but it has no definite goal, and considering the number of constraints and the frequency of chance events, it would be most misleading to call it teleological. Nor is any improvement in adaptation a teleological process, since it is strictly a *post hoc* decision whether a given evolutionary change qualifies as a contribution to adaptedness. (Mayr 1992: 132)

Over the following pages we will see that each of the systems explored here have had within them different competitive advantages and disadvantages. This is partially because they are complex systems, but also because each system retains elements evolved in a bygone era. Only thirty years ago, it appeared, for example that the Japanese model of coordinated capitalism would surely out compete the more liberal models of the west. Similarly in the decade or so before the massive economic collapse of 2009 it appeared to many that the hyper liberal, deregulated economic system developing in

---

[21] Indeed, early modernization theory in political science was the product of the misunderstanding of evolutionary theory (Eisenstadt 2006: 199).

the United States would out compete more regulated and socially oriented systems of Europe in a classical "survival of the fittest" fashion. Needless to say, this argument no longer seems so obvious.

The second reason some social scientists are leery of evolutionary theory is connected to this last point and is both more interesting and more difficult. Social scientists, like most modern individuals want to believe that we make our own destinies. Because evolution is by definition the consequence of the interaction of long series' of unplanned events, many believe that evolution should not be applied to human history. In other words, one might argue or believe that evolutionary theory takes human agency out of human history. But once again, such a conclusion arises from a misunderstanding of evolutionary theory. Indeed, even in the biological world actors matter, what one individual or population actually does can profoundly shape both their own and other's evolutionary paths. Certainly, human beings have the most developed cognitive capacities and far more sophisticated mental abilities to plan/strategize and rationally calculate our individual and collective interests. But it is pure hubris to suggest that humans are unique in this regard or that we are the only creatures that attempt to shape their world to suit their needs or preferences. Following a number of evolutionary theorists, I submit that it is precisely because of human's cognitive capacities and ability to form complex social organizations that our social institutions evolve much more quickly than does biological evolution that relies on sexual selection or gene mutation.[22]

THE CASES: THREE SYSTEMS

In each chapter that follows we will see examples of evolutionary patterns that are commonly understood in a variety of domains. But this is not a book *about* evolutionary theory. *This is a book about three different political economies.*[23] I *use* several concepts borrowed from evolutionary theories developed in other disciplines where I found them useful and enlightening. But in no case am I suggesting that there is a strict or direct translation of the concepts developed in other domains to human social affairs. But I have adopted the ontology and epistemology implied in evolutionary theory. The reader should not look here for a full-blown "theory" of the evolution

---

[22] See (Beinhocker 2006) for a detailed elaboration of this argument. (See also Boyd and Richerson 2005a.)
[23] For readers interested in more detailed analyses of evolutionary theory and its implications and application to studying institutions see Lewis and Steinmo (2008, 2010).

of human social institutions. My aims are far more modest. Instead the following pages' central objective is to explain how and why three different capitalist democratic countries have adapted so differently to some rather remarkably similar pressures.

One should specifically note that I am only exploring a particular branch of the human institutional tree – advanced capitalist democracies. I will argue that while many similar institutions populate each of these countries, they are in fact very different systems. One might even say that the puzzle is: Why would countries as different as Sweden, Japan, and the United States have *anything* in common?[24] After all, Sweden is a large country with a tiny population on the northern border of the complex and historically warring European peninsula. Japan in contrast, is a resource-poor, densely populated, and geographically isolated island that only came into contact with the western world in the late 1800s. Finally, the United States – a continental country – has been the dominant political economy on the earth for almost a century. This country occupies most of a huge and resource-rich continent and has been the prime destination for immigrants, capital, and ideas from around the world and has explicitly and implicitly attempted to use its power to shape the world that it dominates.

Still, these very different nations share a large number of features: They are all democracies with regular elections, freedom of the press, the rule of law, and a wide range of individual liberties. They have market-based economies, with relatively free capital markets, stock exchanges, and strong commitments to private property. In each case their governments intervene and regulate private affairs, tax companies, and citizens through the same set of tax instruments and provide a remarkably consistent set of public programs and social services for its citizens – from old age care and pensions, to unemployment insurance, to support for the needy and systems of higher education. Here I give a brief overview of their political economies.

[24] I am reminded here of a brief argument I had with Ray Wolfinger, one of my professors at UC Berkeley in the early 1980s, when I told him I wanted to write a dissertation on the development of tax systems in Sweden, Britain, and the United States. Wolfinger flatly stated "that is a bad idea." "Why," I asked? He rather sympathetically told me, "Look, less than 10 million people live in Sweden and there are over 250 million Americans. You simply can't compare these two countries." I (rather cleverly, I thought) rejoined, "You just compared them, and if the size of the country is the most important thing that separates them, then I think that is worth knowing!" The truth, however, is that I did not take this rather fundamental and obvious insight seriously in my subsequent dissertation or the book that followed. I was too busy trying to show that all the important action was in the institutions. The fact that the institutions were built in a very homogeneous society was something that I preferred to ignore.

Sweden: How Does a Bumblebee Fly?

Sweden has been the focus of a great deal of academic interest for a number of years for the simple reason that, according to traditional economic analyses, it should not be able to survive. Sweden has the heaviest tax burden, the most generous social welfare system and is the most egalitarian society in the world. At the same time, it is a highly productive and technologically advanced economy, home to some of the world's most successful capitalist enterprises and enjoys one of the highest standards of living in the world. Quite simply, these things are not supposed to go together and, like the bumblebee, Sweden should not really be able to "fly." Yet, somehow it does.

Following many others, I characterize this system as having a social-liberal economic system and a "universalist" welfare state. Very briefly, some of the most distinctive features of the Swedish system are:

- High levels of income equality;
- Universalist social welfare and tax policies;
- High levels of union organization and economic concentration;
- Long history of labor/capital peace and cooperation;
- Highest taxes in the world;
- Highest level of social spending in the world;
- High levels of gender equality.

The reader will see in Chapter 2 that Sweden has been remarkably successful at adapting to changes in the world economy as well as social changes within its own society while maintaining a commitment to a progressive welfare state and egalitarian society. Instead of trying to ignore the fact that Sweden is a small, historically homogenous nation on the northern periphery of Europe, this analysis shows how these factors offered this country several adaptive advantages. Late development, combined with a specific mixture of natural resources led to the rapid takeoff of the steel industry. Her geographic position, combined with the country's particular resources allowed Sweden to remain neutral during both major world wars. In the process a *symbiotic relationship* between organizations representing capital and labor emerged as Sweden struggled to compete in the highly competitive world economy. The result, as many social scientists have noted, was that a dynamic process of *Increasing Returns* (Arthur 1994) developed in which labor, capital and the state found mechanisms for mutual cooperation and advantage. The result has been a remarkably adaptive and flexible system, which apparently can not only fly, but seems to manage the task quite well.

Japan: A Hybrid Struggling to Adapt

Japan was once thought of as the dominant alternative to American "free market" capitalism. This country grew out of the rubble of World War II (WWII) and became the world's second largest and most productive economy in less than forty years. This system can be understood as a kind of hybrid in which liberal capitalist and democratic institutions imposed on Japan after WWII were adapted to a social and economic system based on more traditional forms of authority and hierarchy. The result was what I call a type of institutional *hybrid*. The system was characterized by high levels of intragroup social trust and deference to authority that facilitated the evolution of a highly cooperative and competitive political economy. I argue that this unusual fusion of social, economic, and political institutions created a new kind of capitalist democracy that appeared to work very well for at least the next fifty years.

Indeed, by the 1980s many predicted that Japan would soon dominate the world. Clearly these predictions were off the mark. Instead, the collapse of a property market bubble introduced enormous self-doubt and eventually a series of policies that have worked to eat away at the very foundations of the system itself. Today, Japan finds itself in a situation where it has tried to copy many liberal policy ideas from the West, but has not been able to adapt to the normative or social changes that are concomitants of these ideas. Japan remains a remarkably traditional society in terms of social and gender relations for example, but seems to be abandoning the social-welfare institutions that helped this system work. The result seems to be an awkward fit in which Japan is struggling to adapt.

Some of the key distinguishing characteristics of the Japanese system include:

- Very low taxes and small public welfare state;
- Employer-based welfare state;
- A comparatively traditional and hierarchical society;
- Strong central bureaucracy and weak democratic/representative institutions;
- The Left/Right ideological divide has almost no relevance to Japanese politics.

Today, social, demographic, and economic pressures are impinging on the Japanese system in profound ways: The central bureaucracy is in retreat, confidence in the public sector is almost absent, social values are modernizing, and Japan's aging society is creating massive pressures for increases in social spending and the tax increases they require. How this country adapts to these intense pressures while its democratic institutions are so embattled and weak is the key issue facing Japan today.

The United States: Strong Nation, Weak State

The United States has dominated the world economically, politically and ideologically for most of the past century. I argue that this unique system has benefited enormously from the massive resource wealth into which the American polity expanded. Liberal ideas and institutions emerging in Europe in the eighteenth century found very fertile soil in the new continent. In this case we find a kind of *allopatric* evolution[25] in which a population carrying egalitarian and liberal ideas move into a new geographic space where they found enormous resources and comparatively weak competitors. In this context we see the co-evolution of ideas about limited public authority, a particular individualistic and entrepreneurial ethic. Public authority was institutionally limited and consequently the private sector was able to take advantage of the phenomenal resources available and develop the strongest and most powerful economy in the world. Government was not absent but was forced to play more of a supportive role in which government manipulates the private sector via hidden and often indirect mechanisms.

I also show that many perceptions of the United States and its public policies are wrong. For example it is not true that this is a free market system, even if it is clearly the case that government intervention is less coordinated and more haphazard than that of most other countries. I also show that it is incorrect to believe that America has a small and limited social welfare system. Instead the United States has a massive, remarkably inefficient, but largely "hidden" welfare state.

Key features of this system include:

- Highly dynamic economic enterprises;
- Low taxes;
- High levels of income inequality;
- Targeted welfare state programs;
- Highly particularistic and focused social and economic regulations;
- Low levels of social protection.

[25] Allopatric speciation is where a population splits into different geographic zones, which subsequently evolve along different paths. Over time, these populations can even evolve into entirely separate species.

America's enormous resource wealth on the one hand, and the fragmented political institutions on the other, helped this country evolve into a nation that valued both egalitarian ideals and anti-state sentiments. As the American state began to take on new functions and goals in the last half of the twentieth century, however, the fragmentation of political authority led to the construction of an extensive but incoherent welfare state. Unsurprisingly, public confidence in political authority declined. "Globalization" was never a significant threat to the world's largest economy, but international competition has been used quite effectively to justify a set of policy choices that have further contributed to the growing inequality in this society. More importantly, Americans have become increasingly skeptical of public authority itself. Once heralded as "the land of equal opportunity," America is evolving into a highly stratified society. Not only are income, wealth and power becoming a great deal more unequal than in the past, but also Americans appear to be willing to accept this outcome as somehow inevitable.

Table 1.1 summarizes some of the key features of each of these political economies. We see, as Soskice, Hall, Esping-Andersen, and many others have suggested, that each of these systems is in some sense internally coherent... and that each is systematically different from the others. Sweden's universalist, egalitarian, social-corporatist and progressive democracy is systematically different from Japan's neofeudalist, patronage-oriented system. Each of these in turn is remarkably different from the individualist, fragmented, and unequal systems found in the United States.

Looking at Table 1.1 we see that these are remarkably different systems. At the same time, as we shall see in the following chapters, there is in fact a high degree of coherence within each system. One might even say that while the political, economic, welfare and tax systems are remarkably different, the ways in which they interact provide some degree of functional equivalence. Clearly the state is central to the Swedish system, whereas the family and the corporation are more central to the Japanese. Finally, the individual is more on her own in the American case. Each of these systems evolved according to its own logic – even while they have developed within a broadly common macroeconomic context. They each face significant challenges as they enter the twenty-first century. But because these *systems* are so different we should expect continued divergence and not an unavoidable race to the bottom.

CONCLUSION

Each of the substantive sections/chapters of this book is organized into three basic parts. I open each chapter with a broad overview of the political/

TABLE 1.1. *The Political Economies of Sweden, Japan, and the United States*

	Sweden	Japan	USA
Political System	**Social-Corporatist** Parliamentary/ coalition governments Unitary government Centralized decision Strong political parties Expert/bureaucrat dominated Ideological conflict is muted Cooperative	**Personalist** Faction-based parliamentary system Weak political parties Politicians have local power base Centralized decision Politician/Bureaucrat dominated No ideology Clientelistic	**Pluralist** Single-member electoral districts Federal bi-cameral Decentralized decision making Politician dominated Ideological/ Conflictual
Economic System	**Concentrated** Dominated by large internationally integrated firms Coordinated through employer groups and unions Highly organized and politically powerful unions and employers Flexible Egalitarian outcomes	**Dual Economy** Dominated by small inefficient firms on one hand and by successful, large export-oriented firms on the other. Government has (historically) acted as agent for economic coordination Highly cooperative employer based unions Egalitarian outcomes	**Competitive Market** Dominated by large firms many of which are quite young Uncoordinated Dynamic, Flexible working arrangements Entrepreneur oriented Weak unions Unequal outcomes
Welfare System	**Universalist** Citizenship based Broadly distributed Very high levels of support Highly egalitarian Highly comprehensive State provided social services Very expensive	**Employer/Family** High benefits for core workers and families through firms Very low levels of public aid/support Families/wives provide most social services Strongly advantages employees in big firms and the aged. Expensive for firms but not taxpayer	**Individualist** Targeted Means tested direct benefits High benefit levels for middle class delivered through tax system Mixed private and public social services Costs hidden through tax system.

(continued)

TABLE 1.1 *(continued)*

	Sweden	Japan	USA
Tax System	Universalist Individual taxation Broad base Simple High revenues Heavy on consumers Light on producers	**Traditional Family** Narrow base Progressive (historically, at least) Inefficient Low revenues High corporate taxes Low consumption taxes	Targeted Narrow base Extremely complex Highly interventionist Low revenues Low consumption taxes
Current challenges	Maintaining equality in the context of growing diversity, heavy reliance on small number of successful firms, heavy tax burden/ tax wedge.	Persistence of highly inefficient firms, high levels of distrust of political system and politicians, aging society, Fiscal crisis.	Inequality, declining confidence in government, divided society, fiscal crisis.
Adaptive Advantages	Highly educated workforce, small coherent elite, high levels of public trust in government, high levels of social and economic equality.	Very strong companies at core of the economy, strong traditions of cooperation between firms.	Highly dynamic economy and society, system rewards creative entrepreneurs and firms, incentives for success are very high.

economic model found in each individual country. The idea here is to give an overview of each system by describing the current structure and relationships between the political institutions, economy, welfare policies and tax system. I try to show how each of these subsystems function together and can be seen as parts of a whole – even if they are not necessarily efficient. The second section of each chapter addresses the how and why questions. These evolutionary narratives begin at somewhat different historical starting points for each country. A logical place when trying to understand modern democracies, it seems to me, is in the period where democratic institutions and capitalist economies were being formed. The fact is, however, that these are in very different time periods for Sweden, Japan, and the United States. Indeed, the very fact of the hugely different timings is itself an important part of this story. The final section of each chapter explores the ways in which each country is adapting to the major challenges that it faces today. We will see that while there clearly are common challenges, the fact is that there are also quite different problems in each of these countries today. This is precisely because each individual country has evolved in quite different ways. To take but one example, the challenge of dealing with fiscal crisis resulting from an aging population is a significantly different problem in the United States than it is in Japan – for the simple reason that the United States has a significantly younger population than Japan.

In sum, instead of seeing these different countries as simple variations on a specific type of political economy, this book examines how these countries function and how they are changing by treating them as complex systems which are each adapting to a somewhat common set of pressures. This does not mean that we cannot compare them. This book is fundamentally a comparative exercise. But I believe we learn a great deal more about both the individual countries and the processes and pressures that are shaping them when we understand them as distinct systems.

The aim of this book is almost certainly overly ambitious. I aim to explain both how and why three very different countries have evolved over time, and how and why they are now diverging from one another. Instead of focusing on one policy arena, I try to show how systems and their related subsystems interact and adapt to one another over time. I take evolutionary theory seriously, and consequentially also take context seriously. The analysis emphasizes the structuring role institutions have had on politics and also tries to explain why they developed these different institutions. Finally, we explore how the institutions themselves have evolved over time.

What follows will undoubtedly seem insufficiently detailed for the country expert, for no doubt in the process of compressing each country's narrative I leave out much that is important. The book will also likely be unsatisfying for many political science theorists for whom the objective of comparative politics is to generate powerful deductive and falsifiable theories. In sum, the ambition here is thus likely to be too grand for some, and too limited for others. It is my hope, however, that despite these limitations, this analysis has something to teach us, both about these three rather important and interesting countries and about how we should think about political and historical change.

2

Sweden

The Evolution of a Bumble Bee

There is much to admire about Sweden. Whereas in the late nineteenth century hundreds of thousands of Swedes were faced with the grim choice of either leaving their homeland or starving to death,[1] by the 1970s Sweden had the highest per capita income in the world. Today, not only is the country rich, but virtually everyone shares in the country's good fortune. Swedes are some of the most highly educated people in the world, take the longest vacations, have one of the best health care systems, live the longest, are exposed to very low levels of crime and enjoy one of highest standards of living in the world (see World Bank, Human Development Index). At the same time, the economy is productive, efficient and dynamic. Finally, the government is democratic, highly stable and widely regarded as a model of tolerance and progressive idealism. Swedish Prime Minister Göran Persson nicely captured the irony of Sweden's success: "Think of a bumblebee. With its overly heavy body and little wings, supposedly it should not be able to fly – but it does."[2] It is a small wonder then that a virtual army of academics, labor union officials and politicians from around the world flock to Sweden to see exactly how this surprising system has been constructed. Table 2.1 suggests some of the reasons why.

In recent years, however, some people have come to believe that Sweden's golden era is over; it was great while it lasted, they argue, but such a system cannot survive in a globalized and increasingly competitive world. Just as

---

[1] Between 1840 and 1930, about 1.3 million Swedes emigrated, one fifth of the entire population. See *The Swedish Emigrant Institute*, http://www.utvandrarnashus.se/eng/. See also Stefan de Vylder, "The Rise and Fall of the Swedish Model," Human Development Reports, UNDPR, Background Papers, 1996, and Occasional paper 26 for an introduction to the background of Swedish political economy.

[2] Opening address to party conference, March 10, 2000.

TABLE 2.1. *Sweden: Social and Economic Data and World Ranking*

	Figure	World Rank
Tax as % GDP (2005)	50.7	1 (highest)
Public Spending as % GDP (2006)	54.3	1 (highest)
Social Spending as % GDP (2003)	35.1	1 (highest)
Public Spending on Education as % GDP (all levels)	6.5	2 (from highest)
Global Competitiveness Rank		3 (from highest)
R + D per capita (US $)	1112	1 (highest)
Employment rate (2006)	74.5	6 (from highest)
Internet users per 1,000 inhabitants	320	3 (from highest)
Gini Index	2.52	1 (most equal)
Human Development Index (World Bank, 2005)	.956	6 (from highest)
Life expectancy (2005)	80.6	6 (from highest)
Paid maternity + parental leave (weeks) (1998–2002)	78	1 (highest)
Women's employment rate (2006)	76.0	3 (from highest)
Gender wage gap (%) (2004)	14.8	6 (from lowest)
Poverty Rate	6.5	3 (from lowest)
Infant mortality rate per 1000	3.7	4 (from lowest)

Sources: Adema, Willem, and Maxime Ladaique. 2005. "Net Social Expenditure, 2005 Edition: More Comprehensive Measures of Social Support." In OECD Social Employment and Migration Working Papers No. 29. Paris: OECD Publishing; Dept. of Economic Statistics. 2004. *Statistics Sweden.* Stockholm; OECD. 2001. *Society at a Glance and Social Expenditure Database.* Paris: OECD Publishing; OECD. 2006. *Revenue Statistics.* Paris: OECD Publishing; World Economic Forum. 2004. "Global Competitiveness Index."; Jordan, Jason E. 2006. Who is in? Who is out?: Inclusion and exclusion in Western welfare states. Ph.D. Dissertation, Department of Political Science, University of Colorado at Boulder, Boulder.; OECD. 2007. "Source OECD National Accounts Statistics."; OECD. 2007. "Population and Labour Force Statistics."; OECD. 2007. "Health Data"; OECD. 2006. Society at a Glance. Paris: OECD Publishing; Clearinghouse on International Developments in Child, Youth and Family Policies, Columbia University. Table 1 Maternity, Paternity, and Parental Leaves in the OECD Countries 1998–2002 [cited. Available from http://www.childpolicyintl.org/issuebrief/issuebrief5table1.pdf.]

the Swedish Prime Minister must now have a personal bodyguard, so too must the Swedish political economy adapt to the realities of global competition and "fall into line." Sweden could be egalitarian *and* economically competitive only as long as it remained an isolated country near the North Pole. But now that the world has begun to shrink, many believe that Sweden will be forced to abandon its exceptionalism, cut taxes, roll back its welfare state and accept the huge social and economic inequalities that globalization seems to inevitably bring in its wake.

This chapter will demonstrate that these dire predictions are wrong. I do not suggest that we find no changes in Sweden – or that Sweden has not had to adapt to an increasingly integrated world economy. Quite the contrary, the evidence suggests that Sweden, and the Swedish model more broadly, has evolved and changed in important ways since it was first heralded as "the middle way" between free-market capitalism and state-dominated socialism (Childs 1974). Indeed, Sweden is aggressively adapting to the realities of the twenty-first century world economy. To the surprise of many, however, it appears that the large public sector and extensive welfare state in fact offer the Swedes unique competitive advantages in this increasingly open and competitive world.

In the following pages, I will argue that Sweden's political and economic success is best understood as the result of a number of contingent factors that produced a kind of *symbiosis* between labor, business and the state.[3] Whereas in most capitalist democracies, these three interests are quite separate and often in conflict with one another, in Sweden (for several decades at least) they developed interdependent relationships in which each grew and prospered. These relationships engendered social trust throughout the system, which, in turn, has increased the willingness of both capital and labor to adjust to changing political and economic conditions. The benefits of this system have, importantly, been distributed remarkably fairly, which has also contributed to the willingness and ability of economic and political actors to compromise, cooperate and adapt.

Several factors contributed to these outcomes. First, Swedish capitalism developed rather late, at least compared to several of its Anglo-European competitors. As Gershenkron argued, late development led to both capital and labor being highly concentrated early in the twentieth century (see also, Shonfield 1965). Second, early in the twentieth century the ruling landed elite foresaw that the forces of democratization could not be kept at bay forever. They, therefore, tried to protect their interests by building an electoral/political system that insured that no political party could seize the reigns of government without building coalitions between themselves and other parties. The system that emerged was a kind of Swedish 'checks and balances' which, as we shall see, had very different consequences than those instituted over a hundred years earlier in the United States. Third, for rather specific historically contingent reasons, a *symbiotic* relationship developed

---

[3] Symbiogenesis, the theory made most famous by Lynn Margolis and Dorian Sagan, argues that evolution can occur through cooperation between individuals or populations. The point is not only that organisms can be co-dependent, but that over time, they can co-evolve. "Far from leaving microorganisms behind on an evolutionary ladder, we more complex creatures are both surrounded by them and composed of them. New knowledge of biology alters our view of evolution as a chronic, bloody competition among individuals and species. Life did not take over the globe by combat, but by networking. Life forms multiplied and grew more complex by co-opting others, not just by killing them" (Margulis and Sagan 1993: 18).

between Swedish capital and labor. Late and rapid economic development contributed to the evolution of a highly concentrated capital and labor organization which consequently facilitated the development of a corporatist system dominated by an increasingly self-confident Social Democratic elite who came to view the political economy as something of an engineering problem. This elite was committed to building a rich and egalitarian society and fundamentally understood that these goals required large, successful and internationally oriented corporations (Pontusson 1986; Steinmo 1988). Fourth, the early positive experiences with industrial and economic cooperation, together with Sweden's good fortune in being able to stay neutral during two world wars, allowed the economy to blossom on the one hand, and the beliefs in cooperation and equality to deepen on the other. As a consequence, a system of increasing returns developed in which political and economic compromise was reinforced and the major players in the political economy came to believe that economic change and flexibility were in their individual and collective self-interest (Hancock 1972; Swenson 2002). In this system the Social Democrats used tax policies and public spending as a mechanism to facilitate *both* economic change and economic equality (Elvander 1972; Norr et al. 1959).

In more recent years, Sweden has struggled to maintain its highly egalitarian system and its high rates of productivity in the face of intense international competition and an increasingly diverse domestic polity. As we shall see, demands from labor unions intensified at the same time as competition from newly developing nations grew. Ultimately these competing forces led to a breakdown in the "corporatist" system that had been built up over the past 40 years. Constitutional changes instituted in the mid-1970s led to a realignment of political strategies from both the left and the right. The result was increased acrimony and a resistance to engaging in the kind of compromise that had characterized the Swedish political economy for many years. Nevertheless, it is important to recognize that the large welfare state and the tax system that supports it remained intact and is broadly supported by almost all-important political and economic actors in the system today. Even after the Conservative Party (Moderaterna) took up the reigns of government, the commitment to a relatively equal society remains solidly in place.

This chapter follows a rather simple plan. The chapter opens with a description of Sweden's political economic system. A key argument of this book is that social welfare policies, tax structures and political economies are each part of a *system*. However, this is not a simple descriptive task: each of these countries has enormously complicated social welfare rules, tax laws and economic structures. Hence, although the descriptions below may seem overly simplified for the Swedish, Japanese, or American public policy specialist, it is my intention to step back from the details and attempt to describe and understand each country as a system that can then be usefully compared to others. Sweden has the largest welfare state, the heaviest tax burden, the highest level of union membership and one of the most highly concentrated political economies in the democratic world. I argue that concentration of political and economic power in Sweden is key to understanding how and why this country developed its expansive and universalistic welfare state. In other words, the political, economic and social policy systems *co-evolved* to build one of the most highly successful societies in the world. Before showing how this system evolved, however, I provide an overview of the most distinctive features of the system today. We first examine the "universalistic" welfare state and the tax system that sustains it. We then turn to a discussion of Sweden's "neo-corporatist" decision-making model. In this discussion we explore the inter-relationships between Sweden's economic structure and its political institutions. Having described the system, I present an historical narrative that aims to describe how this unique system evolved over time. Finally, the chapter ends with an examination of how the Swedish system is adapting to the economic, demographic and social pressures it faces early in the twenty-first century.

PART I

A UNIVERSALIST WELFARE STATE

Although most people focus on the high levels of social spending and the heavy tax burden in Sweden, it is essential to understand that the key distinction between this country and most other welfare states is not its size, but its universalism. To be sure, this is not a perfectly universal system, but as we shall see in this and the following chapters, the basic principles underlying this system are quite different from the other countries in this study. The keystone of this system is that rather than attempting to identify the poorest, most needy or most deserving families or individuals in society and then target social spending or tax breaks on them, *the Swedish social welfare system extracts heavy taxes and showers extensive benefits on virtually all citizens regardless of their social or economic circumstances.* In other words, everyone benefits and everyone pays.

Indeed, the very terms "welfare" and "welfare state" have different meanings and associations in Sweden than in many other countries, especially the United States. Whereas in the United States, "welfare" has a negative connotation and implies means tested poverty programs designed for the poor, in Sweden, 'Social Welfare' has a positive connotation and suggests to most citizens a whole range of public programs from free public health care to public education. It may surprise Americans to learn that the kinds of programs that are typically considered "welfare" in the United States, such as Food Stamps, Aid to Families with Dependent Children (AFDC) or Temporary Assistance to Needy Families (TANF), public housing projects, etc., are actually quite limited in Sweden. In fact, means tested programs are relatively small when compared to programs that benefit all citizens regardless of income. Total social protection spending constitutes 31 percent of GNP. But 93.7 percent of this money is distributed to citizens regardless of their income. In 2000 Sweden gave a smaller share of its social transfers to the poor than any other OECD nation (Tanzi and Schuknecht 2000: 96). According to the Central Statistics Bureau, of the 695 billion kronor (30.7% of GNP) spent on various forms of social help, 663 billion was distributed irrespective of recipient's income. Only 30 billion kronor (1.3% of GNP) of social help were means tested.[4] What this signifies in common sense terms is that the vast majority of social spending is given out to citizens with no regard to their economic situation. Thus, for example, the richest family in Sweden receives the exact same amount in standard government child support as an unemployed single mother. Clearly not all social benefits are distributed in exactly this "egalitarian" way,[5] but most social benefits are understood to be a type of social insurance rather than a "welfare" payment in the American sense of the term.

Table 2.2 shows the redistributive effects of taxes and social spending at different income levels in 2007. These data were calculated from actual taxpayer files allowing us to have the most accurate and current picture possible of the total redistributive effects of public social welfare spending and taxation in Sweden. As we can see, the total effect is quite redistributive indeed, individuals with average market incomes between 1/3 and 1/2 of median see their incomes increased from 37,577 kronor a year to 72,732 kronor a

---

[4] The largest categories of social spending of GNP were Health Care (9.0 percent), Disability (3.8 percent), support for the aged (11.3 percent); family support (2.9 percent), unemployment (1.7 percent). These figures include both direct cash subsidies and "in kind" benefits. See SCB Statistiska Centralbyrån, *Total utgifter för sociala förmåner per function.*, http:/www.scb.se.

[5] Though they pale in fiscal terms when compared to the "universal" (non-means-tested) programs, there are still a number of programs in Sweden that may require a means test, including: housing allowances, social assistance, transportation allowances for disabled persons, disability pensions, disability care, active labor market measures, and care for the elderly (in Swedish: bostadsbidrag, socialtjänst, färdtjänst, förtidspension, handikappomsorg, arbetsförmedling, äldreomsorg).

TABLE 2.2. *Distribution of Income and Benefits, minus taxes. Sweden, 2007*
Age groups 20 – 65 only (Swedish Kronor, annual incomes)

	1/3*Med. to 1/2*Med.	1/2*Med. to Med.	Med. to 3/2*Med.	3/2*Med. to 2*Med.	Above 2*Median
Market Income	37.577	103.594	200.271	290.154	529.592
Retirement Benefits	6.507	8.015	9.472	9.622	16.116
Child/Family Allowances	6.785	9.081	4.566	1.908	937
Unemployment Comp.	5.003	8.336	5.519	3.633	1.698
Sick Pay	1.390	6.252	6.059	5.576	3.897
Disability Pay	10.434	16.163	14.618	6.969	4.026
Maternity Pay	7.006	9.511	4.721	2.701	1.246
Means-Tested Benefits	5.734	4.110	2.160	455	133
Total public transfers*	48.109	66.506	55.020	37.776	35.118
Total Gross Income	85.339	169.434	254.307	326.092	560.856
Income Tax	12.607	35.728	61.831	90.764	183.336
Disposable Income	72.732	133.706	192.476	235.328	377.520
Efective Tax-rate	14.8	21.0	24.3	27.5	32.7

Note: Categories refer to averaged income between income groups. Above 2x means all incomes over two times median income averaged. income the median refers to the equivalized household disposible income = household disposible income / sqrt (#household members). *Includes "other," special transfers of various types.

Sources: LINDA data, Statistics Sweden. Computations made by Daniel Hallberg, Institute for Futures Studies, Stockholm. For a detailed description of LINDA, see Edin, P.-A., and P. Frediksson (2000): "LINDA Longitudinal Individual Data for Sweden," Working paper 19, Department of Economics, Uppsala University."

year. Those with twice the average market income (529,592 kronor) have final disposable incomes reduced to 377,520 kronor a year.[6] In short, those near the bottom of the income distribution have their real incomes nearly doubled and those who have twice-average earnings see their final incomes reduced by approximately one third. One should note, however, that these figures do not include 'in kind' benefits, for example the value of free public education, the imputed costs of medical care, or for that matter the emotional security of knowing that even if you become sick and/or old you will most likely be able to maintain a comfortable middle class lifestyle (and take five weeks' vacation).

[6] To be more precise, this category represents the average of the group of individuals that belong to households with at least twice the median of Household equivilized income. I would like to thank Daniel Hallberg from the Institute for Future Studies, Stockholm, Sweden for help assembling this data.

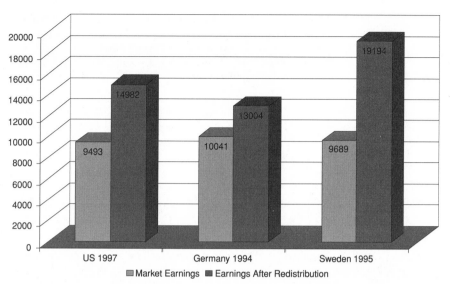

FIGURE 2.1. Income of Median Single Mothers, 1995 US Dollars (PPP). *Source:* Compiled from Luxembourg Income Study. 1998. "Wave IV."

Another way to think of the redistributive effects of the Swedish system is to look at how taxes and benefits add up (see Table 2.2). I include a number of figures and tables that compare countries in this regard in this book, but Figure 2.1 is especially illustrative. If we look at the income effects of taxes and public spending on median income single mothers (a fairly common target for social welfare state, it seems to me) we find that they do substantially better in Sweden than in either the United States or Germany, earning only 5 percent less than median income of all families in the country (we have no comparable data for Japan).

Indeed, as Joakim Palme points out, "The Swedish model is generally associated with low poverty levels, a low level of inequality, a high employment rate, a high level of employment among women, and a situation in which disadvantaged groups such as single mothers and people with disabilities are more likely than in other countries to live on terms that are not very different from those enjoyed by the majority of the population" (Palme 2003a: 1).

One way to understand how a universalist system can have such redistributive effects is to consider the following highly simplified model. Imagine a society with three families (or income groups for that matter). Now imagine a system that taxes each of these families or groups at exactly the same 30 percent rate (i.e., a genuine "flat tax") and then spends the revenues generated by these taxes exactly equally on each of the families or groups.

TABLE 2.3. *The Redistributive Effects of Flat Taxes and Universal Benefits*

Pre-Tax Income	Tax Rate 30%	After Tax Income	Benefit per Individual	Final Income
10,000	3,000	7,000	16,000	23,000
50,000	15,000	35,000	16,000	51,000
100,000	30,000	70,000	16,000	86,000

* 3,000 + 15,000 + 30,000 = 48,000 / 3 = 16,000.
Income Ratio before taxes and benefits 1 to 10 (10,000 to 100,000).
Income Ration after taxes and benefits 1 to 3.7 (23,000 to 86,000).

Table 2.3 shows the consequences would be far more redistributive than one would likely expect. A perfectly flat tax and a perfectly universal benefit system would change the real distribution of income in this hypothetical society from the richest being ten times richer than the poorest to a system where the richest are only 3.7 times richer than the poorest in our society. In point of fact, this system may well be more redistributive than the Swedish because even Sweden does not have perfectly equal distribution of benefits.[7]

Fiscal Churning

It is important to understand (as most Swedes implicitly do) that the high rate of taxation in Sweden is something of a fiscal illusion. The numbers cited here and elsewhere indicate that the government collects over 50 percent of GDP in taxes, but this figure masks the fact that much of these taxes are a product of "fiscal churning." (See Table, 2.4). Fiscal churning occurs when the government pays out a benefit to citizens but then taxes that benefit (Tanzi and Schuknecht 2000). In Sweden, in principle at least, all earned income is taxed equally - even when that income is derived from state benefits.[8] To take but one example, old age social security benefits can be quite generous, but they are also heavily taxed. The logic to this is that all citizens should pay the same tax rates, regardless of the source of that income. Why, for example, should an older citizen pay lower taxes on

[7] There are many reasons for this: family sizes, differential abilities to take advantage of specific socialized benefits and because some benefits are likely to be more readily accessed by those with higher levels of income and/or education (such as free higher education). For a broader discussion of this system, see (Åberg 1989).

[8] There are currently three rates of tax on personal income in Sweden: Capital income is taxed at a flat 30 percent rate. See Swedish Tax Agency 2008 "Taxes in Sweden 2008", URL: http://www.skatteverket.se/download/18.69ef368911e1304a625800017687/10409.pdf, and Skatteverket 2008: Skatter I Sverige 2008. Skattestatistisk Arsbook. URL: http://www.skatteverket.se/download/18.69ef368911e1304a62580001239/15211.pdf.

TABLE 2.4. *Level of Fiscal Churning in Selected Industrial Countries (percent)*

Country/Year	Churning as % of Income Taxes and Transfers	Government Expenditure as % of GDP	Public Expenditures Without Churning
United States 1995	9.0	32.9	23.9
Japan 1994	11.6	34.4	22.8
Germany 1994	15.7	48.9	33.2
Italy 1993	22.7	57.4	34.7
Denmark 1994	28.0	59.3	31.3
Finland 1995	15.5	57.9	42.4
Netherlands 1994	21.1	52.8	31.7
Sweden 1994	*34.2*	*68.3*	*34.1*
OECD Average	18.2	50.0	31.8

Source: Tanzi, Vito, and Ludger Schuknecht. 2000. *Public spending in the 20th century: a global perspective.* Cambridge, UK; New York: Cambridge University Press.

their income than their working child – just because their income is derived from a pension and/or social security? Table 2.4 shows the effects of fiscal churning in several OECD nations. As we can see, Sweden's high levels of spending are not nearly as high as is often thought.

As noted, Swedish citizens are at least implicitly aware of this churning, although certainly few have heard of this economic concept. Survey evidence has demonstrated clearly over the years that Swedish citizens continue to support social spending, even when they think their taxes are too high (Svallfors 1996, 2003; Holmberg and Weibull 2008). We will see the contrast between the Swedish and American systems more clearly when we examine the latter in detail, but it may be useful to draw a brief contrast already here: Whereas the Swedish system attempts to universalize taxes and benefits, the American system targets them on particular groups and constituencies. In other words, instead of distributing benefits widely and taxing them equally, as is done in Sweden, American government keeps direct public spending and tax levels low by offering individuals and companies tax deductions and credits.

Given Sweden's very heavy tax burden, it would seem likely that there would be significant opposition to these taxes. The simple fact is that there is not. Public opinion polls show no strong pressure for tax cuts and none of the major political parties has offered significant cuts in the tax burden in their national platform.[9] How can this be? Are Swedes delusional? Or have they

[9] Only five percent of Swedish voters identified "Taxes" in response to the following question in 2007: "Which issue(s) or societal problems is/are the most important in Sweden today?" (Holmberg and Weibull 2008: 24).

been lulled into what columnist David Brooks has called a "delicious life," unaware that these taxes will ruin their country (Brooks 2005)? Perhaps they have been lulled, but a better explanation is that Swedes are tolerant of their heavy taxes because they feel taxes are applied fairly (Hadenius 1985; Laurin 1986). Even while the average Swede pays nearly fifty percent of income in taxes, considering all taxes combined, very few people fill out a year-end tax declaration. Why? Because the tax system is so simple that unless the individual has extraordinary income other than salary and bank interest, the taxes are calculated monthly by the employer and by their banking institutions. Whereas tens of millions of American taxpayers find it necessary to consult a professional tax advisor because the United States tax code is so complicated, the majority of Swedes receive their annual tax declaration from the revenue authorities in a text message on their mobile phone. If the individual does not have unusual or special circumstances, taxes for the year are completed simply by pressing 'reply' on the their mobile phone (Swedish Tax Agency, 2008). Given this system, there are very few opportunities to cheat and most people seem to accept that they must pay in order to receive the substantial benefits they each receive (Svallfors 1996).

In sum, the Swedish tax and social welfare system is quite distinctive and as we will see in the other chapters of this book, quite different from any other system we examine here. Taxes and public spending are extremely high, to be sure. But there is a widespread sense among Swedes that the system is fair. This is, in part, because virtually everyone pays into the system and virtually everyone can directly see the benefits they receive from the state.[10] It may drive the small number of Swedish neo-liberals crazy, but apparently most people don't mind paying so much in taxes - at least as long as what they pay continues to support some of the world's best public education, child care, maternity leave, medical care and vacation pay and as long as the economy continues to prosper.

The Social-Liberal Economy

"Sweden, for instance, is today very much less socialistically organized than Great Britain or Austria, though Sweden is commonly regarded as much more socialistic" Friedrich A. Hayek, Preface to the 1976 edition of The Road to Serfdom.[11]

---

[10] It appears, in short, that the Swedes have partially solved Down's classic dilemma, where citizens in democracy do not directly feel the benefits of public spending (clean air, etc.) but do directly feel the costs of government spending (in their paychecks). (See Downs 1960).

[11] Hayek does argue, however, that the institutions of the welfare state are a new kind of "imperfect" socialism whose "ultimate outcome tends to be very much the same" (Hayek 2007).

Some non-Swedes may find it surprising that the country is not, and has never been, a "socialist" system. Though the dominant political party, the *"Social Democraterna,"* often refers to itself as "Socialist," the government *does not* play an active role in managing or directing the private economy. I refer to the Swedish political economy as "social-liberal" in order to try to describe the unusual system that combines enormous social protection for the individual with a remarkably liberal economy. Sweden historically has had very low levels of public ownership (SOU 1977; Södersten 1987; Steinmo 1993), has suffered a less onerous regulatory burden (Lindquist 1980), and maintains significantly more flexibility in terms of the hiring and firing of employees when compared with companies in most other capitalist countries (Swenson 2002; Davidsson 2008).[12] Indeed, *Forbes* magazine described it as a "booming economy bubbling with entrepreneurial activity" (Heller 2001) and the World Economic Forum consistently ranks it as one of the most competitive economies in the world and one of the most attractive sites for international investment (Lopez-Claros 2005).

I do not mean to suggest that Swedish public policy does not effect, or is somehow unrelated to, the private economy. Neither Sweden nor any other country in the world has a truly *free market*. But rather than attempt to control or direct the private economy, public policies have often been designed to coordinate with and effectively support the private economy. Whereas Americans and Brits in particular often see government and the private sector as natural enemies, the Swedes have a system where they have been more likely to refer to each other as partners. To be sure, there have been significant and important changes in business-state relations over the past twenty years in particular. Indeed, it is probably less cooperative today with the Conservative Party holding the reigns of government than it used to be when the Social Democrats were in power. But in general we can say that the Swedes have developed tax and social policies that have generated enormous revenue *and* have minimized the unintended distortions, which one might expect from a country with such heavy taxes and social spending. Taken together, this system has contributed to economic growth *and* income equalization.[13]

---

[12] In Europe, only Britain and Denmark offer greater labor market flexibility than Sweden (See Davidsson 2007).

[13] Many economists argue that taxation by definition creates economic distortions and, logically then, the higher the tax level the greater the distortion. What is meant here is that the Swedes have built a tax system that is quite successful at minimizing the distortions given the level of revenue generated.

Joseph Stiglitz argues similarly:

Yet Sweden and the other Scandinavian countries have shown that there is an alternative way to cope with globalization. These countries are highly integrated into the global economy; but they are highly successful economies that still provide strong social protections and make high levels of investments in people. They have been successful in part because of these policies, not in spite of them. Full employment and strong safety nets enable individuals to undertake more risk (with the commensurate high rewards) without unduly worrying about the downside of failure. (Stiglitz 2006)

Though a few movie producers, popular writers and sport stars left the country due to the high tax rates on their income and wealth, in the 1960s and 1970s capitalists and large companies were offered such generous tax expenditures that they generally pay very little taxes in fact.[14] Contrary to many people's expectations, it was never true that Sweden used taxes to directly redistribute income between social classes. Quite the contrary, to the extent that the tax system has redistributed income it has been *from wage earners to capitalists* (Steinmo 1993).

Economic Concentration

In the final section of this chapter we will explore how this system is changing, but it is important to recognize here that for most of the twentieth century successive Social Democratic governments have pushed policies that have significantly benefited large companies and unions (See Table 2.5). The most important of these has been tax policies that have helped concentrate capital and unemployment insurance policies that have aided in the union's ability to attract members. Because these policies worked to concentrate labor and capital, this in turn, has made it easier for the organization representing these interests to meet, find common interests and cooperate effectively.

The other side of the concentration coin is the remarkable extent to which a relatively small number of industrial firms and their owners have dominated the Swedish economy (Israel 1978). Here too we see significant changes in recent years. But there can be no doubt that capital has been controlled by a relatively small number of individuals and firms who were

---

[14] Sweden was widely known around the world for possessing "an arsenal of revenue devices" (Norr et al. 1959), designed to lower the costs of capital, concentrate resources, encourage domestic investment in plants and machinery, and, thus, keep the Swedish economy competitive and dynamic. In fact, tax write-offs available to companies and capital were so generous that the Swedish tax authorities almost never bothered to audit large companies, knowing that these companies had easy access to more write-offs than they generally took advantage of (See also Steinmo 1984).

TABLE 2.5. *Union Density and Collective Bargaining*

	Percent of Workforce Who are Union Members		Percent of Workforce Covered Under Collective Bargaining Agreements	
	1980	2000	1980	2000
Sweden	80%	79%	80%	90%
Japan	31%	22%	25%	14%
USA	22%	13%	26%	14%

Source: Pontusson, Jonas. 2005. *Inequality and prosperity: social Europe vs. liberal America.* Ithaca, N.Y.: Cornell University Press, p. 99.

key to the construction of Sweden's "Historic Compromise" (Hancock, 1972; Swenson, 2002).

One example of the kind of policies generated through industrial cooperation is the famous "Rehn-Meidner" plan. In this system, named after the two labor union economists who initially proposed it in 1951, the basic idea is that the government would pursue fiscal and monetary policies supporting full employment while maintaining open international trade in order to expose the economy to international competition. At the same time, the major trade union confederations and the main employers would negotiate national annual wage and would attempt to equalize wages across sectors in the economy. This system was explicitly intended to advantage the most successful Swedish companies (because it held wages in these firms lower than the individual unions might have been able to negotiate). On the other hand, it essentially guaranteed wage increases to employees even in sectors that were suffering economic stress because the system pushed the less competitive enterprises in Sweden out of business. The *goal* of this system was to push capital and labor resources out of underperforming economic arenas and into those areas where Sweden could gain competitive advantage. Though the government was not explicitly involved in the annual wage negotiations, its cooperation was also essential to the system because it depended on low trade barriers to insure competitive pressures on the Swedish economy and active labor market policies so that workers displaced by economic change could be retrained and relocated if necessary (Elvander 1988; Meidner 1980).

It may be impossible to disaggregate the redistributive effects of labor market institutions from the effects of specific social policies (Pontusson 2000). There can be no doubt, however, that labor market policies were enormously important in creating the egalitarian society for which Sweden became so famous.

In sum, I have called the Swedish political economy a "social-liberal" system. It is social in the sense of being the most egalitarian society in the world. It spends more on social programs and has the highest levels of taxation in the world. It is liberal in that state ownership has been quite limited, it is one of the world's most open economies, and the state has played a remarkably limited role in actively directing the private economy.[15] The key features of the Swedish model have been the remarkable levels of cooperation between capital and labor (called 'social partners' in Sweden), the high degree of economic concentration, the high levels of unionization and its large universalist welfare state. Sweden had both the highest level of union membership in the world, the highest percentage of workers covered by collective agreements and the lowest strike levels in Europe. Finally, Sweden is one of the most highly concentrated private economies in the world, it is home to several of the world's largest and most successful international corporations and for most of the post-war period it has had extremely low taxes on capital and profits (Israel 1978; Steinmo 1984, 1988).

In the following section we examine how this system came about. As previously noted, I develop what biologist Ernst Mayer calls an historical narrative that attempts to give an evolutionary account of Swedish political and economic development. As such, this narrative emphasizes the *co-evolution* of political and economic development, how the unique relationship between the major actors in this political economy can be seen as an *emergent* phenomenon and, finally, the role that *contingency* has played at several junctures in this development. It does seem to be rather like a bumblebee. In the next section we will see how it learned to fly.

PART II

THE EVOLUTION OF THE SWEDISH MODEL

Sweden has long been known for its "Politics of Compromise" (Rustow 1955). But it is important to see that this has not always been so. Indeed, many saw Sweden as a particularly conflictual political economy at the beginning of the century. In the following analysis we will see a prime example of the fate of unintended consequences resulting in the evolution of

---

[15] The Japanese government has a more limited welfare state and much lower tax burdens, but the government has been far more interventionist in private economic decision-making than have the Swedes. Indeed, if we consider the tax system as economic intervention, by many measures, one can argue that the American system is more interventionist than the Swedish (Steinmo 1993).

a symbiotic relationship between social interests that in most countries are bitter antagonists. This story is one of contingency and, in Sweden's case, good fortune.

Our evolutionary story begins at the end of the nineteenth century. This was a period of enormous change throughout the modernizing world, but particularly so for Sweden where industrialization began in earnest at this time. Three basic facts then are profoundly important for understanding Sweden's particular developmental path: First, in terms of its industrial and political modernization, Sweden was a "late developer" (Gershenkron 1962). As a result, its social, economic and political development were in a sense compressed in time when compared to other industrializing and democratizing nations of Europe and America. Second, Sweden was (and is) a very large resource-rich country with a small but homogenous population. Thus, on the one hand, there was significant demand for Swedish commodities and products from other countries further along this path, but at the same time Sweden was able to escape many of the internal political disputes that challenged many other nations as they moved through their 'Great Transformation' (Heckscher and Heckscher 1954). Finally, Sweden's geographic position north of the main European landmass, but closely connected to it by easy transport across the Baltic, allowed it to engage in active commerce with its neighbors while allowing it to escape some of the entanglements and eventually wars that soon plagued the rest of the continent.

In many ways Sweden was similar to several other European states as the industrial revolution took off. It was poor, mostly agricultural and essentially peripheral to the major centers of economic and political power of Britain, Holland, France and Germany. In Sweden, as in many other countries in the nineteenth century, changes in food supply and transportation contributed to a massive population explosion – from 2.5 million in 1815 to 5.1 million in 1900 – despite the emigration of nearly one million people, mostly to America (Hadenius 1966: 28).[16] But in the space of less than half a century,

---

[16] They left for several reasons: First, Sweden had experienced a huge population expansion in the previous 100 years (nearly doubling), which resulted in the peasant's land holdings being increasingly divided into ever smaller and smaller shares. By the mid 19th century, many parcels had simply become too small to sustain the large families that were common in the day. Secondly, the expansion of agriculture in the Americas drove food prices down, making it ever more difficult to survive in small-scale farming. Finally, the United States was opening huge tracts of land for homesteading – and even Swedes who could neither read nor speak English could get high quality arable land for free – if only they could make it across the sea. The more Swedes who immigrated, of course, the easier it became for other family members to follow. The novel *The Emigrants*, by Vilhelm Moberg, offers a fascinating and quite accurate rendition of this history (Moberg 1951, 1975).

TABLE 2.6. *GDP Per Capita, Sweden. Market Prices (Index, 1930 = 100)*

1870	1880	1890	1900	1910	1920
31	34.7	38.0	50.2	62.7	75.3

Source: Krantz, Olle, and Lennart Schön. 2007. *Swedish Historical National Accounts 1800–2000*. Vol. 41. Stockolm: Almqvist and Wicksell, table 4.

the country grew from this poor agricultural monarchy on the periphery of Europe to an industrializing democratic nation that had developed very significant industrial strengths. Heckscher remarks in his classic text, *An Economic History of Sweden* (1954), that, "[t]he first thing to be noted in this hasty survey of the basic characteristics of the development of this period, is the international orientation of the modern Swedish economy" (Heckscher and Heckscher 1954: 209).

Compared to western and central Europe, then, the country's economic development began late and when industrial take-off finally began in the later part of the nineteenth century, it was both extremely rapid and concentrated on key industries where Sweden could gain some comparative advantage. "For Sweden, it was especially important that the change to more 'capitalistic' methods of production created a tremendous demand for iron, one of the commodities Sweden was particularly fitted to produce" (ibid, p. 213). Capital and technology flowed into Sweden as it attempted to catch up to Europe at the same time that significant resources were invested in both human resources and communications technologies. GDP per capita, while virtually stagnant for most of the nineteenth century, exploded at century's end, nearly doubling in only twenty years (see Table 2.6).

Sweden, it turned out, was relatively advantaged in this stage of European industrial development by the fact that it had plentiful iron resources as well massive forests which could be used for making coal and coke. Thus peasants not only moved to the United States, but many also moved to the iron and coke mining towns and eventually to the cities to find work in an economy that was accelerating as the country developed the ability to produce steel for the booming world economy (Koblik 1975). As the industry became increasingly successful, the demand for workers also grew. This was particularly marked during World War I, at which time Sweden found itself in the fortunate position of being able to provide key ingredients for war making without having to suffer the hardships of war itself. Being at the northern periphery of Europe, it was able to escape the bitter entanglements that dragged most European countries into war, remaining neutral throughout. This fact had important political as well as economic consequences.[17]

In sum, Swedish industry emerged at a particular moment in world history that offered Sweden specific advantages. No one planned this outcome. And while certainly one can find individual actors pursuing self-interests and maximizing profits, it is also a story of adaptation and emergence.

The Electoral Origins of the Politics of Compromise

Though universal suffrage was not introduced until 1921 (1909 for men) the foundations of Sweden's particular form of political democracy were laid much earlier. Rapid industrial expansion brought together huge numbers of a new working class in unfamiliar and often hostile living conditions. As a consequence, it was relatively easy to mobilize the new working class. The old guild system had been broken down in mid-century and the transformation of the economy helped create a more coherent working class identity, one relatively unencumbered by the multiple divisions found in the United Kingdom. Swedes were a relatively homogeneous people, thus the kinds of ethnic, linguistic and cultural divisions that could work to undermine a working class identity were minimal here as well. Though in Sweden, as in all industrializing countries, there were serious efforts on the part of employers to prevent the working class from organizing itself and thus initiating lock-outs, strike breakers and even violence. The *Landsorganisationen (LO)* the National Labor Organization was formed in 1898 after only two decades of trade union activity and it quickly grew to be a dominant force in economic and political life.[18] Membership in LO unions grew rapidly from 43,575 members in 1900 to 186,226 in 1907 (Hadenius et al. 1967: Table 8 A), as did their demands for better wages and working conditions. The first national strike called in 1909 proved to be a defeat for the unions.[19]

Clearly the writing was on the wall. Even if employers were able to win this particular battle, given the enormous changes ongoing in the Swedish economy and the broader intellectual shifts occurring throughout the modernizing world, no one doubted that the working class would continue to

---

[17] See (Berman 1998) for a detailed and fascinating analysis of the evolution of Social Democratic ideas during this period.

[18] Interestingly, the Swedish Employers Federation *(SAF)* only organized four years after the LO and mostly in response to labor's increased activity (Heckscher and Heckscher 1954: 235).

[19] As Bo Stråth points out, "When the threat of the poor en masse was transformed into a threat of a labour shortage due to emigration, the problem of integration of the lower classes became quite different in Sweden than in Bismarck's Germany" (Stråth 1996: 75).

grow, nor that they would eventually be given the right to vote (Verney 1957). Sweden was clearly on the cusp of massive political change and the only real questions were how would this change be structured, and for the old ruling class at least, how could they best protect their interests from the masses?[20] Certainly the franchise would have to be extended and ultimately universal manhood suffrage would inevitably arrive. Like elsewhere, the right to vote was slowly being extended to different groups (property holders, veterans, etc.), but as the vote was to be extended to the masses, the traditional elite came to worry that they would be a minority in any specific electoral district and thus could find themselves totally powerless in very short order. As Verney shows, the conservatives fully understood this problem and therefore instituted a proportional representation electoral system in order to provide what was called a "conservative guarantee" against working class dominance (Verney 1957; Castles 1978: 115). The Liberal Party, which represented mostly middle class interests, bought into this idea and took the reigns of government after the next election, but the young Social Democratic Party (SAP) "categorically" argued that the bill was "unacceptable" because it was a trick design to keep the rich in power.[21] Luckily, as we shall see, the Social Democrats were simply outvoted.[22]

It turned out that the move to the PR system had consequences for the strategies of the SAP. The reform enhanced incentives for it to moderate its rhetoric and ultimately its program, but there were many bitter fights within the Left and the working class over just how moderate they should be (Berman 1998). Socialism in the traditional meaning was a concept that many were just not willing to abandon simply in order to gain electoral advantage (Tingsten 1973: 167).[23] Already in the 1911 election the SAP received 28.5 percent of the vote and by the 1921 election it increased its vote share to 36.2 percent, thereby becoming the largest single party. Though there were several shifting coalition governments for the next decade or so, by the time of the economic crisis of the early 1930s it was hard to deny that

---

[20] We will see in chapter 4 that while the timing was very different, the "Founding Fathers" of the United States Constitution faced a similar dilemma.

[21] According to Branting, the Social Democratic Party leader, the technical features of this reform would insure that 1/7th of the people possessed 90 percent of the power (Verney 1957: 164–5.)

[22] Some Social Democrats continued to fight against the PR system well into the 1920s but by the time the SAP was nearing real political power, the party elite apparently came to see the practical benefits of the system. (See Verney, 1957: 215–216; Immergut 1992a).

[23] For broader discussions of the evolution of Social Democratic ideology away from its Marxist principles see (Castles 1978; Pontusson 1992; Steinmo 1988).

the Socialists would soon become a near permanent fixture in government.[24] The great irony was that the very same "conservative guarantee" that the Socialists had once decried now became a "Social Democratic guarantee." Because of the very complicated rules which were designed to protect the conservatives' hold on power even if they did poorly in an election or two, all parties and interests soon had to accept the political reality that for the foreseeable future they would be dealing with a Social Democratic government – even if their electoral fortunes turned temporarily sour. This had obvious implications for the political parties, but in the end the more important lesson was being learned by organized capital and labor.

Given the particular electoral rules on the one hand and the reality of the evolving Swedish economic and thereby social structure on the other, it was perfectly obvious that the Social Democrats would be the dominant party in politics for quite some time. At the same time, and for the same structural reasons, it was equally obvious that the Social Democrats would not be able to form a majority government in the Riksdag anytime in the foreseeable future. In other words, coalition governments would be necessary and, quite simply, compromise would be necessary as well.

The deal eventually hit upon was what to become known as the "Cow Deal" and was made between the SAP and the Center Party, which represented small farmers. Sweden was still very much in the midst of what Heckscher (following Polanyi, 1944) called its "Great Transformation," and small rural farmers remained a huge political and social force. The problem, of course, was that the interests of farmers and industrial workers were often deeply at odds (Weir 1989: 141). While farmers wanted protection from foreign (especially American) agricultural products, industrial workers wanted low cost imports and open trade barriers so that their products would be more competitive in international markets. The "Cow Deal" gave them both. But most importantly, it resulted in the introduction of a new unemployment insurance system called the Ghent system. Under the Ghent system labor unions themselves were given authority to manage the unemployment insurance program.[25] Both Social Democrats and union officials understood that if the unions could control the system it would work to build union membership and prevent unemployed workers from being used

---

[24] Between March 30, 1917 and September 24, 1932, Sweden had ten different coalition governments. The SAP participated in four of them. From September 1932 the Social Democrats were the dominant party in every government (except for four months in 1936) until October 1976.

[25] Rather bizarrely, then, one of the few "social" programs in Sweden that is *not* universal is unemployment insurance.

as strike breakers, as was commonly the case up to that point (Rothstein 1992: 47–49).[26] Though the insured did not necessarily have to be a union member to buy unemployment insurance, the fact that the very same people who registered you for unemployment insurance also registered you for union membership in fact provided a powerful recruiting tool for the unions.

Saltsjöbad – The Historic Compromise

In the first decades of the twentieth century Sweden had one of the most conflictual labor markets in the world (Korpi and Shalev 1979). As unions were mobilizing the workforce, capital was becoming more highly concentrated and better organized. The direct result was that the Swedish economy became the most strike prone in Europe. Fortunately for both sides, the very concentration of power eventually resulted in their ability to sit down together and negotiate.

The major breakthrough occurred in a series of meetings beginning in 1936 held at a summer hotel in *Saltsjöbad*, just outside Stockholm. These meetings eventually led to what has become known as the "Historic Compromise" between unions and employers. It is important to remember that at the beginning of this decade, Swedish labor and capital were engaged in bitter conflicts in the early 1930s. Elites on both sides of these conflicts eventually came to realize that they could fight back and forth year in and year out, but as Hjalmar Van Sydow, head of the Swedish Employer's Federation (SAF), eventually recognized, in the end, "it will end as it always did, with a new agreement" (Rothstein 2005: 170). It is unclear exactly who initiated the next round of negotiations between 1936 and 1938, but the idea was to break the cycle of conflict and instead build a new relationship.

Ultimately, capital and labor came to understand that they had common interests in increasing productivity and employment levels. Sweden, let's remember, was a large country with a relatively small and homogenous population. In stark contrast to the United States, the working class was neither divided along racial and/or ethnic lines, nor was capital divided along regional or even product lines. Indeed, it is fair to say that the very small number of people in top positions worked to facilitate compromise and helped them see that they had common interests. In short, they eventually developed a type of *symbiotic* relationship (Sapp 2003: 231–251) in which the particular mechanism was a system of cooperation over wages and

---

[26] Though of course virtually everyone signed up for the generous program, it was never mandatory, nor financed by tax dollars.

employment. From then on they would view themselves as "labor market partners" rather than antagonists.

It is interesting to note that at first leading Social Democrats were *not* in favor of the close cooperation between labor unions and big business. These were deals between capital and labor, not the state. In the end, however, the Social Democrats began to see their mutual benefit from the new system. Rothstein emphasizes the extent to which the Social Democrats were not involved in the negotiations, but "[a]fter the agreement was reached, Prime Minister Hansson stated in the Riksdag that its chief virtue was the "new spirit" that had sprung up between the parties (Lower House, 1939-01-18). The editor of the principal management-side newspaper, Axel Brunius, believed the central aspect was the "mental reorientation" that the agreement represented" (Rothstein 2005: 170).

In short, the Saltsjöbad agreement changed the political context in which the Social Democrats came to govern. Governmental policy soon came to be used to help facilitate the Historic Compromise. For example, as long as large corporations and wealthy capitalists kept their capital in productive assets, they were offered tax incentives that essentially insured that they would pay relatively low taxes. On the other hand, smaller, privately held firms shouldered much heavier tax burdens.[27] From this point forward Swedish corporate tax policy was used to squeeze capital out of smaller enterprises and into the large, internationally competitive manufacturing industries (Elvander 1972; Rodriguez 1980; Swenson 1989; Steinmo 1993; Pontusson and Swenson 1996; Rothstein and Bergström 1999: 101–109).[28]

It is important to remember that as the Swedish economy modernized and became more successful, the middle class was also growing. This point was not lost on the Social Democratic elite. If the Social Democrats were going to be able to govern over the longer run, they would have to appeal to middle class voters as well. In this light, their thinking about redistribution also evolved. Rather than fight a class war and define taxes and benefits in zero-sum ways, it made better electoral and moral sense to build on traditional visions of Sweden as an inclusive "people's home."

---

[27] For small privately-held firms and self-employed individuals, the intersection of income tax rates of over 80 percent, steep wealth taxes, and heavy mandatory social insurance charges meant that total taxes could exceed 100 percent of annual income.

[28] At the same time, Sweden maintained an open international trade policy that was explicitly aimed at forcing Swedish firms to maintain international competitiveness. These firms were, of course, precisely the firms dominated by Sweden's large centralized union organization (LO) and were also the same firms that had by now developed a working relationship with Social Democrats in classic corporatist arrangements.

Already before the beginning of World War II, a series of highly particular and contingent events offered the Social Democratic Party opportunities to build and broaden their position in Swedish politics. Sweden's size, its geographic position, natural endowments, small and relatively homogenous population, as well as the specific choices made by labor and business leaders yielded opportunities not available to leaders in other countries. At the same time, the Social Democratic elite took advantage of these opportunities to begin building a cross social class compromise that would keep them in power for almost half a century.

In sum, the foundations of Sweden's famous historical compromise are not simply the result of strong unions and left parties, foresighted employers, clever politicians, or even political institutions.[29] Instead, the particular outcome was the product of a complex interaction of interests and individuals adapting to the choices available to them in a highly contingent context. The result of which was the establishment of a set of co-dependent and symbiotic relationships that proved to be the cornerstone of what we now describe as the Swedish Model. As we shall see, future developments depended on this foundation, but they were not pre-determined by them.

War and Its Advantages

Perhaps the Swedes are just lucky: the reawakening of European hostilities and war once again provided Sweden with significant economic advantages. As in 1914, the country remained neutral during World War II and profited enormously by selling to both sides. As shows, the Social Democratic base was in many ways divided in its ideological commitments in the pre-war years and thus choosing sides could easily have split the party (Berman 1998).[30] At the same time, there were strong economic incentives to straddling the fence during this second conflict. Sweden and Germany were developing an interdependent relationship with Swedish iron ore (and later manufactured products) necessary for the German war efforts and German coal necessary for Sweden's own iron and steel industries. "Coal was regarded as the most important import good, partly because the supply of

---

[29] Recent contributions to these debates include: (Korpi 2006; Paster 2008; Rothstein 2005; Swenson 2002).

[30] Berman notes that some of the foundational ideas in Sweden's version of social democracy proved to be key to this countries rejection of fascist ideology. Even while many Swedes were clearly attracted to fascist rhetoric the more deeply embedded egalitarianism in Swedish Social Democracy helped them take a different path from their German counterparts. (See Berman 1998).

energy was of crucial importance for the ability of the engineering industry to contribute to rearmament" (Fritz and Karlsson 2003:120). Joining with the Allies, even if this had been politically possible, would have lead to Sweden suffering heavy economic losses. But whatever the consequences for the hallowed "neutral" self-image, there can be no doubt that remaining neutral once again proved to be a huge economic advantage for the country. In the context of the rapidly changing technologies driven by massive war spending, as well as by the enormous international demand for manufactured goods, Sweden was able to use its position to move up the technological ladder and become a leader in highly sophisticated engineering products rather quickly (ibid, p. 121). Moreover, when the end of hostilities came, Sweden was well positioned to export even more of these products, as the rest of Europe tried to rebuild from the wreckage of war.

An equally important consequence of Sweden's wartime experience was the tightening of the relationships between labor, capital and the state. Bo Stråth summarizes this relationship as follows:

The experience of World War II reinforced and institutionalized the compromises of the 1930s. The Swedish labor movement accepted the overall responsibility of wartime management and eventually got the credit for this by and large successful undertaking. At the institutional level the huge wartime administration was designed as an apparatus with competence and responsibility that did not lead to any substantial increase in its power and influence, rather on the contrary. At the political level the enormous resources mobilized because of the war opened up an entirely new perspective for Social Democrats. The war demonstrated that the rate of taxation, public spending, public consumption and compulsory accumulation of capital went far beyond their wildest dreams of the prewar Social Democrats. This was a lesson they would never forget. (Stråth 1996: 93–4)

When the end of war came, unlike many other capitalist states, Sweden was in a prime position to benefit from the inevitable surge in world trade. Spectacular economic expansion across the western world in the aftermath of the war disproportionately advantaged the Swedish economy. This also had the effect of confirming Swedes' beliefs in the benefits of cooperation and conciliation in the economy. Moreover, concentration of industry in the form of further centralization, or 'rationalization' as they called it, continued.[31] At the same time, exports exploded growing from 1,765 million kronor in 1945 to 5,710 in 1950 (see Table 2.7). Thus in Sweden, as in many

---

[31] By the early 1960s, the 100 largest Swedish companies produced 46 percent of value added for all industry in the country (Magnusson 2000: 214–5). For a discussion of the increasing concentration of economic power and their relationship with the three main Swedish banks (see also Magnusson 2000: 215–20).

TABLE 2.7. *Swedish Export Growth 1945 to 1960 (by sector) mill. Swedish Kr.*

Year	Agriculture	Forest Prod.	Iron (raw)	Steel	Manufactured Products	Paper Products	Total Exports
1945	96	7	28	108	432	618	1765
1950	239	36	428	349	1573	1764	5710
1955	173	196	857	713	2479	2338	8935
1960	278	80	1095	1289	4714	3204	13237

Source: Ohlsson, Lennart. 1969. *Utrikeshandeln och den ekonomiska tillväxten i Sveriga 1871–1966.* Stockholm: Almqvist och Wicksell, table B 5.

countries in Europe, employment expanded, incomes grew and consumption rose dramatically. By the mid-1950s, the two biggest problems facing the economy were an *employment* crisis (e.g., too many jobs and not enough employees) and the corollary problem of expanding inflation.

Crucially, in the context of these twin problems Sweden made three fundamentally important choices that dramatically structured the future evolution of its political economy. First, it embraced the famous "Rehn Meidner" labor market model, in which unions and employers set national wage deals that explicitly and intentionally worked to squeeze out companies and sectors that could not afford to pay higher wages.[32] Second, the Social Democrats re-introduced consumption taxation even while there was no immediate fiscal pressure on the Treasury for these revenues (Steinmo 1993). Finally, the government chose to initiate measures (most importantly, the introduction of individual taxation) that encouraged women into the labor market instead of importing foreign workers to help meet the burgeoning demand for labor (Jordan 2006a).

To be sure these were unusual choices. One would not expect a Social Democratic government or their labor union allies in the 1950s to agree to or implement policies that explicitly taxed workers more than capitalists, held down wages in the most economically profitable sectors of the economy, or pass tax laws that discriminated against women who chose not to take employment outside the home. But by the 1950s there was a very strong belief that the government could *and should* manage the economy and society as if it were a kind of engineering problem.[33] Perhaps it was

---

[32] This model discussed, the major point to note here is that those who lose their jobs are retrained and even relocated if necessary so that the individual worker does not bear the costs of economic change.

[33] Norwegian economist Knut Elgsaas recalled that when he was a student at the University of Oslo in the mid-1950s, his economics class was taken to Sweden on a study tour. They spent one day with economist Gunnar Myrdal, who explained to them that rationalizing the Swedish economy was a technical issue. As just one example, he cited the "million

the relative political and economic stability that their system had provided them, or perhaps it was the relatively small size and ethnic homogeneity of Sweden that made it easier for them to look out into the future. But by the end of the 1950s, Swedish policy elites could see quite well that society and the economy were changing and that to facilitate these changes a larger state would be necessary. A larger state would require more workers and higher taxes. These were in some senses seen as "technical" issues, rather than as fundamentally political ones. As Mark Blyth suggests, the power of the Social Democrats by this point allowed them to frame the boundaries of political debate (Blyth 2002).

The fact that the Social Democrats, and the labor unions for that matter, had come to believe in cooperating with capitalists and employers did not imply that they had abandoned their beliefs in a more fair or equal society. Clearly, as a number of Swedish academics have shown over the decades, they *did* abandon their belief that the only way to insure justice was through state socialism (Tingsten 1973). The Swedish Lefts' ideas had now evolved to the point where 'Socialism' in the traditional meaning of the word was no longer the goal. Instead, they now believed that a compromise with capitalism was not only necessary but genuinely to be desired. Capitalism, as Marx also understood, was the most productive system for generating wealth and economic growth and it was now seen as the best system for generating the resources needed to build programs and policies that would most benefit Swedish workers and citizens. Moreover, as Sweden became more economically successful, larger numbers of Swedes moved into the middle class and, it is quite clear, the working class was hardly poor itself.

The Social Democrats, both for electoral and philosophical reasons, increasingly came to argue for and develop policies that benefited the whole society, rather than just the traditional working class. We will see in subsequent chapters that unions and working class representatives in Japan and the United States repeatedly fought for tax and social policies that benefited their specific members and even sometimes specifically opposed policies that generalized benefits outside their members. In my view, this outcome should not be understood as simply a product of individual actors or organizations maximizing their narrow self-interests, but instead should be seen as

apartment program" where the Swedish government – understanding that continued economic prosperity would bring more people from the countryside to the cities – embarked on an ambitious program where it built 100,000 new apartments each year for ten years to accommodate this massive demographic shift. The young Elgsås returned home deeply frustrated believing that the Norwegian government would never be so efficient and organized (Interview with author, Oslo, June 2001).

example of the emergence of a new level of cooperative behavior. Clearly the game would be iterated and in this sense could be described in classic game theory terms. But, as we have seen repeatedly in this case, the actors' preferences adapted to the context as it also evolved. Thus there was no a priori way to deduce these preferences.

As Robert Axelrod points out in *The Complexity of Cooperation*, "[t]he main alternative to the assumption of rational choice is some form of adaptive behavior. The adaptation may be at the individual level through learning, or it may be at the population level... Either way, the consequences of adaptive process are often very hard to deduce when there are many interacting agents following rules that have non-linear effects" (Axelrod 1997: 4). Given this fact, one option is to open your models and to attempt to build adaptive agents and/or learning into the model. But as he notes, these techniques do not aim to provide an accurate representation of any particular empirical application (ibid: 4–5). The current study you have before you agrees with Axelrod in many respects. But in this case we are interested in exploring the real world with the aim of examining both some of these principles and substantive historical cases. In the Swedish case we once again see an example of the emergence of a form of social cooperation that evolved in a particular historical context that eventually had increasing return benefits to the system as a whole.[34]

Women, Employment, and Equality

It is worth specifically noting here the gender-specific consequences of the policy choices taken in the 1950s and 1960s. We will see in the following chapters that the United States and Japan have each pushed policies designed to protect the traditional family. Sweden has taken a quite different route. But as Ruggie noted over two decades ago, "women workers in Sweden are in a better position than elsewhere (with certain qualifications) because the state intervenes not for the sake of women alone, but for the sake of the economy and labor market as a whole" (Ruggie 1984: 29). The authorities decided to encourage more women into the workforce both because it would be fairer to working women and because it would have less socially disruptive effects than beginning a full-fledged 'gaestarbeiter' program. Gunnar Sträng, minister of finance in the 1950s and 1960s, justified his battle for eliminating family taxation in the following way: "We

---

[34] For discussions of the evolution of cooperative behavior see (Boyd and Richerson 2005a; Pennisi 2005).

TABLE 2.8. *Women in the Workforce, 2000*

	Employment Rate	Gender Gap*
France	69.6	17.7
Germany	71.1	16.3
Japan (1999)	62.7	31.6
Sweden	81.7	4.1
United States (1999)	74.1	14.8
OECD unweighted average	69.0	18.6

Note: * Gender Gap refers to the difference between male and female employment rates.
Source: OECD. 2002. *Employment Outlook, July.* Paris: OECD Publishing, Table 2.4.

needed more workers in Sweden. The job market was very tight. Also, as I thought about it, and I thought about the future. In the future I saw Swedish women's marching into working life even for working class women. And I also represented a district with lots of textile workers. There, women in the job market were already a reality... Soon, I could see that women would go into all areas" (interview with author, May 21, 1984). A family neutral, individual income tax system was introduced that treated each individual as a separate tax unit (e.g., the family unit is not advantaged). Yet while it is true that this fits with the general idea of Swedish equality, this policy was not particularly popular with the LO. Sträng strongly believed that it was preferable to bring women into the labor market than to import workers from less developed countries. Sweden already had employment agreements with the other Scandinavian countries and the experience with these workers was that they often stayed longer than their original work contracts. It was one thing to have large numbers of Finns and Norwegians setting up permanent residence, but to import very large numbers of workers from Poland or Turkey was another thing altogether.[35] As Table 2.8 indicates, these policies have been remarkably effective at bringing women into the workforce. They have also worked to continue to build on the idea of equality in Sweden. Today, gender equality is taken just as seriously as economic equality.

There have been several important consequences of these decisions. First, as Table 2.8 shows, Sweden has one of the highest rates of female employment in the world. This means of course that women can find work (and have child care paid for while they are at work) are much less likely to need social assistance and therefore much less likely to be poor (Jordan

[35] The motivations for this policy were explained to me by Mr. Sträng in an interview in 1991.

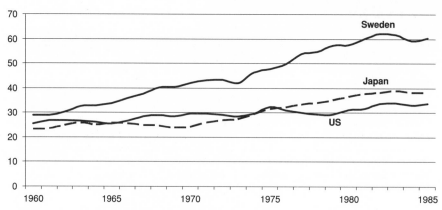

FIGURE 2.2. Total Government Spending, 1960 to 1985. *Source:* OECD Economic Outlook 2000 available online: www.sourceoecd.org.

2006b). Second, there have been growing demands for even more "family friendly" policies, such as extended maternity leave, child-sick leave and increased subsidies for child care programs. Finally, a significant share of employed women work in the public sector.[36] Thus, these policies have had direct consequences for public support for the welfare state, cutting back on government will consequentially have direct negative effects on women in particular. In Sweden, as elsewhere, women are the voting majority.

Another result was that, rather than fight for childcare subsidies designed to target the working class or the poor, generalized child subsidies for all families were introduced (Sainsbury 1996). Similarly, rather than fight for health insurance to be provided for by employers, Social Democrats built a universal healthcare system benefiting all citizens (Immergut 1992a). Of course these kinds of policies are far more expensive than programs targeted directly at the needy, but they also are much more likely to be seen as fair both by those who pay the taxes and those who receive the benefits (Rothstein 1998). Certainly, however, they also mean a massive expansion of the state and employment by the state. Figure 2.2 shows the expansion of state spending between 1960 and 1985 compared to the United States and Japan. Table 2.9 shows the implication of this spending in terms of employment.

---

[36] Women made up 73 percent of total public sector employment in 2006. Source: LABORSTA Labour Statistics Database, compiled by the International Labour Office, Geneva (International Labour Office. Bureau of 2009)URL: http://laborsta.ilo.org.

TABLE 2.9. *Sweden: Number of Employees in Different Economic Activities (thousands)*

Year	Agriculture	Manufacturing	Services	Government
1945	886	1061	285	290
1960	585	1204	339	462
1975	261	1201	323	1045
1990	167	1012	375	1434
2000	134	863	441	1237

Source: Edvinsson, Rodney. 2005. *Growth Accumulation Crisis*. Stockholm: Almquist and Wicksell. Edvinsson, Table P.

In sum, here we see another case in which a choice made in one historical context has had enormous unforeseen consequences in quite another. Women were specifically encouraged into the labor market both for reasons of gender equality and because they were a ready made workforce that could be used instead of imported immigrants from abroad. No one knew in the 1950s and 1960s, however, that Sweden was about to build the largest public welfare state in the world. But as it did so, it was women who largely came to take these positions. As we can see in Table 2.9, by the early 1990s government employed more people than any other sector of the economy. The political reality of this fact has meant that 'cutting back the state' would have a disproportionate consequence for women and their families. Not something that Swedish politicians of any political party are eager to do. If Sweden needed to change in the face of global competition and demographic pressures, alternative strategies would eventually have to be found.

Politicization and Decline of the Corporatist Bargain

By the mid-1970s, Sweden had become one of the richest countries in the world and had done this while also building one of the most egalitarian societies. It had essentially eliminated poverty and educated one of the most dynamic and flexible workforces found in any capitalist economy, while achieving high levels of economic growth. At the same time the economy was quite productive, efficient, dynamic and dominated by major internationally competitive firms such as Volvo, ASEA and Eriksson. Finally, the government was democratic, highly stable, efficiently run by a well-trained and well-insulated technocratically oriented elite that possessed an arsenal of policy devices designed to keep the Swedish economy open, competitive and dynamic. In this context, no one should be surprised that the Swedish economic and policy elites became increasingly confident in their ability to manage the economy.

In retrospect it seems that no sooner had Sweden become recognized as the premier example of 'the Middle Way' between the individualizing and inegalitarian capitalism of the West and the deadening and inefficient socialism of the East, than the system began to experience difficulties. Sweden's prominence and image in the world led many elites to believe that they had developed the most successful, egalitarian and democratic society in the world. The main problem with this image, however, was that Swedish institutions were in fact not really that democratic. Not only was economic power far more concentrated in the hands of a small number of business and labor union elites than in any other country in the democratic world, political power had also been held by a very small group of individuals for nearly forty-four years. The "Conservative guarantee" introduced early in the century worked instead as a kind of "Social Democratic guarantee" and had essentially secured their electoral dominance for four decades. This was *not* an unreflective "predatory state" (Levi 1988) more interested in retaining power and collecting taxes than in governing well or providing services to their citizens. These elites genuinely believed they were doing the best for their society. The rub was that by the mid-1970s, it was hard to deny that they had somehow gotten out of touch.

The beginning of the end can be traced back to the early 1970s. Certainly the watershed event was a massive wildcat strike beginning in the iron mines in the north of Sweden (Kiruna) in 1969. These strikes were exceptional because they originated in the heart of the working class *against the union organization and their political allies in Stockholm.* Though the strike itself was eventually settled, satisfying many of the miners' demands, the more basic accusations implied in the strike left serious self-doubt in the minds of the labor movement and Socialist leadership. What kind of union and what kind of Social Democracy is it that workers themselves feel they must strike against?

These doubts led to significant self-examination and rethinking both within the Party and inside the LO: Unions became less quiescent and began to demand higher wages from employers in their national wage negotiations. At the same time, the Social Democratic Party itself (at least significant portions of the Left within the Party) came to question its own legitimacy. Clearly the most important result was the constitutional change introduced in 1974 intended to make Swedish democracy more direct and more responsive to citizens. Several changes were introduced into the new Constitution, including the elimination of the Upper Chamber of the Riksdag, which had previously been extremely slow to change.[37] The reform had almost instantaneous effects that transformed Swedish governance so that now a relatively small change in election outcomes could actually change who held the reigns of government. The Social Democrats, in fact, lost power in 1976. But unfortunately for the first bourgeois coalition government in forty years, the constitutional reform also meant that any government would be less able "to take unpopular decisions," and to "distance itself from special interests" (Ruin 1981). The result, was a dramatic increase in public spending and in the tax burden that was necessary to finance it.

Also, as Pontusson and Swenson point out, Solidaristic wage policy arguably became too egalitarian during the course of the 1960s and 1970s, producing a generalized profits squeeze, and ultimately, an employer campaign to decentralize wage bargaining in the 1980s (Pontusson and Swenson 1996).

This weakening of the state's autonomy worked to significantly increase the level of conflict both in politics and in the labor market. The LO began to demand structural changes both at the workplace level[38] and later even in terms of the public ownership of Swedish capital.[39] Perhaps unsurprisingly, the Swedish Employer Federation (SAF) came to believe that the LO and the Social Democrats could no longer be trusted. For their part, they demanded the loosening of the national wage bargaining system and eventually its end. Thus, at the same time that trust between the former partners declined (Rothstein 2000), the ability of the Social Democratic elite, particularly the Ministry of Finance, to act as guardian of the public purse also weakened.

The growth of public programs also dramatically expanded the number of public employees, which in turn had numerous implications for the character of the Swedish Model itself. Sweden, which had once been noted for its

---

[37] Under the traditional two Chamber system, the Upper Chamber elections only effected approximately 1/8th of representative. Thus, even if the ruling party suffered significant losses in any given election, they were very likely to continue to be in control of the Upper Chamber and thus the government. (See Sydow 1989; Sydow and Riksbankens jubileumsfond 1997).

[38] A series of policies were demanded and implemented (such as health and safety policies) but the most significant specific reform was the demand for worker co-determination policies designed to include unions in corporate decision making.

[39] "Wage Earner Funds" were to be created though both increased profits taxes and increases in wage taxes. Though never fully implemented, the idea behind this policy was to create a huge public fund which would essentially "buy out" Swedish capital and thereby realize the socialist ideal of workers owning the means of production. (See Åsard 1984).

highly centralized wage negotiation system and unified and disciplined union structure, was now developing a substantially fragmented union structure. The blunt truth is that it is far easier to find a common front between the interests of miners and auto workers, for example, than it is to find a common interest between these groups and medical doctors, or, for that matter, daycare employees. Ironically, in many ways, a consequence of building a big welfare state was to undermine worker solidarity.

These developments had direct consequences for both wage demands and public spending. In the old Model, union wage demands could be tempered by the economic realities of the international marketplace and decisions once reached at the elite level could be implemented at the local, shop floor level due to the high degree of power of the central union organization. But by the late 1970s and early 1980s the Swedish political economy was quite different. Whereas unions in export-oriented industries had once been willing to practice wage restraint on the logic that their jobs depended on international competition, the newly powerful public employees unions did not have the same international market discipline to temper their demands. By 1989 the two unions representing salaried employees and those with higher academic degrees, (TCO and the SACO-SR) represented 41.7 percent of the workforce.[40] Given these basic facts, Sweden quickly developed even stronger inflationary proclivities. The government, desperately trying to maintain international competitiveness, felt that its only alternative was to periodically devalue the Swedish Krona. The result, as Ton Notermans has argued, was that "[t]he Swedish Model collapsed when, due largely to internal pressures, employers and unions had become unable to deliver any kind of wage moderation" (Notermans 2000: 24).

The very centralization of Sweden's wage negotiation system contributed to the demise of the system. As early as 1983, the Swedish Engineering Employers' Association (Verkstadsföreningen, or VF) began to chafe against the system. The Solidaristic wage system did not allow for the kind of wage flexibility that employers felt they needed to meet the changing demands of the international marketplace (Thelen 1993: 28–30; Swenson 1991).

In sum, in my view at least, Sweden's very successes led many actors within the system to pursue strategies that effectively worked to undermine the efficiency of the system as a whole. Even the policies that were designed to make the country more democratic, served to undermine the system's symbiotic

---

[40] The TCO and SACO-SR represented just 18.2 percent of unionized workforce in 1950. See (Jonung 1999) for a detailed analysis of the politics of inflation/devaluation during the 1970s and 1980s. See also (Moses 2000).

relationships. By the late 1970s and early 1980s, Sweden was in the process of undergoing substantial changes in both its political decision-making institutions and its economic structure (upon which the political institutions in many ways depended). These changes were partially a result of exogenous changes (i.e., the maturation of world capitalism), but it is equally clear that endogenous forces were also at work: The symbiotic relationship between capital and labor began to break down because this relationship was built within a particular domestic and international context. As these contexts changed, the relationship and trust between the organizations changed as well. In other words, the evolution of the relationships between subsystems in one area eventually created unsustainable friction within other parts of the system.

As we noted in Chapter One, evolution is "progressive" only in the sense that events build on one another, but this is not a teleological argument suggesting that each development is necessarily efficient. At the same time, humans *do* have extended capacities to learn and adapt using our (sometimes) advanced cognitive skills. Consequentially, feedback effects of a trial and error process can move quite quickly in some cases at least. We will see in later sections just this type of adaptive process. There is nothing predestined about these outcomes, but it is obviously also true that the history of cooperation on the one hand, and the high levels of trust in central authorities on the other, certainly yielded adaptive advantages to this small country.

Rethinking the Swedish Model

Once again, by the early 1980s, many members of the Swedish elite saw these developments in terms of an impending crisis. The crisis was both economic/fiscal and a crisis of confidence. Of course the most bitter critiques came from outside the Social Democratic Party (Lodin 1982; Agell et al. 1995; Lindbeck 1997). But the Social Democratic elite was also becoming increasingly aware of underlying problems with the Swedish economy and even more broadly with the Swedish Model itself (Feldt 1991). Whereas in the past these elites believed they could manage their economy quite effectively, now they were increasingly convinced that such management was no longer possible. Inflationary pressures were intensifying and economic competitiveness was waning (See Table 2.10). Slowly but surely, Sweden's position as one of the richest countries in the world was beginning to disappear.

What were once thought of as "labor market partners" were now increasingly acting like typical interest groups. In addition, whereas the political

TABLE 2.10. *The Percentage Change in Labor Costs (Per hour – including Payroll Taxes) from Previous Year – Sweden*

1970	1971	1972	1973	1974	1975	1976	1977	1978	1979	1980	1981	1982
10.2	13.6	10.2	11.5	17.0	22.2	16.9	12.1	9.2	8.7	11.8	9.6	6.1

1983	1984	1985	1986	1987	1988	1989	1990	1991	1992	1993	1994	1995
9.0	10.0	7.7	7.8	7.8	8.0	11.2	9.1	8.0	2.4	−2.1	3.3	5.0

Source: Lindbeck, Assar. 1997. *The Swedish experiment.* Stockholm: Studieförbundet Näringsliv och samhälle.

system in the earlier era insulated the fiscal elite and gave them enormous policy autonomy, now political demands on both the tax side and the spending side were increasingly difficult to ignore. In the words of one senior Ministry of Finance official, "I was taught in college that we could manage the economy via fiscal manipulations. But now in Sweden, and other countries too, we have less faith in politicians. We now realize that political asymmetries are so large that you have to be careful about what you recommend. Politicians don't only do what their economic advisors recommend. They also have to listen to interest groups... If economists think that political decisions are symmetric, then they use false assumptions. Politicians have short time horizons."[41]

One example of this rethinking was a policy campaign championed by Minister of Finance, Kjell Olof Feldt, designed to question the long-term viability of the tax system that had been built up to that date. In his view, Sweden's high tax rates caused a set of interrelated problems. First, the system of high marginal tax rates, effectively reduced by deep tax expenditures (loopholes), was creating a system of false economic incentives. For example, since taxation on interest income was deductible, this effectively meant that people could buy homes (or vacation yachts) and could deduct up to 80 percent of their interest payments from taxes. In short, the government essentially financed the purchase, and the housing (and boating) industry therefore experienced an unprecedented boom.[42] Second, high marginal rates created incentives for Swedish taxpayers to send their earnings and wealth abroad. As an open economy, it was virtually impossible to stop the flow of capital out of the country. Finally, many feared that high tax rates gave people strong incentives to cheat the system and this would ultimately undermine Swedish citizens' basic belief in the fairness. Sweden's iconic

[41] Anonymous interview with the author, April 2000.
[42] Almost exactly the same thing occurred in the United States in 2008. But as we will see, the response in Sweden was quite different than in the United States.

economist, Gunnar Myrdal, wrote that the system was creating *et folk av fifflare (a people of cheaters)* (Myrdal 1982).

For the bulk of the 1980s, tax and tax policy stood at the center of an enormous political battle inside the SAP. Indeed, some saw this battle as an ideological conflict over the very meaning of social democracy in Sweden. However, in this author's view, the struggle is better understood as a fight over the *means of achieving* the basic goals of an egalitarian social democratic society. This was a battle over *ideas* and not *values*. The critical issue for the Ministry of Finance was what kinds of public policies would allow Sweden to continue to compete and succeed in the world economy in order that the economy could provide sufficient economic well being to be distributed amongst its citizens (see also Blyth 2007).

The Crisis of Swedish Capitalism

The internal fight within the Social Democratic Party and its general inability to implement an effective economic policy strategy eventually led to a crisis of confidence among voters in the late 1980s. The Left in the party became increasingly alienated and suspicious of the Ministry of Finance in general – and the Minister of Finance Kjell-Olof Feldt – in particular. At the same time, the more Centrist voters feared that the growing vociferousness and bitterness within the party implied a return to the more traditional Leftist policies of the earlier years. The result, unsurprisingly, was that the Social Democrats were turned out of office in 1991 just as they were putting the final touches on *The Tax Reform of the Century*.

The new government, a Center-Right coalition between Conservatives, Liberals and the Center Party, was easily persuaded to continue the tax reform agenda. The key problem, however, was that each of the coalition partners also wanted to cut taxes for their particular constituencies. As a result, contrary to the original plan, the reform was under-financed and contributed to a spiraling deficit. The new government also found itself politically incapable of resisting the demands of the many constituencies that clambered for support: How could they cut housing support, child payments, social welfare payments, sickness benefits, or any other major social program in the context of an economic decline of this magnitude? In fact, these years actually witnessed an *increase* in public spending, despite the fact that a bourgeois government was at the helm.

The new government was also extremely unlucky. By far the most important part of the reform was the removal of the deductibility of interest payments from the national income tax. The central idea was quite reasonable: Lower tax rates and cut major tax expenditures. No matter how good the original idea, however, the immediate policy consequences were disastrous. It was the bourgeois coalition government's bad timing to come to office at the beginning of a recession, as they did in 1976. Clearly, the policies pursued by this coalition government (i.e., with each party trying to pay off its particular constituency) substantially worsened Sweden's economic situation. The tax reform, for example, dramatically exacerbated the collapse in the real property market.[43]

The result was that the budget deficit increased to 13 percent of GDP. At one point, international confidence in the Krona sunk so low that the central bank was forced to increase the overnight lending rate to 500 percent in a vain effort to protect the currency. Eventually, two of Sweden's three largest banks effectively went bankrupt. The government, whether it wanted to or not, was required to come to the rescue of Swedish banking industry.[44]

Capital taxation was also radically reformed. All capital income now faced a flat 30 percent rate while deductions were substantially rolled back. In addition, the corporate profits tax rate was reduced from 57 to 30 percent and many of the most generous tax expenditures available in the code were eliminated.[45] Finally, a series of other rather specific reforms and adjustments were instituted (such as taxing the percent return on assets in private life insurance and pension funds) which were designed to either balance the negative redistributive effects of rate reductions, close specific loopholes and/or to raise revenue.[46]

Many analysts saw this as the beginning of the end of the Swedish Welfare State. Many feared that though the tax burden remained quite high, the public commitment to maintaining a (nominally) progressive tax system was now gone. Moreover, since the tax reform was underfinanced, many analysts (including this author) assumed that the lost revenues would eventually have

---

[43] By substantially eliminating the deductibility of interest even on owner occupied homes, those who had borrowed to finance purchases now found they could not afford their loans. Given that this occurred during a general recession, the result was a collapse of the market. I do not mean to suggest here that the tax reform was specifically responsible for the economic collapse in these years. Indeed, other policy failures, including the government's commitment to tie the krona to the ECU, as well as the very poorly executed banking deregulation, were undoubtedly far more important factors (See Agell et al. 1996).

[44] Banks were recapitalized through a general government guarantee for all creditors *except shareholders*. The government also set up a separate public authority to effectively manage the banking industry through the crisis. For a concise discussion of this crisis and the government's responses (see Bäckström 2007).

[45] Now the income tax was essentially a flat rate income tax for most income earners, (average 30 percent, depending on the commune) with a second rate of 20 percent affecting only higher income earners.

[46] For a balanced analysis of this tax reform and its fiscal effects (See Agell et al. 1996).

to be made up with increases in taxes on lower income earners, or cuts in the social welfare state, or both. These predictions, of course, fit very well with the "End of the Welfare State" analysis that became so popular in the mid-1990s (Lindbeck 1997).

Not only did the traditional Swedish Model look dead, it now appeared that the Swedish economy was lying on the deathbed next to it.

PART III

CHALLENGES AT CENTURY'S END

The "Socialists" Adapt

Perhaps unsurprisingly, the dire economic performance of the early 1990s soon brought the Social Democratic Party (in coalition with the Left Party[47] and the Green Party) back to office (1994). Sweden's unofficial "Party of Government" quickly set about re-stabilizing Sweden's financial position. At first it appeared that the Socialists had accepted the basic neo-liberal logic as they began cutting back several social welfare policies. But careful analysis of these policies suggests that rather than slash programs, most of these reductions were in fact designed to make them more fiscally reasonable and remove some of the opportunities for abuse that had been created earlier by the stunning generosity of these policies.[48]

Rather than simply accepting neo-liberal ideas wholesale, they adopted some of the liberal's insights and tried to adapt them to Social Democratic goals. In short, Social Democratic policy adapted to and evolved with the realities of the changing world economy. Rejecting the idea that government was by definition inefficient and/or wasteful, they came to accept the argument that *some* government programs were inefficient and wasteful. Similarly, they eventually came to agree with the basic point made by many critics of the large welfare state that the monopoly power of the state created incentives for public employees to treat citizens as clients rather than customers (Kumlin 2002b).

---

[47] Former Communist Party.

[48] Thus, for example, employees were no longer eligible for full pay for up to seven days sick leave even when they had no slip from a doctor. A number of similar benefits were reduced as well. Some, of course, cause considerable financial hardship in specific public bureaucracies. The health care sector appears to have been particularly hard hit. For an overview of the social security in Sweden after the changes in the 1990s see: SOU, *Välfärd Vid Vägskäl [Welfare at the Crossroads]*.

In the mid-1990s, then, Sweden found itself facing difficult problems. On the one hand, the world economy was changing quite rapidly. New technologies, lowered international barriers and greater levels of international mobility increased competition in the traditional manufacturing/engineering industries where Sweden had been so successful for so long. But on the other hand, some of Sweden's social programs had become less service-oriented and/or inefficient.

Once one gets passed the obtuse arguments that government spending is, by definition, bad for the economy and that globalization must necessarily drive down taxes and social spending, one is quickly led to the more difficult questions: Where should public investments go to help the economy and society best adapt to capitalism as it also evolves? In other words, how should public monies best be spent? Viewing globalization as an adaptive problem rather than as simply an insurmountable challenge to the public sector evokes dramatically different responses.

To be sure, Sweden's longstanding exposure to the world economy and its historic reliance on large internationally oriented firms effectively advantaged this country as international pressures intensified. Not only was a move to protectionism an unrealistic option given the internationalization of Swedish firms (e.g., they would simply leave), but also precisely because the economy was internationally oriented the Swedish elite were attuned to the changing world economy earlier and to a far greater extent than most other advanced nations. Due to the fact that this was a relatively small elite that has tended to view policy making as more of an engineering problem than as a political problem, globalization was treated in a completely different way by Swedes than by other countries in this study. As Anders Bergh argues, Sweden's ruling elites chose a strategy of incremental adaptation to in a changing environment (Bergh 2008).

From this perspective, Sweden's highly educated workforce, efficient public service and especially its high levels of social trust could be seen as *advantages* in a more dynamic and flexible world economy. Eventually, the Swedish elite came to believe that Sweden's comparative advantage in the twenty-first century would be in knowledge production rather than in traditional manufacturing. As Jenny Andersson notes, "Knowledge is created through learning – and learning is a social activity, one that depends on trust, communication and reciprocity" (Andersson 2007: 9). As we have previously seen, these are factors that Sweden has in abundance. In short, as the world economy evolved it would advantage those with higher level skills and education toward a knowledge-based economy. Sweden, in this view, was already in a better position to adapt because of her large and generous welfare state and its high levels of equality.

> The old Left, or so the New Labour story goes, thought that it could steer innovation and change and did not realize the individualism and the private nature of creativity and entrepreneurship, while neoliberalism with its atomistic theory of economic man and free market did not see the fundamental social logics of processes such as learning and creativity. To that extent, the Third Way contains a firm rejection of both socialism and neoliberalism, both with reference to knowledge as a good with specific social alternatives, fostered in trust and not in conflict. (Andersson 2007: 10)

Social Democrats understood that they could not "buck the trend" (Steinmo 2003) and instead searched for new ways to embrace it. Rather than fighting against globalization, Swedish elites decided that Sweden had the possibility of using globalization to their country's advantage. Sweden, after all, was already highly integrated into the world economy and already had some of the world's most successful global corporations, a highly educated workforce and very high levels of social trust and cooperative capacities built into their political economy. Globalization, in short, could provide a niche into which Sweden's small, technologically advanced and highly competitive economy could fit into and thrive within. Knut Rexed, an advisor to the Prime Minister, summarized the implications of this perspective well when he told me in an interview in June 2000, "There will be increased competition between countries due to internationalization, but it won't be the country with the lowest tax rates that wins. It will be the countries which have the most efficient use of resources that win" (Knut Rexed StatsSecretar, Stockholm, June 8, 2000).

To use its resources more efficiently, however, required both investment and return to fiscal balance. This meant tax increases.[49] Perhaps surprisingly, at least to those ideologically committed to the idea of a small state, these tax increases did not choke off Sweden's economic recovery. By decade's end, Sweden's economic and fiscal picture had instead improved markedly: Unemployment had been reduced, though not to the levels common during the heyday of the Swedish Model. The budget was now in surplus. Investment had returned to levels not seen in many years (Finance 2000: 2). Finally, GDP growth was now at a healthy and sustainable rate. Indeed, the first budget in the new century was widely heralded (and decried) as, "A Classic Social Democratic Budget" (Wettergren 2000).

---

[49] For a more detailed analysis of this period from a fiscal view see (Steinmo, 2003).

Instead of using the budget surpluses to cut taxes on mobile capital as was demanded by the Right and predicted by many analysts, the Finance Minister chose to *increase* public spending on child support yet again and to continue using the surplus to pay off Sweden's substantial public debt. The government does not envision scaling back on the state anytime soon. If anything, the picture drawn by the government with its own pen is one of continuing high taxes, as well as high social welfare expenditures. As one Ministry of Finance official told this author "We love Sweden the way it is. That may be difficult to sell politically, but it is the simple truth. We think things are pretty good here and we want to keep them that way. Of course we want to keep up with and stay ahead of changes in the world economy, but we see no reason why we should have to cut back tremendously on taxes or spending at this point" (anonymous interview with the author, Stockholm, June 9, 2000). In fact, relatively small adjustments in taxes have been made since 2000. But positive economic growth, low interest rates and a budget surplus have meant that relatively small tax cuts could be sustained while concomitantly reducing public debt *and* maintaining public spending at over 50 percent of GDP (Finansdepartementet 2002).

In sum, the Social Democrats have embraced a new set of policy instruments. Rather than roll back their welfare state, they have committed themselves to making it more efficient and a better service to Swedish citizens. In several cases this may mean adopting the liberal idea of introducing market competition. Recall that early in the century, Social Democrats came to terms with big capital and came to see capital as something that could not only be cooperated with, but could in effect be used for the party's idealistic and political goals. Today, it appears that something analogous is going on with their approach to markets and market competition. As Andersson points out, from this new perspective the market is seen "as provider of public value, for instance through more efficient delivery of welfare services, but also through more complex things such as the fostering of creativity and entrepreneurship through public/private partnerships in schools and other public institutions." Specifically in education "the market emerges not only as the efficient provider, but also as an injection of creativity, entrepreneurship and best practice, and in the end, as the arbiter of what knowledge, skill and creativity are useful in society" (Andersson 2007: 12).

Education in a Global Economy

The most obvious policy area that has benefited from the new thinking has been education. The 1990s saw a major emphasis in spending for all levels

TABLE 2.11. *Total Public Direct Expenditures on Education as a Percentage of GDP, 1990, 2000*

	All Institutions		Primary and Secondary		Higher Education	
	1990	2000	1990	2000	1990	2000
Sweden	5.3	7.4	4.4	4.9	1.0	2.0
Japan	3.6	3.6	2.9	2.7	0.4	0.5
USA	5.3	5.0	3.8	3.5	1.4	1.1

Source: Snyder, Thomas D., Sally A. Dillow, and Charlene M. Hoffman. 2008. *Digest of Education Statistics 2007* (NCES 2008–022). Washington D.C.: National Center for Education Statistics, Institute of Education Sciences, U.S. Department of Education.

of education (See Table 2.11). As we can see, Sweden increased spending on education overall and doubled its investment in higher education funding between 1990 and 2000. There has also been particular attention paid to adult education and the need to re-train those who have lost work due to the changing world economy (Palme et al. 2003:19). The "Adult Education Initiative" (Kunskapslyftet) was enrolling more than 150,000 students each year by the mid-1990s.

Another surprising policy initiative embraced by the Social Democrats in the 1990s was what Americans call "school choice." Sweden has a long tradition of providing free public education to all levels of society. Traditionally this system has been based on the idea that the best school was the local school, where all students could learn together. Beginning in the 1960s, primary schools, especially, eschewed the idea of competition and instead emphasized cooperation and group learning. Even grades were eliminated.[50]

In recent years there has been a growing movement to introduce more competition in the public school system in Sweden.[51] School choice was

[50] The national curriculum (Läroplan) that came in 1980 meant that students received their first grades during their eighth school year (normally the year they became fifteen). Before that, from 1969, grades were given in school years three, six, seven, eight and nine (the basic school "grundskolan" is nine years). However, local school districts could decide to replace grades in year three and six with other types of information to parents (usually oral information). It is unclear how much this was used. Grades are now replaced by extended oral and written information to parents – usually you have a meeting with one or several teachers for about twenty minutes each semester when they present the students results and achievements. How well this works varies of course a lot. The new center-right government has a new policy – grades will be given from year six (See "Svensk utbildningshistoria," Gunnar Richardson. Lund: Studentlitteratur 2004). (Thanks to Bo Rothstein for this information.)

[51] Similar reforms have taken place in health care, where choice and competition have been introduced to deliver a diverse set of services to citizens (See Olessen 2010).

first introduced in the "Skolpeng-reform" in 1992 and has since grown and developed to where today it is widely accepted that parents and students should be able to choose different types of schools. The government has even gone so far as to pay private companies to operate schools *for profit*, as long as they do not discriminate against students in any way and as long as they use *only* public money to fund the school. In other words, they may not take the public subsidy and allow parents to "top up" the funding through private donations. Today over 10 percent of Swedish students attend these privately run schools, with the largest school chain, Kunskapsskolan ("Knowledge Schools"), owning 30 schools and teaching nearly 10,000 pupils (Economist 2008b).

Of course this new system and these new ideas have not been implemented without controversy. Many are worried that this system could result in a multi-tiered education system in which the most educated and middle class students will migrate to particular schools and lower income and immigrant children could migrate to quite different schools. While the curriculum is still regulated by the government (e.g., schools must teach religion but cannot preach a particular doctrine), there is certainly reason to be concerned that the long run implications of these (and other) reforms might be to undermine traditional Swedish solidarity, as shown in the discussion in the following section.

SUBVERSIVE NEO-LIBERALISM?

Claes Belfrage argues that the liberalizing reforms introduced by both the Social Democrats and the Conservatives in recent years will have "subversive" effects on the Swedish Model. He notes, for example, that the pension reform's individual fund was meant to encourage people to take care of their own financial futures.[52] While this fund will be relatively small in fiscal terms, the argument here is that it can or will have long-term consequences for the Swedish model precisely because it encourages people to think of themselves first and the society second. "What I think has changed the most in Sweden in the past twenty years," a former Left Party member of the Riksdag told me, "is that idea of 'solidarity' has been removed from the agenda."[53] Similarly, when asked, "What does Social Democracy mean in today's context?" a high level official in the Social Democratic Party said the following: "We know what we want, but we have to be flexible as to the

[52] Belfrage borrows this phrase from Martin Rhodes' important essay, "Subversive Liberalism: Market integration, globalization and European Welfare states," (Rhodes, 1995).

[53] Hans Petersson, interview with author May 15, 2008, Stockholm.

methods we choose. The most important thing today is that people should have more personal choices – more personal freedom. For example, people want to be able to choose the schools their children attend and not have the government telling them where they should go or how that education should be structured." When I commented that it was interesting that she did not mention solidarity or equality, which would certainly have been very important goals for a person in her position in the past, she responded that she was not an expert on Social Democratic history. But she was adamant that equality is still an important goal. Later in our discussion, she suggested that over the longer run the movement toward individual choice and privatization could indeed cause problems for the cherished goal of equality. "We have to fight against this," she said. "If I were able to do anything I want today, I think I would take back these reforms. But I can't see this happening now. It is politically impossible."[54]

Torbjorn Lundqvist's analysis of the history of competition policy in Sweden draws similar conclusions. While there have long been policies that have encouraged particular types of competition and anti-trust in Sweden, Lundqvist argues that there was a philosophical change in the 1990s. "The new competition policy," he argues, "was a part (sic) of an attack on the 'inefficient' Swedish model. This was more than a shift in economic policy. When the competition authority at the time tried to explain why competition was a problem in Sweden the answer became a description of the Swedish model." In the end he believes that the entire political culture is in transition. Sweden is moving from a "culture of negotiations, interest participation and pragmatism" to a political economy of "clear rules of the game, legalism and competition. The idea was to take Sweden into an economic liberal era" (Lundqvist 2006: 19–20). Still, he argues that the overall story suggest both "change and continuity," for, in the end, the "change from regulation to competition as an organizing principle in the economy is fundamental however not absolute. Still there is a lot of regulation and competition that has been important policy since at least the 1850s... Perhaps the most striking change is in the role of the state from a participator to an enabler of the game" (ibid: 20).

Jessica Lindvert captures one of the key changes in the Swedish model in recent years in her essay, "The Political logics of Accountability: From 'doing the right thing' to 'doing the thing right'" (Lindvert 2008). She describes

---

[54] Anonymous, interview with author, May 15, 2008, Stockholm. On the same day a highly successful Swedish entrepreneur proposed the idea that private companies that operate long-term care facilities should be allowed to accept extra payments from individuals who want extra care at the facilities. The Social Democrats strongly opposed this idea arguing that it would lead to a two-class system for older people (See Ibison 2008).

what might seem like a subtle change in rhetoric to a significant evolution in the ways in which Swedish administrators and bureaucrats conceive of their role and position in society. Throughout this chapter, I have emphasized the profound centralization of power in the Swedish state. I have suggested that the Swedish has been the most "autonomous" of democratic states and that this has in fact been one of the keys to the remarkable social and economic success of this small, relatively homogeneous nation. Indeed, it was precisely the centralization of power in this system that made the kind of elite deal making possible that eventually resulted in the "win-win" outcomes for which Sweden has become so renowned. But the recent reforms in the direction of more transparency and openness may indeed have the unintended consequences of forcing a kind of juridical legalism that is, in the end, quite antithetical to the Swedish model in which authorities become accountable not for the general outcomes but for having followed prescribed processes and rules. If Sweden continues down this path we may well find that these small seemingly inconspicuous administrative reforms have, in the end, the most profound implications for the forces that keep the bumblebee flying.

As we have previously seen, the Swedish welfare state has been deemed in crisis before. In each case some argued that the Swedish economy was near collapse and massive reforms were necessary, while others insisted that reform would fundamentally undermine the logic of the Social Democratic system. In the end they compromised. This does not mean, however, that the Social Democratic welfare state has not adapted and cannot change. Indeed, quite the opposite is true. Like any complex system it *must* adapt to survive (Bergh 2008; Olessen 2010). The reforms in health care, pensions, education, etc. are only the most recent iterations in this process. The more puzzling and perhaps loaded question is whether these adaptations will ultimately undermine the egalitarian norms for which Swedish Social Democracy has become so famous. Of course, we cannot know the future, but as illustrated in the following section, there are additional reasons to have concern in this regard.

Adapting to Demographic Change

One of the most difficult issues facing all advanced industrial democracies today is demographic change. Simply put, there are two faces to this demographic change: First, most advanced societies are becoming significantly more diverse. Second, the populations of all rich countries are aging. These two changes deeply intersect with one another in Sweden, as in every modern society. I will discuss each of these in turn.

In recent years, Sweden has become a nation of immigrants. Sweden's economic success on the one hand, and its self-perception as a generous and egalitarian land on the other, led this country to be one of the most generous immigrant and refugee systems in the advanced world. Interestingly, much like when the Social Democrats reformed the constitution in 1974 and thereby opened the door to opposition parties gaining real power, the Swedish sense of self required that they open their borders to huge numbers of political refugees and immigrants. Whereas Sweden was one of the most racially and culturally homogeneous countries in the world only a few decades ago, today it is becoming remarkably diverse. Currently 12 percent of Sweden's population is foreign born – which is near the level reached by the United States at the peak of its immigration boom in 1913, when foreigners constituted 14 percent of Americans. By some estimates, non-Scandinavians (i.e., people whose family lineage originates outside of Scandinavia) constitute nearly 25 percent of Sweden's population today. In some districts in cities like Malmö and Stockholm, darker skinned citizens hugely outnumber Scandinavians.

This demographic change presents significant challenges for the Swedish welfare state if it works to undermine public support for the welfare state. As Mauricio Rojas, Swedish immigrant and now a member of Parliament, warns, "The welfare state presupposes a strong community. When you take tax you must redistribute to a community near you. The difficult problem is that immigration is resented by some Swedes who say, 'they are taking our money.' For a welfare state to exist, you need a close community" (Roberts 2003b).[55] To their credit, Swedish authorities are making tremendous efforts to confront these issues. Some of these include public awareness campaigns and educational programs in the schools. The government is also encouraging (via subsidies) immigrant families to move into and integrate within more typically 'Swedish' communities and away from the more ghetto-ized communities, which originally sprung up in the publicly financed housing projects just outside the major cities. It is impossible to tell at this point how, whether, or if these demographic trends will evolve into a more generalized

---

[55] One should note that while Sweden can fairly be characterized as a universal welfare state, is *not* perfectly "universal" in the sense that all programs are equally distributed. On the contrary, social assistance, *socialbidrag*, does play a role in even the Swedish model. Social assistance can also add up to quite a lot of money in Sweden. The basic cash allowance (in 2006) for an individual without children was 3450 SEK (about $430) is meant to cover food, shoes, clothing, etc. While another fund pays rent, electricity, etc. depending on the actual expenses. "Because rent and electricity benefits alone can easily sum to 4000 SEK for a single adult, the total benefit level is very high by international standards" (Bergh 2006).

resistance to social welfare programs. But there is little doubt that this issue will become a far greater challenge for the Swedish welfare state than the threat that capital will no longer want to do business in the country.

Many argue that while racism is an important issue, it does not pose nearly the challenge to the Swedish welfare state implied by authors like Rohas. Although racism is indeed a threat in Sweden, as in all OECD countries with increasing immigration, there is evidence that it is less so in Sweden. Like all advanced western countries, Sweden faces the challenge of increasing ethnic diversity, but there is reason to believe that Sweden may meet this challenge more gracefully than many of its European neighbors. The government has been very up front in informing its people that immigration is helping fund the welfare state as Swedish society ages. Moreover, though there is growing mistrust of government in all advanced capitalist nations, this problem does appear less severe in Sweden than in most other countries.[56] Perhaps this is because this country has rather steadfastly held on to its commitment to egalitarian values – even in the face of an international economic competition (Kumlin and Rothstein 2010).

The second demographic challenge facing Sweden, and all rich capitalist democracies, is population aging. One of the apparent facts of the social and economic successes of the modern welfare state is that families, or more specifically women, both delay childbirth and choose to have fewer children. In the long run, of course, this can cause serious social and fiscal problems. Quite simply, as our societies age, there are fewer and fewer workers supporting more and more retirees. Importantly, there are also very strong correlations between women's educational attainment and fertility: As women's education improves, they choose to have even fewer children. As Figure 2.3 indicates, these trends might ultimately invert what was once called the "population pyramid."

As societies advance and modernize they develop what Ronald Inglehart has described as "post-material values" (Inglehart 1997, 2003). As societies become wealthier, citizens worry less about meeting their basic needs (i.e., housing, food, security, etc.) and become more concerned with what one might call the "better things in life" (i.e., leisure, health, the environment, etc.). In Sweden, as elsewhere, the political pressures from these changes have worked to create a very generous social insurance system for older citizens. Across Europe today, it is widely expected that one should be able

---

[56] It is interesting to note that trust for politicians and political parties has increased in recent years, but confidence in government and public institutions remains very high. (See Kumlin and Rothstein 2010)

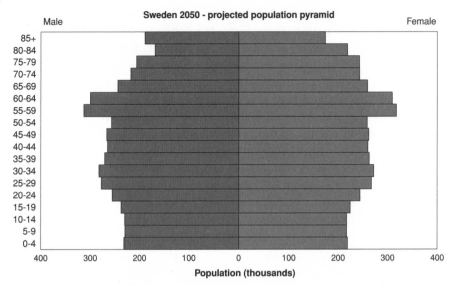

FIGURE 2.3. Projected Demographic Situation in Sweden 2050. *Source:* U.S Census Bureau, International Statistics (retrieved Nov. 26, 2009).

to retire at a relatively young age (late 50s or early 60s) *and* be able to live essentially at the same standard of living that was enjoyed while fully employed. These expectations are not peculiar to Sweden. The problem is that these preferences and past policy choices are creating two distinct policy dilemmas. First and most obviously, high social security benefits necessitate high taxation on the working population.[57] Second, people no longer need large families to support themselves financially in their old age, and consequentially, younger families have fewer children today than they did in past generations. Finally, to achieve the life-style demanded by most middle class citizens, more and more young families are deciding to have fewer children, or perhaps none at all. The combined effect of these multiple trends is that as there are fewer young people in the workforce, there are fewer people paying into the social security system. The result is an impending fiscal crisis. Figure 2.3 illustrates the changing age demographics in Sweden. Whereas in 2005, 17.5 percent of the Swedish population are 65 years or older, by 2050 there will be more people over the age of 60 in Sweden than those under the

---

[57] It is sometimes wrongly assumed that social security benefits are paid out of some kind of fund or account that has essentially saved the tax payment individuals paid in over their lifetime. The reality is that old age social security funds are based on a "Pay as You Go" system in all countries. Generally, there is a small fund when payments are higher than benefits paid out. But in no country are current payments/taxes "saved" for decades.

age of 30. By one United Nations estimate, pensioners will equal 54 percent of the working-age population of Sweden by 2050 (Roberts 2003a).

This problem presents policy makers with difficult fiscal dilemmas in all rich countries.

Unless you somehow randomly began reading this book on this page, you will probably not be surprised to learn that the Swedes have adopted policy mechanisms that, at least in the medium term, have substantially worked to mitigate this social security crisis. In typical Swedish fashion, the government set up a commission with academic experts and members from key interest organizations and asked them to make specific policy recommendations. Taken as technical issues, these problems were far less overwhelming than taken as political issues. Clearly solutions were possible: encourage young families to have more children and encourage working people to save more and retire later.

The first of these solutions was already largely in place. Sweden already had the world's most comprehensive public family support systems through heavily subsidized day care for children, long maternity leaves for parents, and substantial time off allowed, with pay, to care for sick children. These benefits are too numerous and too complex to list here, but some of the most important include direct child allowances, paternity leave for twelve months with salary replacement of 75 percent of income (one month of this leave must be taken by the husband), 90 days of sick leave so parents can take care of their children when ill, the right for parents to reduce their work schedule to 75 percent of full time and subsidized high quality child care available to all parents.[58]

The second set of policies - designed to reduce public spending on old age security – is more surprising. Many readers will be familiar with the (failed) attempts of President George Bush to reform the American system of Social Security. Readers will unlikely be aware of the fact that the Swedish Democrats confronted this problem with policies remarkably similar to some of those proposed by the Republican administration in the United States in years prior. In 1994, after three years of cross-party negotiations in the so-called Pension Working Group and consultations with the various interest

---

[58] Though there has been some considerable controversy over whether pro-natal policies work generally (Esping-Anderson 2002), the evidence in the Swedish case is that these policies have indeed had the desired effects (Björklund 2006). No one who visits Sweden today can fail to notice the remarkable numbers of young people walking their babies in prams, nor the large numbers of overflowing schools and child care centers throughout the nation. For more detailed descriptions of these policies see (Lindvert 2002; Sainsbury 1996).

organizations, guidelines for a radical reform of the mandatory pension system were passed with an overwhelming parliamentary majority, consisting of the bourgeois government coalition and the Social Democrats. With the continued support of the same five parties that had agreed on "the big pension compromise" four years earlier, two more bills regarding the concrete implementation of the reform were adopted in 1998. Note, however, that this time around the Social Democrats held government office. I will not detail the entire reform here, but two factors stand out. First, they divided the mandatory pension system in three compulsory parts: A tax-financed *guarantee pension* for those with pension rights below a certain threshold; An *income pension* linked to the lifetime contributions; And, finally, an individual *premium pension* account. This premium pension bears remarkable resemblance to the 'privatized' social security plan promoted by President Bush. In this system 2.5 percent of the social insurance contributions went to an individually owned pension account that is invested by (or for) the income earner. The second important feature of the social insurance reform was a change in the automatic growth mechanism built into this (like most other) system. This was called a fiscal "balancing mechanism." What this essentially meant was that benefits in the income pension scheme would be adjusted to the development of demographic as well as economic variables. Thus, if the total amount of pension payments due in the system are not matched by incoming contributions, benefits are adjusted to remain at a financially sustainable pace.[59] Moreover, pension benefits are indexed to wages not to inflation or economic growth, as is common in most other countries. In short, retirees benefit from the growth of the Swedish economy, but do not have their benefits increased unless the society at large sees a growth in income.

This reform has drawn enormous interest and approval both within Sweden and around the world, because by most accounts, it has solved the critical fiscal dilemma facing all advanced countries.[60] Because this new system offers strong incentives for workers to stay in the labor market longer and directly ties old age benefits to economic performance, it is expected to be fiscally viable in the long run. Few advanced societies can make this claim.

[59] If overall entitlements exceeds contributions, the indexation is adjusted downwards until the system is again in balance. (I would like to thank Mi ah Schøyen for assistance with this section.)

[60] See (Die Bundesreigerung (German Federal Government) 2003; Palme 2003b; Social-departementet Ministry of Health and Social Affairs/Riksfoersaekringsverket (RFV) National Social Insurance Board 2003; OECD 2002).

The Social Democratic Consensus

After more than ten years of remarkable political and economic success, Swedish voters evicted the Social Democrats from power in 2006. To some observers at the time, this election suggested that Swedes no longer supported the high tax/big welfare state policies of the Social Democrats and would mark the return of neo-liberalism to Sweden (Economist 2006). The truth however, is that the Conservatives won the election essentially by arguing that they would be better at achieving the goals of social democracy than the Social Democrats. Indeed, in the run up to the election the Conservatives renamed themselves the "New Moderates," campaigned as the "New Labor Party," and vowed to protect the social welfare state and not undermine it. Professor Bo Rothstein called the election a "Triumph for the Social Democrats."[61]

The New Conservative Prime Minister, Fredrik Reinfeldt, is highly cognizant of the electoral disaster his party faced when it tried to reform the social welfare state the last time it was in office. Reinfeldt re-branded his party the "New Moderates" and was, effectively, elected by promising that they would act like Social Democrats. As he says, "We are not pushing a neo-liberal reshaping of Swedish society. People don't like revolutions. If you ask somebody, 'do you want change?' he will say that my neighbor needs it, but not me" (Economist 2007).

Indeed it appears that a new consensus has settled in Sweden in the early twenty-first century. On the one hand, the Social Democrats have embraced ideas of making the public sector more efficient and consumer oriented by imposing market forces into the public sphere (Kumlin 2002a) and, at the same time, the parties on the right of Swedish politics promise fealty to the egalitarian welfare state and the high tax burdens that support it. To be sure, the Right wants lower taxes on high income earners and capital income while the Social Democrats focus more on the long term revenue consequences of tax cuts and these differences are constantly aired in the Swedish press. But from a comparative point of view, it is difficult to see these as much more than differences of opinion on how to achieve a common goal, not evidence of a deeply divided country. When we see how politics in the United States has evolved later in Chapter 4, we should recall the low level of conflict apparent in the Swedish system today. At the end of the first decade of the

---

[61] "Valet en triumf för socialdemokraterna" *Dagens Nyheter*, September 20, 2006. http://www.dn.se/DNet/jsp/polopoly.jsp?a=574004.

twenty-first century, neo-liberal/anti-state ideology and rhetoric is virtually absent in Swedish politics. "It is interesting," notes Sören Holmberg, the director of the Swedish National Election Studies program, "you just don't hear people demanding a roll back of the state anymore. It seems like the neo-liberals just disappeared."[62]

The Swedish Model and the Social Welfare State

The economic and political crises of the 1980s and 1990s clearly forced the Social Democratic elite in Sweden to change its ideas about how to achieve the goals to which the party has long been committed. But there is little evidence to suggest that this elite has changed its values concerning an egalitarian society, a large distributive welfare state and a successful capitalist economy. The Swedish Social Democratic Party elite has never been socialist in the traditional anti-capitalist sense of the term.[63]

Only a few years ago a large number of popular reports predicted that the high tax rates and overall tax levels in Sweden would drive high-income earners and capitalists out of Sweden. Today, these same publications announce the rebirth of the Swedish economy and sometimes curiously ponder why capitalists aren't rational actors (i.e., Why don't they follow their "rational self-interest" and abandon this high tax country?) (Economist 2001b). These analyses dismiss too easily the fact that a strong social welfare state helps finance a quality of life that citizens in these societies prefer.

High-income Swedes are well aware of this choice. When faced with the question, "Why don't you leave? Certainly, you would pay a lot lower taxes and probably also have a higher salary in the United States," a Volvo executive responded as follows: "Certainly, you would pay a lot lower taxes and probably also have a higher salary in the U.S. But I would also almost never get home before 7 o'clock and I certainly would not have the vacations everyone has a right to here. And you know what else? I would have to spend a lot more money on insurance, college for my kids and travel back home to my family. In the end, I'm not really sure I would be any better off." (anonymous interview with the author, Gothenburg, Sweden, May 10, 2000) Recent analysis of migration patterns of highly educated Swedish workers conducted in house by the government suggests that, though a large number of Swedish engineers work abroad immediately after graduating

---

[62] Interview with author, Gothenberg, May 13, 2008.
[63] For historical elaborations of this argument see (Pontusson 1992; Steinmo 1988).

TABLE 2.12. *Attitudes toward Public Expenditures*

Answers to the following question: "Taxes are used for various purposes. Do you think the revenues spent on the purposes mentioned below should be increased, held the same, or reduced?" The figures in the table represent the percentage of those wishing to increase expenditures minus the percentage of those wishing to reduce them.

Program	1981	1986	1992	1997	2002
Health care	+42	+44	+48	+75	+77
Support for the elderly	+29	+33	+58	+68	+69
Support to families with children	+19	+35	+17	+30	+26
Housing allowances	−23	−23	−25	−20	−40
Social assistance	−5	−5	−13	±0	−7
Primary and secondary education	+20	+30	+49	+69	+70
Employment policy	+63	+46	+55	+27	+15

Sources: Svallfors, Stefan. 1998. "Mellan risk och tilltro: Opinionsstödet för en kollektiv välfärdspolitik." Umeå: Department of Sociology, Umeå University; Hadenius, Axel. 1986. *A Crisis of the Welfare State?: opinions about taxes and public expenditure in Sweden.* Stockholm: Almqvist & Wiksell International. (2002 Data courtesy of Stefan Svallforss.)

from university, the vast majority return to Sweden when it becomes time to start a family.[64]

Most non-Swedes find it surprising that Swedes did not revolt against their tax burden long before it reached 50 percent of GDP. Few non-Swedes can understand how and why a people could tolerate paying over half of their income to the tax authorities. But what we, non-Swedes, fail to understand is that most Swedes clearly believe they get a lot for the high taxes they pay. Survey after survey has shown that while Swedes, like virtually all citizens in modern welfare states, agree that taxes are too high, only a minority of citizens support tax cuts if they are forced to choose them in exchange for reductions in public spending.

It is also difficult to overemphasize the political implications of the fact that at least 65 percent of Swedes receive a direct public subsidy from their government. Thus, to *average* Swedes, cutting back on public spending means cutting back on benefits they directly receive from the government (Hadenius 1986; Edlund 1999a; Svallfors 1989, 1997). In many areas, at least, they are actually willing to pay more. In fact, as Table 2.12 indicates, public support for *increases* in public spending has *grown* in most areas in recent years.

---

[64] Interview with Knut Rexed StatsSecretar, Stockholm, Sweden, June 8, 2000).

As we can see from Table 2.12, politicians who wish to win elections have few incentives to begin rolling back the universal welfare state. Clearly, social assistance and housing allowances (the two main needs based/income tested programs in Sweden) lack public support. But programs that benefit the middle classes, which, once again, characterizes most public spending in Sweden, seem to be even more popular today than they were ten and twenty years ago.

Clearly the worldwide recession of 2008–09 has had significant implications for the Swedish economy. GDP declined, investment slowed and unemployment set record levels. Interestingly, however, no banks were brought into receivership and the financial sector appears to have weathered the storm relatively well.[65] In the wake of the crisis a new consensus is emerging in Sweden: Activate the labor market, but certainly not through massive deficit increasing tax cuts or a significant scaling back in the welfare state. Once again, the contrast to the United States is especially striking.

Conclusion: Still Flying, But is it Still a Bumble-Bee?

Well before the assassination of Prime Minister, Olof Palme, in 1986, Sweden had already begun to change. Two things were happening at once: Sweden's world famous corporatist wage and policy negotiation system was crumbling. At the same time, the Social Democratic Party elite were re-evaluating the policy instruments that they had long cherished as essential features of the Social Democratic state. These changes were obviously related and taken together they led many to suggest that the Swedish Social Democracy was coming to an end (Lindbeck 1997; Pontusson and Swenson 1996; Schwartz 1993; Lash 1985). In this chapter I have argued that these dire predictions were wrong. It is absolutely clear that the Swedish political economy is changing, and in large part this is in line with major changes in the world economy. But these changes do not mean the end of Sweden's large state or egalitarian ambitions. Instead, what was once known as the "Swedish Model" has evolved. This does not imply that the system is in a race to the bottom or that the leadership must give up on its egalitarian and progressive policy ambitions. But it does appear that the relationships

---

[65] According to Enrique Rodriquez, senior vice-President of SwedBank, the largest Savings and Loan bank in Sweden, the banking crisis was less severe in Sweden because the bankers and regulators had developed close working relationships since the crisis of 1991–2 and consequentially they had taken far less risky positions than their counterparts in many other nations – especially Britain and the United States (Interview with author, November, 8 2009, Stockholm, Sweden).

between labor, business, and the state can no longer be described as symbiotic, as they once were. Clearly they co-evolved, but as the international
context in which they all operated changed, so did their relationships. Each
of these interests has been profoundly shaped by its past, but as in any evolutionary history, when the ecological context in which relationships emerge
changes, so can the relationships – even symbiotic ones. Social Democrats,
labor unions, and business alike have had to adapt the means by which they
achieve their goals in order to remain true to those goals.

Viewing the Swedish case as an evolutionary narrative reminds us that
Sweden in the twenty-first century *must* be very different from Sweden in
the later half of the twentieth century. To remain successful Sweden must
adapt as the world economy evolves. Sweden's traditional reliance on large
high quality manufacturing is clearly giving way to more dynamic, more
service, and more highly skilled political economy. Competitive pressures
from the newly industrializing countries will continue to provide significant
challenges to the Swedish economy just as the growing diversity of Swedish
society offers challenges to Sweden's traditional sense of common identity.

Still, there can be no doubt that Sweden has achieved remarkable economic success *and* egalitarian outcomes over the years and that the commitment to these twin goals are deeply embedded across society and the
political spectrum. It is clear to virtually all analysts that the key to these
redistributive outcomes has been the universalistic social programs which
provide benefits to all citizens regardless of wealth and income (Rothstein
1998). Because they are universalistic, however, they are very expensive.
At the same time, because they are universalistic they generate enormous
popular support. Thus even in the event of slow economic growth, recent
history demonstrates that it is exceptionally difficult to cut these programs.
In the case of economic expansion, like that witnessed recently, there are
even fewer incentives to move in this direction.

Clearly competitive economic pressures have contributed to a variety of
changes in Swedish social welfare and tax systems, but the new model that
is evolving appears to be both economically robust and politically popular.
As Joakim Palme has noted:

The crisis that the Swedish model has undergone has presented different aspects. The
financial crisis was deep but could be overcome relatively quickly. The political and
ideological crisis that this model underwent for much of the 1980s and early 1990s
appears to have been superseded by greater backing for major public undertakings
in the various areas of social policy. Furthermore, the number of people who feel
that the various systems are being over-exploited declined in the early 1990s. Public
faith in the model now appears to be strong on the whole, but an element of distrust

remains. It is expressed in dissatisfaction with healthcare services and with the returns on taxes. Faith in private alternatives, however, does not appear to have increased. (Palme 2003a: 5)

The Swedish welfare state will certainly continue to evolve as new challenges emerge. How well the system adapts to these challenges, of course, remains to be seen. But there does not seem any *a priori* reason to predict that it cannot continue the remarkably healthy evolutionary process that it is currently engaged in.

In the crisis period of the 1930s and 1940s it was quite common to hear both pundits and scholars argue that capitalism had come to a crossroads: Either economic change or political demands (or both) had brought about a transformation of capitalism as it had been known. Looking back, however, one could instead argue that it was the very policies developed in these decades that effectively saved capitalism (Lindblom 1973; Schumpeter 1947). Instead of killing the market, the regulatory and welfare state programs that so many feared had the opposite effects: By redistributing wealth and dampening the swings of the free market, state policy effectively increased aggregate demand and reduced uncertainty. The result was, contra the chicken little hystericists, a virtuous cycle of growth, productivity and increasing prosperity.

At the beginning of the new century, modern capitalism is undergoing enormous change. Not only are capital and labor more internationally mobile than they have been at any time since the end of World War I, but new technologies of production also increasingly pressure capitalists and policy makers alike toward more flexible regimes (Economist 2000; Brooks 2000; Drucker 1986). These changes, however, do not spell the end of the welfare state any more than changes earlier in the century spelled the end of capitalism. Instead, we are witnessing another "Great Transformation" (Blyth 2002), one in which the specific relationship between public and private power is once again a subject of contestation.

As Fritz Scharpf has suggested:

There is, in other words, no one best way through which advanced welfare states could maintain their economic viability in an environment of international capitalism without abandoning their employment, social security and egalitarian aspirations ... [and] there is no reason to think that economic viability should be incompatible with the successful pursuit of these aspirations. (Scharpf 2000: 224)

Sweden's leading expert in public opinion, Sören Holmberg, put it this way: "Well, the citizens don't want to cut back on social spending or social programs, and the New Moderates don't want to roll back the welfare state, so I don't see who would do it. If any politicians propose this," he argues, "they will lose elections. So, I don't see where the incentive to cut back will come from. You just don't hear that kind of neo-liberal talk anymore here in Sweden. Not in the media, not from the parties" (May 12, 2008, Gothenburg).

Anders Borg, Conservative Minister of Finance in a speech in Spring 2008, sounded very much like a Social Democrat when he said that "Globalization" requires public investment. Note that he does not suggest that Sweden should compete in a globalizing world by cutting taxes.

The ability to adapt easily is necessary in a globalized economy. It requires not only lifelong learning but also social security systems designed so that the incentives for re-entering the labour market are strong. Only then is it possible to reduce the risk of individuals becoming trapped in permanent exclusion with few possibilities of affecting their income development. (Borg 2008)

Sweden clearly faces important and very difficult political and economic challenges ahead. As in all advanced democracies, the aging of the population will mean an increasing share of its workers will become recipients of social benefits instead of contributors. As we have seen, potentially more troubling is the possibility that the growing ethnic heterogeneity of this nation will one day undermine the traditional Nordic Swedes willingness to pay taxes for social programs that may increasingly go to racial and ethnic minorities. At this point, however, we see little direct evidence of this problem erupting in Sweden to any extent like that seen in several other European countries.[66]

No one can predict how Sweden or any other country will adapt in the future. At the time of this writing (November, 2009), Sweden appears to be weathering the current economic crisis remarkably well. Indeed many economists and advisors have pointed to the way Sweden handled its economic crisis in the early 1990s as a model for other countries today. I do not doubt that there are many things that others can learn from the Swedish experience. But as I believe this analysis has demonstrated, we must also remember that Sweden is unique. Sweden was advantaged by many factors early in the twentieth century and, consequentially, capital, labor, and the

---

[66] In Fall 2009 an explicitly anti-immigrant political party (Sweden Democrats) is attracting enough popular support that many serious observers are worried that they may enter the parliament in the next national election (September 2010). Quite bluntly, no one can predict the consequence if this does come to pass. But the history of compromise, cooperation, and trust between the traditional parties, interest groups, and elites in Sweden suggests that Swedes will not abandon their commitment to social equality – even if a fringe gets into the Riksdag.

Social Democratic Party co-evolved and even developed symbiotic relationships over time. Though the specific relationships have continued to evolve, in the process, they created a powerful and confident state that has had the legitimacy to act authoritatively in times of crisis and uncertainty. As we have seen, Sweden is changing, but it seems that with these changes come new institutional adaptations within the system. We do not know if this system will continue to be sustained, but from the vantage we have at the end of the first decade of the new millennium, the probabilities look very good indeed.

We will now turn to a very different story.

3

The Japanese Hybrid

One of the most difficult issues I have had in trying to write this book has been to confront the many ways that Japan is both different and similar to the other countries that I have studied. Quite frankly, Japan is not an easy country to understand. This is because Japan is both one of the most modern countries in the world and at the same time it is a remarkably traditional society.

Let me give you a few examples: Japan is clearly a successful democracy with universal suffrage, competitive elections and freedom of the press. Still, until 2009, a single party dominated politics and controlled the government for over 60 years.[1] That party, the Liberal Democratic Party (LDP), however, never offered Japanese voters a coherent or programmatic policy agenda.[2] Similarly, the economy is highly competitive, but at the same time it has been run like a giant cartel. This county is widely known for its hugely successful technically sophisticated international firms, but in reality small and inefficient producers, farmers and retailers dominate much of the economy. Japan has some of the largest and most modern cities in the world, yet throughout Japan one sees farmers and their families standing knee-deep in their rice paddies, hand-planting individual stalks of rice on their small one to two hector farms. Until very recently at least, the distribution of wealth in Japan has been almost as egalitarian as in Sweden. At the same time, Japan is one of the most socially hierarchical countries on earth. Finally, Japan has a reputation as a "strong state" in which its intrusive state bureaucracy has managed and directed the economy so successfully that it grew from the ashes of World War II to the second richest country in the world in less than

---

[1] In 1994 a minority government took the reigns of power for nine months.
[2] This is not to say that there has been no political conflict. For example, there has been intense disagreement over the constitutional prohibition against militarization and nuclear arms.

forty years. But, if you look closely, especially at fiscal and social policy, you find a government that appears incapable of making authoritative decisions or imposing costs on almost anyone in that society. Japan is indeed an enigma (Wolferen 1990).

I believe that the best way to understand this country is to see it as a kind of hybrid.[3] I will argue that Japan really *is* different from the other countries studied here, in part, because it did not go through the slow evolutionary process of developing its own domestic institutions and building those institutions in the context of simultaneously evolving social values and norms. Instead, Japan was forced to adopt (and then adapt to) political and economic institutions that were literally imposed on them from abroad.[4] The result has been a system that is something quite different from the liberal democracies of the Anglo/European world *and* quite different from the traditionalist Asian society from which it evolved. Of course neither these foreign institutions, nor Japanese society and culture have remained frozen (or been held in equilibrium).

Once again, political institutions are at the center of this story. They are in many ways the genes of the state. In Japan's case, however, these institutions were spliced into the body politic and the country has spent much of the last 60 years adjusting. I will show that the peculiar electoral system established after World War II contributed to the creation of a political system in which the classical fight between organized political parties over economic issues or classical redistribution is virtually absent in Japan. Politicians are elected by local constituencies to press local issues. What are normally called political parties are, in fact, coalitions between remarkably autonomous political entrepreneurs. These politicians join together in factions *not* to promote a common ideology or agenda but, instead, join forces in order to serve clientelist objectives. As we shall see, this system is heavily biased in favor of the rural periphery and, rather ironically, disadvantages the productive centers of economic power.[5]

---

[3] Toshimitsu Shinkawa has argued that we need to be careful with the use of the term "hybrid" when describing Japan, because in some senses, we can think of almost any country as a hybrid. To be sure, no country is a pure ideal type and all have in fact had ideas and institutions imported from elsewhere. Still, I argue that Japan is demonstrably different from either Sweden or the United States in this regard (see Shinkawa 2004b).

[4] The biological analogy is a kind of "symbiogenisis." This is a process in which the genes of one organism literally infect another organism and then the new hybrid passes on this gene mix as a new type of organism. Indeed, in micro-organisms, some argue that this is the primary evolutionary force rather than gene mutation (see Margulis 1998; Carrapico 2009; Sapp 2003).

[5] We need to note specifically here the Democratic Party of Japan (DPJ) which came to power in Fall 2009 has promised to change this pattern and is clearly trying to build a more coherent

Part II is an evolutionary narrative describing how this system absorbed *two* great exogenous shocks and then quickly adapted to the realities of a new world that was literally imposed on it. In this narrative, we see a very different story than we read in the last chapter: Sweden developed quickly too. But this relatively late developer was advantaged by the plentitude of iron and charcoal and its position on the northern edge of a rapidly expanding (and warring) European continent. And, as a small and resource rich country, it was able to adapt to successive evolutions of the international political economy. Japan, in contrast, is a geographically isolated nation with almost no natural resources but with a large population spread across an island chain on the eastern edge of the Asian continent. For over 200 years, Japan had isolated itself from the west only to have its feudal system punctuated by the rude arrival of an American admiral and his small fleet of iron warships. The system crumbled and was rebuilt with enormous speed and efficiency as the country engaged in a period of empire building. The result was another major system disruption, this time punctuated with mushroom clouds. But, yet again, the country organized itself with remarkable speed and soon returned to a position of economic prominence, relying on its hierarchical discipline and commitment to growth.

In Part III we will see how this system is struggling, trying to adapt to the new economic realities of a globalizing world economy and an aging society. Here too, our story differs quite dramatically from the Swedish case. Though far more homogeneous than Sweden, Japan appears to have fundamentally more difficulty in adapting and changing to the political and economic realities of the twenty-first century. Although Japan's social, fiscal and economic systems appear to have been quite successful in an era of easy economic growth, it is far from clear how this country can adjust to a more uncertain and more complex world.

PART I

THE JAPANESE MODEL: JAPAN INC.

The Japanese system, like all the other countries studied in this book, is currently undergoing significant changes. But in order to understand these ongoing changes, we must first get a sense of how this complex system fits

and programmatic party system in favor of a more "Westminster" model of government. If they succeed in this goal, they will almost certainly transform the Japanese system. At this point, however, it is far to early to tell whether they will succeed in breaking the traditional patterns of Japanese politics.

together in the first place. First, we will examine its particular economic structure, often referred to as the Japanese Model and sometimes as "Japan Inc." To be sure, there are some significant misunderstandings about this system, but there can be no denying the powerful role the state played in supporting and directing the economy for much of the post-war era. Next, we turn to a discussion of how the unique political institutions developed in post-war Japan. We will see that the structure of the electoral system contributed to a clientelistic system that allowed for the centralization of economic power into the hands of the bureaucratic officials. Finally, we turn to the Japanese welfare state and tax system. Here we will see that Japan never developed a modern "state centered" welfare system, but instead subsidized families and encouraged companies to provide many of the services that in other countries are provided by the state.

Japan Inc.

Much has been written about the "Japanese Model" and particularly the ways in which elite bureaucrats managed a system that emphasized long-term economic growth over consumption and short term profits. Its general outlines are likely well known to the reader: The Ministry of Finance (MoF) and the Ministry of International Trade and Industry (MITI) directed a sophisticated industrial policy in which tariffs, industrial subsidies, market manipulations and export promotion policies were used to promote a number of hugely successful companies and industries.[6]

Although it is easy to overstate the degree of power or control these bureaucrats have had over individual firms, the economic model was very different from that of the other countries examined in this book. A cornerstone of this difference, as Yamamura and Streeck point out, was dependence on a "firm conviction of the superiority of political-economic and social institutions that promote long-term economic performance and on a widely shared assumption that market forces cannot bring about such performance" (Yamamura and Streeck 2003: 5). In this system, large export-oriented manufacturing firms were explicitly promoted in a variety of ways, including trade protection, tax incentives, export promotion, favorable interest rates and, perhaps most distinctively, an explicit system of coordination and cooperation fostered between firms and the central

---

[6] Certainly the most noted work to identify this model was (Johnson 1982). Other works to build on and expand or refine this basic analysis include (Zysman 1977; Borrus et al. 1982; Zysman 1983; Sandholtz and Berkeley Roundtable on the International Economy 1992).

TABLE 3.1. *The Degree of State Control of Economy in Japan, Sweden, and the United States*

	Use of Command and Control Regulation	
	1998	2003
Japan	3.9	3.0
Sweden	1.5	2.3
United States	1.5	1.5

Note: The numbers refer to the OECD's index (0–6 scale from smallest to largest control).
Source: Conway, Paul, Véronique Janod and Guiseppe Nicoletti. 2005. "Product Market Regulation in OECD Countries: 1998 to 2003." In *OECD Economics Department Working Papers*, No. 419. Paris: OECD.

bureaucracy. "To achieve this," Yamamura and Streeck suggest, "the state with its proactive bureaucracy and many private organizations engage in activities that foster mutual trust and cooperation among economic actors" (ibid: 5).

Though Japan is sometimes compared to Germany as a "coordinated market economy," because both countries have "non-liberal" or "coordinated" forms of capitalism, it is important to understand that these systems are different in important ways (Estevez-Abe 2008; Hiwatari 1989). Though both allowed for a much higher degree of economic cooperation than would even be legal in American law, the role of the state has been quite different. Whereas the central commercial banks coordinated much economic activity at a general level in Germany (through, for example, interlocking directorships of the large firms and their banks), in Japan *central government bureaucrats* have played a much more active and specific role in economic management and promotion.

The OECD recently attempted to quantify state intervention in the economy along a variety of measures. As we can see in Table 3.1, even in 2003 (after a decade of reform) the Japanese government has substantially more "command and control," as well as more extensive price controls than so-called "socialist" Sweden. See Table 3.1.

In sharp contrast to the Swedish system, Japan has combined a strong and intrusive state in economic affairs with a remarkably weak state in social affairs. Whereas Swedish governments (even "Socialist" governments) intervened in the economy (mostly) through supportive social policies and only rarely attempted to micro-manage or specifically shape private enterprise decision making, Japanese government actively intervened in the private sector but did not develop extensive social welfare programs either on redistributive or economic efficiency grounds (Estevez-Abe 2008).

The Dual Economy

When most people think of the Japanese economy and Japanese products, we tend to think of the highly efficient and successful export-oriented companies like Mitsubishi, Toyota, and Sony and the technologically advanced products of these companies.[7] These firms are most certainly responsible for the phenomenal growth of the Japanese economy since World War II, but it would not be entirely correct to say that these firms dominate the Japanese economy. In fact, these large firms employ less than twenty percent of the workforce (Katz, 2003: 40).[8] It is surprising to most non-Japanese to discover that Japanese workers are far more likely to work for small companies and/or be self-employed than Americans (see Figure 3.1).

Japan has a large number of small highly productive and innovative firms. The key problem, however, is that Japan *also* has a large share of its economy tied up in small *inefficient* retailers, construction firms and farms. Although it is difficult to accurately measure their drag on the economy – there is no objective way to define firms as "efficient" or "inefficient" in the aggregate – few experts would argue with Richard Katz when he says, "[l]arge swaths of manufacturing, from food processing to materials industries such as glass and cement, lag far behind world standards . . . Construction and the service sector together employ twice as many workers as manufacturing (twenty five million workers) yet offer only half the output per worker" (Katz 2003: 401). Japan's farming and retail sectors are considered to be even more inefficient (McKinsey 2000).

---

[7] These are also known for the interconnectedness within the large banking/industrial/trading groups. For example, the Mitsubishi group (sometimes called a *Keiretsu*), which is lead by the Tokyo-Mistubishi UFJ Bank, consists of: Mitsubishi Corporation, Kirin Brewery, Mitsubishi Electric, Mitsubishi Fuso, Mitsubishi Motors, Nippon Yusen, Nippon Oil, Tokyo Marine and Fire Insurance, Nikon, Mitsubishi Chemical, Mitsubishi Estate, Mitsubishi Heavy Industries, Mitsubishi Rayon Co., Ltd., Mitsubishi Materials Corp., Mitsubishi Paper Mills Ltd., Pacific Consultants International Ltd. These firms are highly interconnected through complex networks of finance, trade and often personal relationships.

[8] This figure should be taken with a grain of salt. Many of these firms hire part time or temporary workers in periods of expansion and also sub-contract with a huge array of other firms.

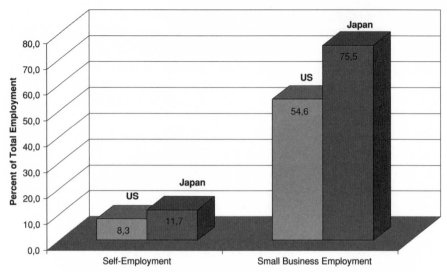

FIGURE 3.1. Self-Employment and Small Business Employment 1996 (As Percent of Total Employment). *Note:* "Small Business" defined as private corporations employing less than 100 workers; Small Business Employment shown as percent of total private employment. *Source:* Statistics Bureau, Ministry of Internal Affairs and Communications. 2000. *Japan Statistical Yearbook.* Tokyo: Japan Statistical Association; U.S. Census Bureau. 2000. *Statistical Abstract of the United States.* Washington, D.C.: Government Printing Office.

Indeed, one of the first things that strikes many new arrivals to Japan is seen in the bus ride from the new Tokyo airport into the city: Just outside the densely packed urban center are small groups of farmers knee deep in tiny half acre rice fields, hand planting individual stalks of rice. If you weren't just a few minutes outside one of the world's most advanced urban centers, you might think you were in the wrong place . . . Until, that is, you go shopping and discover the price of rice.

This "dual economy" can be understood as the product of an implicit deal between the large and highly competitive export oriented manufacturing firms in the major cities, on the one hand and small business and farmers, on the other.[9] The productive sector was to be promoted as world class

---

[9] The relationship between small business, large corporations and the LDP can be difficult for outsiders to understand. Hiroshi Kato, former chair of the Government Tax Council explained it in this way: "In Japan the system is so that big firm creates small and middle-sized firms. So . . . in Japan they are a member of this big corporation system, so they don't think that they are in the bottom, so they actually are in support for the LDP" (Interview, Tokyo, May 28, 2002).

competitors while the backward sectors, especially farming, retailing and construction, were to be protected and subsidized so they did not have to adapt or change. T.J. Pempel describes the system in the following way:

This post-war coalition in Japan is far from self-evidently logical, particularly given the rapid industrialization of Japan and the high domestic costs of the protection afforded... The government maintained an extensive system of price subsidies to Japanese farmers, as well as unnecessarily high levels of government spending in rural areas, both of which kept faming incomes as high as in those in urban areas... Much the same strategy prevailed with regard to small business. (Pempel 1989: 172)

In recent years, this part of the economy and society has acted as a leaden anchor on the more vibrant and dynamic export sectors as Japan faced increased economic competition from its Asian neighbors. Surprisingly, however, after more than fifteen years of recession and economic stagnation, little has been done to modernize and restructure the backward and inefficient sectors of the economy.

"Welfare Through Work"[10]

A key reason why cutting back on the dual economy has been so difficult is that these companies create jobs. Japan's public social welfare system is tiny when compared to other rich industrialized countries and in this context one should think of employers as an integral part of the welfare state. "Japan has over 2.5 million corporations today – most of which are very small companies and a large share of which do not make profits and are instead operating at a loss," a senior official in the Ministry of Finance explained to me. "The people who run the business receive the salary from the corporation, so it's deducted from the company, making a loss at the level of corporation. The company then gets loans from the banks to support itself." This happens year after year, even when there is no turnaround in sight. "In the US, I don't think the company making seven years consecutive losses would be able to borrow money from outside" he concluded. "But in Japan, this is how we support our society" (Oka, April 15, 2002). The result is that even companies that have no hope of paying back their loans are simply extended further credit so they can continue to pay salaries. Japan has long been known for the lifelong relationships between employer and

---

[10] This phrase is drawn directly from Mari Miura's excellent dissertation, "From Welfare Through Work Through Lean Work," University of California, Berkeley, 2002.

employee, though this too is changing rapidly.[11] This means that you keep your job even when the company is losing money by employing you. Indeed, traditionally at least, the relationship continues even *after* the employee leaves the firm. It is widely accepted that one of the fundamental reasons that Japanese firms have done so well in international competition is that their workers were just as committed to the long-term success of the firm as were the managers (Morishima 1982; Thurow 1992).

Miura characterizes the Japanese system as "Welfare through Work" (Miura 2002). It is *not* that the Japanese political economy does not provide what many westerners would consider social welfare, but rather a large measure of this welfare, at least for the salaried employee, is provided in his or her (usually "his") relationship to the employer.

The problem, of course, is that in slack economic times jobs can be scarce. The way to solve this problem has been to increase spending on public infrastructure and construction projects and then contract with small and medium sized firms who then hire the most economically vulnerable. These jobs are often part-time and/or temporary, but they do provide work to able-bodied persons and, thus, should be considered part of Japan's unique social welfare system. The much maligned public works programs in Japan must thus be understood as *both* pork-barrel spending projects and "make work" welfare.[12] It is often noted that Japan spends more on "capital fixed investment" (a.k.a., public works programs) than does any other rich democracy, which is why Japan has sometimes been called a "construction state" (*doken kokka*), one that redistributes national wealth through regional spending on infrastructure.[13] In the mid-90s, the percentage of Gross Domestic Product

---

[11] One should note here that there have been a number of changes in these traditional relationships in recent years. We examine many of these changes and their implications for the Japanese political economy in Part III of this chapter.

[12] The famous *Fiscal Loan and Insurance Program (FLIP)* was one of the many ways this was accomplished: Through a highly complex system of savings incentives and personal local relations, Japanese citizens were encouraged to invest their personal saving in the Postal Savings System. These savings accounts were collected into huge funds that accounted for up to 40 trillion Japanese yen at their height in the mid-1990s that were then redistributed out for special projects around the country (roads, harbor protections, recreation centers, hospitals, bridges, etc.).

[13] Japanese officials defended the system arguing that over 20 trillion yen in annual FILP funds go to social purposes (according to a report by MOF as much 77 percent are spent on "areas that directly to improve people's lives"). These funds, once again, are not included in the annual budget figures, even while they are collected by the public post office, loaned to public authorities and controlled by the Ministry of Finance. (see FILP Plan for FY2000, Ministry of Finance: 2.) Critics and others who analyze the political economy of state spending in Japan, highlight the extensive pork-barrel role of public works (see McCormack 1996). The Post-Office Bank was technically privatized in 2007 though many of its traditional practices are said to remain.

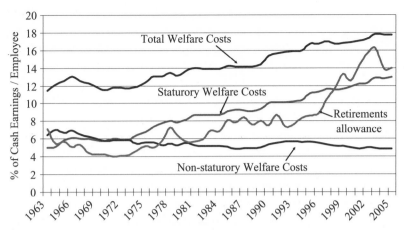

FIGURE 3.2. Japan's Corporate Welfare Expenditures. *Source:* Keidanren. 2004. "Survey on Corporate Welfare Expenditures for FY 2001.

consumed by general government sector fixed capital formation, which is largely public works, was 6.6 percent, which was nearly twice that of Sweden at 3.3 percent, which is itself noticeably greater than the rough average of 2.0 percent for the rest of the OECD. Indeed, gross capital formation constitutes almost a third of Japan's local authorities' expenditures. In 1994, for example, the "Fixed Capital Formation" constituted 31 percent of subnational expenditures in Japan, but only 7 percent in Sweden, 9.1 percent in the United States and 10.1 percent in Germany.[14] Surely, much of this spending was wasteful. Examples of "bridges to nowhere" and highways that do not connect to any major urban area are easy to find. But as Greg Noble points out, on the one hand, there has been a significant scaling back on these expenditures since the end of the century and, on the other hand, they did help take up much of the social welfare functions that the traditional welfare state could not absorb (Noble 2006).

Figure 3.2 shows the "welfare" costs paid by employers to employees in Japan in 2001. As we can see, these payments equal nearly 20 percent of the cash earnings of the employee.

Workers and unions have to a large extent cooperated in the system through what are called "enterprise unions." Whereas organized labor in most capitalist democracies often defines its interest in class terms, Japanese unions are organized along enterprise lines and often see their self-interest

---

[14] Fixed capital formation by national government was also high by international standards accounting for 6.6 percent of total expenditures in Japan in 1994, but only 3.3 percent in Sweden, 2.0 percent in Germany and 1.6 percent in the United States. Source: *OECD: National Accounts, Detailed Tables, Volume 2, 1982–1994.* Paris: 1996.

tied to their firm's economic success. This does not mean that companies and unions always agree. But because workers are organized *within* particular companies, they have been more likely to fight for very specific company based benefits rather than more generalized collective goods, such as unemployment insurance or public pensions. To be sure, the system can be over-characterized, but until recently at least, companies and employees have had "cradle to grave" relationships.

One of the more difficult things for an outsider to understand about the Japanese firms (and the system more generally) is that they have been both egalitarian *and* hierarchical. Observers have long been surprised by the fact that, until recently, Japan has had an economic structure that had near Swedish levels of economic equality.[15] At the same time, the level of deference to seniority, authority and position is palpably greater. Indeed, many have argued that this unique combination has been a key to Japan's success. Professor Toshiaki Tachibanaki, for example, argues that the "egalitarian principle accepted for both blue-collar and white-collar workers seems to have worked to infuse the factory floor with team spirit, which increased productivity of all workers" (Tachibanaki 2005: 61). Economic egalitarianism also encouraged hard work and limited the incentive for "shirking." It encouraged workers to feel that they were members of a family that would take care of them even when times were hard. As we will see, it also contributed to the sense that citizens and consumers should sacrifice for the sake of the betterment of society, especially in the difficult years following World War II.[16] Advancement still follows seniority, although there are several quite notable exceptions to this today. The principle seems to be that if you work hard and are patient, you also will benefit. The individual is not seen as the keystone of this system, instead it is the group. Indeed, the Japanese expression, "the nail that sticks out will be pounded down," is commonly used to help foreigners understand group mentality in this country.

Economic equality does not mean social equality. Rather, the system is governed by a set of hierarchical relationships that assume and demand deference and respect. This system is probably the most alien to Americans who have virtually no traditions glorifying hierarchy. (Before my Japanese

[15] We will see below that this picture is no longer accurate and Japan has become much less egalitarian over the past two decades.

[16] According to World Bank statistics from 1993, Japan was the third most egalitarian country in the democratic world (after Denmark and Sweden) with a Gini index of 24.9. The share of national income that went to the poorest 20 percent was 10.6 percent whereas the share going to the richest 20 percent of the population was 35.7 percent. This ratio (4.5 percent is the lowest of any country they examined (World Bank 2005). As we shall see below, most of this equality is explained by the relatively even distribution of incomes. We will also see, however, that this picture has changed dramatically in recent years. See (Garon 2006a).

friends and colleague jump up here and shout, "that's an old fashioned view," let me say that I know this is changing. But the fact is that Japan still, at the beginning of the twenty first century, is more traditional and hierarchical than any Anglo-European advanced society.) The point here is not to make cultural stereotypes but to admit that the norms of deference to authority, respect for hierarchy and economic equality have gone together in Japan to create a remarkably successful economic model.

Political Structure: Politics without Ideology

In Western democracies it makes good sense to describe politics on a "Left/Right" scale with the Left representing workers, consumers, and the poor/middle classes and the Right representing producers, capitalists, and the middle/upper classes. In Japan, at least for domestic politics, this scale simply does not apply. Although there have been occasions in which far Left socialist/communist parties have made a significant amount of noise in Japan, they have traditionally taken policy positions that would be difficult to explain to a Western "socialist" (e.g., demanding tax cuts for small businesses and objecting to the expansion of many public programs). The class based ideological battles that have defined and driven politics in much of the industrialized world have simply been less important in Japan than elsewhere. Indeed, until very recently at least, there has been a virtual consensus that the fruits of Japan's economic growth should be shared and that the kind of inequality witnessed in pre-war years should be avoided at virtually all costs. While there is a very vocal and important "Right wing" in Japanese politics, these activists represent militarists and social traditionalists from a wide swath of economic interests, including workers and rich capitalists.[17]

It is tempting to explain the lack of clear ideological choices in Japanese politics as a product of the hierarchical or deferential culture, but to do so reifies culture to the point where the concept no longer makes any sense. Instead, the key to understanding the political dynamics of Japanese politics is to understand it as clientelistic system. Japanese politics is clientelistic because of the structure of its political institutions *not* because Japanese people don't have strong political views (even if it can be difficult to get them to express these views to foreigners). We will discuss recent changes in the electoral system later in this chapter, but for the first five decades

---

[17] The major ideological divide between what is called 'Left' and 'Right' in Japan is over foreign policy. The Japanese Left has traditionally demanded an anti-militarist (pro-constitution) stance, while the Japanese Right favors more investment in the military and a more assertive foreign policy (see Shinkawa 2000).

following World War II, Japan's electoral structure was biased against ideological politics. The system of multiple-member electoral districts and "single non-transferable votes" (SNTV) meant that politicians acted as independent political entrepreneurs. Each candidate effectively ran his/her own (again almost always, 'his') electoral campaign, which was largely independent of the party to which he was nominally affiliated.[18] *Parties* are coalitions of politicians who build relationships between themselves and the bureaucracy in order to distribute specific benefits to their constituencies. Americans will be familiar with the 'pork barrel' politics of the United States system; the Japanese system, in comparison, is more like an industrial hog farm (DeWit 2002).

The lack of a clear ideological Left/Right divide helps explain how and why much of the details of policymaking have often reverted to administrators in the central government. Politicians focus on protecting and promoting their local constituents' interests rather than advancing broad policy platforms or introducing long range plans. As we will see, this institutional fact has been enormously consequential for the development of the Japanese welfare state. Faced with these electoral realities, on the one side and with a virtual national consensus on the need to develop strong and successful industries and corporations, on the other, central government officials built a system that used the economic success of Japan's internationally competitive export firms to subsidize an enormous number of small and medium sized inefficient farms and businesses. Unsurprisingly, these groups make up the electoral core of the Liberal Democratic Party (Ramseyer and Rosenbluth 1993; Pempel 1982b).

The personalized structure of the Japanese electoral system also yielded heavy electoral bias in favor of rural districts. Most democracies tend to overweight the political value of rural voters. Industrialization typically works to drive more people from rural communities to urban centers. Rarely does an electoral system keep up with this demographic shift. But in Japan this bias has been extreme.[19] This has meant that politicians face strong incentives to cater to the interests of rural communities that have older and poorer constituents than those in the urban center (DeWit and Steinmo 2002). As

---

[18] For good discussions of the Japanese electoral system and its implications (see Itoh 1973; Johnson 1995; Curtis 1999; Pfarr 2000; Pempel 1982a; Reed 2003).

[19] Before 1972 one electoral district had *five times* as many Diet members per capita as some urban districts. In 1976 a Japanese Supreme Court ruling declared the radical malapportionment extant in Japan unconstitutional. As a result a series of reapportionments have been put into place. Still the system persists to the point where one persons vote in a rural district can be worth as much as 2.3 urban votes (Katz 2003: 286).

TABLE 3.2. *Prefectures' Per Capita Tax Burdens, Receipt of Subsidies, and Effective Rate of Return in 1998 (Units: Y1000)*

Prefecture	Tax Burden			Revenues			Rate of Return
	National	Local	Total(A)	L. Tax	Subsidies	Total(B)	B/A
Tokyo	1,410	533	1,943	533	87	628	0.323
Osaka	625	341	966	341	130	474	0.491
Aichi	515	351	866	351	45	460	0.531
Kanagawa	369	313	682	313	93	408	0.598
Chiba	274	267	541	267	133	404	0.747
Okinawa	199	145	344	145	560	709	2.061
Nagasaki	165	177	342	177	526	708	2.070
Kagoshima	172	175	347	176	653	737	2.124
Kochi	202	186	388	185	765	857	2.209
Shimane	197	211	408	211	729	949	2.326
National Average	416	286	702	286	263	554	0.789

Note: Minor revenue sources are excluded and hence the sum of local taxes and subsidies is slightly less than the total in B.

Source: Adapted from Tokyo Tax Commission (2000), Reference Section, p. 18.

Table 3.2 shows, the per capita tax burden in the largest city, Tokyo, is nearly *five times* as heavy as in more rural prefectures, while public per capita transfers from the central government to local authorities can be nearly twice as high in rural areas than in the largest cities.

The contrast with Sweden – a country dominated by a single political party for most of the past half century with a bureaucratic elite playing a key role in developing long term plans to achieve their fundamental ideological goals – could not be more stark.[20] Whereas the Social Democrats entered government with an ideological agenda, the LDP has been far less clear about what holds members together other than the desire to get re-elected.[21] There has been almost no mechanism for elected officials to see beyond their short-term electoral needs or to build comprehensive solutions to long-term

[20] For an interesting comparative analysis of one party regimes with a specific look at Japanese and Swedish comparisons see (Pempel 1990).

[21] Muramatsu and Krauss emphasize the flexibility and openness of the LDP as what they call a "catch-almost-all" party. For them the party is not ideologically vacuous, but rather open to many ideas and interests. They point out, for example, that the party is primarily conservative in its leanings, but as citizen concern over the environment and welfare inadequacies grew in the 1970s, the party championed both a "welfare revolution" and some of the most stringent antipollution laws in the world (Muramatsu and Krauss 1990).

problems (Reed 1993). This function has been left to the bureaucracy. In both Sweden and Japan, central government elites, especially in the Ministry of Finance, have had to balance the interests and demands placed upon them by elected officials, but as we saw earlier, Swedish elites have been repeatedly able to convince their members of the need to sacrifice short-term electoral incentives in favor of longer term ideologically informed agendas. Absent strong political parties, Japanese officials have been far less successful in this regard.

This does not mean, however, that politicians are outside the policy making sphere in Japan. Quite the contrary, just as in the United States, elected officials can be very active policy makers. The electoral system in Japan can also work to give politicians enormous job security (Scheiner 2005). Once in office for several elections, politicians often develop extensive, substantive knowledge over particular policy domains *and* extensive contacts with the bureaucratic machinery. In this way they can extend their sphere of influence in the Diet. Consequentially, a kind of symbiotic relationship often develops: Bureaucrats rely on politicians to introduce policy initiatives they favor and politicians rely on the bureaucratic support (and expertise) to insure that their districts continue to be happy. Most important areas of public policy have a group of senior politicians, a *Zoku*, who wield significant expertise in their fields and, consequentially, no small amount of respect from the agencies with which they interact (Curtis 1999: 53–55).[22] LDP politicians can participate in these *Zoku* for many years and, over time, can become highly expert in these policy areas.[23] Given the very long tenure in the Diet, this can sometimes mean that the politicians can know and understand particular policy domains as well or better than the bureaucrats. Senior members of important *Zoku* are also very likely to be selected to important ministerial level positions in the government, which of course enhances both their policy expertise and their power to distribute largess to other members of the Diet.

[22] The well-known practice of *"Amakudari" (Descent from Heaven)* also contributes to the policy expertise in the Diet. A significant number of politicians are one-time senior bureaucrats. Senior bureaucratic elites are expected to retire from administration by the age of 55 at the latest. Typically the most senior officials will become executives in major Japanese private firms and public enterprises, or they will run for elected office. For a excellent discussion of this process see (Johnson 1982) see also (Pempel 1974). Voters will support former bureaucrats because they believe that the bureaucrats will be most successful at "bringing home the bacon" since they have well-established networks inside the bureaucracy.

[23] We will see in the following chapter that a similar, but more formal, committee system has been established in the United States as well.

It is important to note, as Andrew DeWitt skillfully does, that one should not build a false dichotomy emphasizing *either* strong bureaucrats *or* strong politicians in order to understand the development of Japanese fiscal policy:

Thus I would emphasize that my argument is not another partisan challenge from the "statist" side of the highly polarized and ultimately pointless debate on whether bureaucrats or politicians run Japan. Parties and politicians are powerful actors in contemporary Japan, but it is a non sequitur to insist that bureaucratic interests and influence are therefore irrelevant. The reverse equation is equally illogical, as presuming bureaucratic power does not require that one also assume elected politicians are thus enfeebled, barely able even to wield a rubber stamp. In researching intergovernmental fiscal politics such gross methodological reductionism is of little value (DeWit 1998).[24]

In sum, the Japanese political economy can be characterized as being a system in which large export oriented firms have been promoted and supported by a highly sophisticated interventionist elite bureaucracy through detailed industrial policy tools. The fruits of this economic success have been redistributed rather broadly throughout the society through a complex clientelistic and non-ideological political system and not, as we shall see in the following section, through traditional welfare state mechanisms.

Japan's Small (Public) Welfare State

"Japan is not a country of the welfare state." (Tachibanaki 1996:283)

Perhaps one of the most interesting features of the Japanese post-war political economy is that Japan developed one of the most egalitarian countries in the world, without the growth of a large welfare state. This fact does not suggest that Japan resembles a more liberal free market society, like the United States. Quite the contrary, it has accomplished this goal (and social equality has clearly been a goal)[25] by maintaining high levels of employment

---

[24] Examples include journalistic assertions of bureaucratic dominance, the "Japan Inc." model, Marxian theories of state monopoly capitalism and the effortless *post hoc* claims of political control from the rational choice principal-agent school. By contrast, note Peter Evans's defense of the eclectic messy center of comparative politics; in Atul Kohli *et al.*, "The Role of Theory in Comparative Politics," *World Politics* 48, October 1995, p. 2. See also John C. Campbell's comments on the rational choice versus statist debate in Japanese politics in *Social Science Japan*, No.8, 1997.

[25] Indeed, as Sidney Verba's study on elite attitudes toward equality, Japanese elites were the most egalitarian in the world (Verba 1987).

where employees receive good wages with excellent benefits, relying on net-works of family social responsibility, restricting immigration and, finally, tremendous spending on "make work" public construction projects.

Many people believe that the United States has the smallest welfare state in the advanced world. Although the United States has the lowest level of public spending, the highest levels of inequality and a political culture that emphasizes individual responsibility, it actually has a more developed and extensive set of public programs targeted at the poor than does Japan. In fact, welfare programs targeted on low-income earners and/or programs designed to aid the poor are smaller, relatively underdeveloped and less funded in Japan than they are in any other advanced democratic state in the world. The total number of people receiving some type of public assistance in Japan in 2001 was 805,000 households. The majority of these were the aged (370,000) or households with disabled family members (304,000).[26] In a country of over 120 million inhabitants, only 68,000 "households of mother and children" received public aid. Many American cities have more public aid recipients than the whole of Japan.[27]

Consider the plight of an unemployed housewife living in a rented apart-ment with two children whose husband abandons her without resources. In most welfare states this family would be eligible for a variety of different types of public assistance. The household would most likely have its rent paid for and be given direct cash subsidies to pay for the costs of living. In the United States this family could become homeless, but there are also a variety of programs (food stamps, public assistance, etc.) that would, at least temporarily, help the family in this situation. In Japan, if the woman went to the public authorities to ask for assistance, she would be told that

[26] (DeWit and Steinmo 2002) See also: Statistics and Information Department, Minister's Secretariat and Social Welfare and War Victims' Relief Bureau, Ministry of Health, Labour and Welfare. "Public assistance" accounted for only 2.5 percent of social spending in Japan in 2001. Family allowance, public assistance and "social welfare" combined consumed 6.4 percent of total Social Security expenditures (Health Insurance = 18.2 percent, Health and medical services for the aged = 13.3 percent, Long-term care insurance = 13.3 percent, Pensions = 49.9 percent). Data from Department of Home Affairs.

[27] Another significant feature of the Japanese system is the very low 'take up rates' for welfare and public health. Both because of social stigma and very strict bureaucratic rules, Japan has a very small percentage of citizens who take advantage of social welfare policies. In fact, the take up rate in Japan actually declined from 2.30 percent in 1950 to 1.3 percent in 1970. In the United Kingdom, the take up rate increased from 3.9 percent to 7.7 percent over the same period – and the United Kingdom had relatively low take up rates when compared to other European countries (Tachibanaki 2000: 200). In recent years the country has been scandalized by cases where individuals who were rejected by public welfare officials have been found dead from starvation (Onishi 2007).

TABLE 3.3. *Public Expenditure on Wage-Related Income-Transfer Programs, 1992 (Percent GDP)*

Japan	0.91
France	5.39
Germany	6.31
UK	7.84
US	2.64

Note: Unemployment payments excluded.
Source: Tanzi, Vito and Ludger Schuknecht. *Public spending in the 20th century: a global perspective.* Cambridge, UK; New York: Cambridge University Press, Table II. 11.

she must first contact all of her relatives (mother, father, brothers, uncles, etc.) to ask for their help. Only after she can demonstrate that her family members are not able or willing to help would the state step in with direct support. It is highly unlikely that this family would become homeless, as they could eventually do in the United States, but it is less obvious that this is because of the public programs protecting the poor than because families do in fact take greater responsibility for their members in this society than they do in Europe and America.[28]

As Table 3.3 indicates, Japan spends only slightly more than a third as much on income transfer programs as the United States and almost eight times less than the United Kingdom.

The point here is *not* to suggest that this system does not provide social welfare to its citizens. Instead, there are highly complicated and often very extensive mechanisms through which social welfare is essentially funded by companies and provided by family networks – which in reality effectively means by wives and daughters (Shinkawa 2004a). As Table 3.4 shows, income inequality was relatively low by international standards fifteen years ago, despite the fact that government taxes and transfers resulted in comparatively little redistribution.

One of the key differences between the Swedish welfare state and the Japanese is that in Sweden women are generally paid in public service to perform many of the functions that they provide "for free" in Japan. The first consequence of this is that women have more limited life choices in Japan than in Sweden. In Japan women's social welfare functions are tied to

---

[28] See (Gill 2001), for a broad account of this growing problem in Japan.

TABLE 3.4. *Gini Coefficients and Redistribution, Selected Countries, 1995*

	Before Taxes and Transfers	After Taxes and Transfers	Percent Changes Due to Taxes and Transfers
Sweden	48.7	23.0	−52.9
France	39.2	23.1	−41.0
Germany	43.6	28.2	−35.3
Japan	34.0	26.5	−22.0
USA	45.5	34.4	−24.5

Source: OECD 1999. "Economic Surveys, Sweden," Table, 13.

particular individuals, their children and their parents in-law. Certainly, the Japanese social welfare system has significant advantages from a state/fiscal point of view. Basically, it is much cheaper, in the short run, than the Swedish system: The government does not need to raise tax revenue to pay women when they stay at home and care for children and grandparents. But this system fundamentally shapes women's employment and career opportunities, as women are *expected* to leave the workforce immediately upon having children.[29] The virtual absence of subsidized day care, combined with the low average salaries earned by women, makes this almost a necessity at any rate. Finally, as we will see, the tax and wage systems also discriminate in favor of male-breadwinner families and against women who wished to stay in the workforce.[30]

Taxation Japanese Style

The Japanese tax system has co-evolved with its dual economy and its small welfare state. It has a number of surprising features. The first is that Japan has had the smallest tax burden of any rich country since World War II. The second is that, until very recently at least, it collected a higher share of its revenues from corporate profits and property taxes with a lower share from consumption taxes than any other country in the OECD. These general revenue outcomes are the product of a system that has advantaged specific groups such as farmers, small businessmen, the aged and workers while taxing heavily the largest and most successful firms. The result has been a

[29] In fact, it is still quite normal for women to leave paid work immediately upon getting married, even before they become pregnant.

[30] Once again, we should note that the new DPJ government in Japan has promised reforms in this area. It is too early to tell if they will be able to implement these especially given the economic crisis this country now faces.

TABLE 3.5. *Personal Income Tax Payments by Income Class, 1999*

	Income Class (units: ¥ 10,000)					
	500	700	1000	3000	4000	5000
Japan	11.5	32	86	890	1,365	1,840
France	24.5	54	123	1,055	1,558	2,060
Germany	53.2	125	250	1,268	1,780	2,291
UK	91.8	168	288	1,088	1,488	1,888
USA	54.0	97	202	1,011	1,464	1,913

Note: The data reflect tax payments for a worker with 2 children and a non-working spouse.
Source: Ministry of Finance, Japan. Retrieved from http://www.mof.go.jp/jouhou/syuzei/siryou/028.htm.

tax system that by economic standards has been highly inefficient, but by most accounts an effective instrument through which the state could and did influence private sector decisions (Akaishi and Steinmo 2003; Johnson 1982). Japan has had one of the most nominally progressive personal income tax systems in the world. This is not because the rich pay so much more in Japan than elsewhere, but rather because the poor pay so little (See Table 3.5).

The Japanese have, in short, taken virtually the opposite approach to taxation from the Swedish. Whereas the Swedes have a remarkably flat tax system that generates huge amounts of revenues to the state (which are then spent mostly on universal programs), the Japanese have developed a tax system with a very narrow tax base that generates comparatively little revenue.

This system is particularly favorable to the key constituent groups of small business owners and farmers (Estevez-Abe 2002; see also Hiwatari 1991). Professor Hiromitsu Ishi, perhaps Japan's most eminent fiscal economist, famously described the Japanese system as a "Ku-ro-yon" (90–60-40) tax system, meaning that due to tax loopholes and inefficiencies in tax collection/administration, different types of income are collected at radically different rates. Salaried workers who have taxes withheld at source pay taxes on approximately 90 percent of their income (Ku). The self-employed pay taxes on only 60 percent (ro) and farmers pay taxes on only 40 percent (yon) of their income (Ishi 1992: 140–43).

It will surprise many to learn that, despite the power and interconnections between Japanese large export-oriented firms and central government officials, these large companies carry a higher percent of the total tax burden than do companies in any other capitalist democracy (See Table 3.6). In

TABLE 3.6. *Revenues from Major Taxes as Percent of Total Taxation,*
1998

	Income	Profits	Soc. Sec.	Property	Goods & Services
Japan	18.8	13.3	38.4	10.5	18.8
France	17.4	5.9	36.2	7.3	26.6
Germany	25.0	4.4	40.4	2.4	27.4
UK	27.5	11.0	17.6	10.7	32.6
USA	40.5	9.0	23.7	10.6	16.2
OECD avg.	27.1	8.9	24.7	5.4	31.3

Source: OECD. 2001. *Revenue Statistics, 1965–1999.* Paris: OECD Publishing.

other words, the large and profitable export oriented companies have traditionally carried substantial welfare costs for their employees and at the same
time paid very high profits taxes. Taxes on small firms, personal income and
consumption, on the other hand, have been very low in Japan due to the
large numbers of deductions and exemptions available to small businesses,
farmers, pensioners, and employees with families.[31]

Summing Up

The Japanese political economy is a complex hybrid *system.* On the one
hand, there can be no doubt that the formal democratic and economic
institutions bear strong similarities to those in the West. On the other hand,
it is clear that these institutions do not function in the same ways as they do
in the West. Initially, it can be difficult to understand how this system fits
together, but my argument here is that it *has* fit together. While it has built a
very small public social welfare state, it has had high levels of public welfare;
and while tax and social spending have not been particularly redistributive,
this county has been one of the most egalitarian societies in the capitalist
world. Japan grew from a country devastated by nuclear war and firebombed
cities in 1945 to the second richest country in the world in less than 40 years.
It has spawned some of the richest and most successful international firms
and concomitantly retained a very large and very unproductive economic

[31] 67 percent of small firms in Japan (under 100 million yen in initial capitalization) paid no
taxes in 2005 (a year or economic recovery) for the simple reason that they had no reported
profits. In addition, small retailers are able to collect the 5 percent sales tax and it is widely
known that they often do not report these taxes to the authorities. In other words, they can
legally pocket the sales tax revenues they have collected from their customers. Data provided
by MoF. Sept. 2008.

core. It taxes its most successful firms extremely heavily and subsidizes the least successful. It has passed laws promoting women's rights at the same time that it relies on wives *(okusan)* to serve as the major delivers of social services in a state with few formal social services. It modernized and it didn't.

In the next section I present an evolutionary narrative that is intended to help the reader better understand how and why this system evolved down the path it has taken. Then, in the last part of this chapter, we will explore the enormous challenges facing Japan economically, politically, and socially and how it is adapting to them (or not).

PART II

THE EVOLUTION OF THE JAPANESE MODEL

On July 8, 1853, Commodore Mathew Perry of the United States Navy sailed four black-hulled, modern, steam powered frigates into Uraga Harbor near Edo (modern day Tokyo) and shook Japan's world. For more than two hundred years the Japanese regime had protected itself and its rule from outside influences by refusing to allow foreigners to enter the country or even trade with its people.[32] Perry's intention was not to conquer Japan, in the normal sense of the word. Instead, he simply insisted that he be allowed ashore to present a letter from President Millard Fillmore that demanded that Japan open itself to trade and commerce with the United States. There are differing interpretations of exactly the turn of events and also over how biased the eventual treaty would be against Japanese interests. But the fact that the hitherto all-powerful Samurai military was flatly incapable of confronting a few iron ships and their modern cannon, proved to be a humiliating defeat. The eventual result was a crumbling of the Tokugawa Shogunate and the profoundly hierarchical and traditional society on which it had depended.

It is difficult for us to appreciate today just how hierarchical and structured Japanese society was at this point. As in European feudalism, there were profound differences between different ranks of society, but by most accounts, the strict hierarchy and demands for obedience were far higher in Japan than in medieval Europe. For example, peasants were required to show deference to their superiors to the point that if a lord felt that a peasant had not shown him proper respect, he had the legal right to behead him on the spot. In contrast to European knights of the middle ages who took

---

[32] Exceptions were allowed for trade through the extreme southwestern port of Nagasaki.

pride in chivalry, Japanese Samurai held women in extremely low regard. Indeed, the principle of *danson-johi* (respect for the male, contempt for the female) was deeply embedded in the structure of the social order (Hurst and Notehelfer 2009).[33]

I will not elaborate here on the history of the next several decades other than to note that in response to the massive shock to their system, the Japanese proved remarkably capable of adapting to and absorbing the technologies to which they had proven so vulnerable. A virtual army of its young men traveled the world in search of ideas, patents and machinery that they could bring home to build Japan back to its rightful place as a great (rather than servile) nation. The pace of the transformation was awesome: Japan was transformed from a pre-industrial nation in the 1870s to an aspiring empire in the early decades of the twentieth century.[34] These ambitions and technologies combined contributed to military expansionism and war (Smitka 1998). In a matter of a very few decades, Japan was in a position to challenge the great powers that had once humiliated it.[35] In 1941, Japan attacked the American Navy at Pearl Harbor. The military dictatorship hoped that one swift blow to a country already at war would allow Japan to continue its expansion and domination of Asia (Mosk 2001). It did not work out exactly this way.

It would be an understatement to say that defeat in World War II was a critical juncture – or "punctuated equilibrium" – in the evolution of the Japanese political economy. In the following pages, we will examine how this country adapted and changed after its defeat. This is a remarkable story of evolutionary symbiogenisis in which entirely new institutions were transferred and integrated into the old. But as we also shall see, this story offers examples of *exaptation*, where old institutions take over new functions and,

---

[33] See (Ikegami 1995) for a fascinating and sophisticated analysis of the role of the samurai in the transformation of Japan from a traditional feudal society to a modern political economy.

[34] At the core of the industrial expansion of Japan were large family held integrated enterprises called *Zaibatsu*. These zaibatsu were highly integrated firms consisting of a holding company, a controlling bank and several industrial enterprises, which generally dominated specific sectors of a market, either solely, or through a number of sub-subsidiary companies. The four main zaibatsu, in particular (Sumitomo, Mitsui, Mitsubishi, and Yasuda), had significant political influence, especially in the years after 1920. These four firms alone controlled between 30 and 50 percent of many key industries in pre-war Japan (chemicals, mining, machinery and equipment, as well as over 50 percent of merchant shipping and 60 percent of the Japanese stock market.)

[35] Not only did they defeat the Chinese in the first Sino-Japanese War in 1895, but more importantly, the Japanese became the first Asian nation to defeat a European power in the Russo-Japanese War of 1904–5.

ultimately, create new hybrids.[36] Japan became a democratic and capitalist nation. Although there were elements of progressive and democratic politics in Japan before the war, these forces were weak at best. Quite possibly, the country might one day have reached a level of economic development that might have evoked more powerful demands for democratic electoral institutions, redistributive taxation and social welfare programs, just as Western countries did. But the fact remains that Japan lost the war and in its aftermath democratic institutions *were imposed*. Japan had to adapt to these new institutions, but the institutions also had to be adapted to Japan.

Occupation

The American occupiers did not know exactly what kind of political institutions they should bring to Japan, but they clearly believed Japan would become a better country and friend if they developed a more egalitarian democracy (Pempel 1982b). They struggled with the question of whether they should establish an American style system replete with "checks and balances" or a more centralized parliamentary system as in Britain. In the immediate post-war years, a multi-member electoral district system was brought in on the European parliamentary model. But, by 1947, this system was repealed and Japan introduced a system of Single-Non-Transferable Votes (SNTV), which resembled the electoral system used in Japan before the war. This system was neither the "single member district" system as found in Britain and the United States, nor a directly proportional representation system (PR) like that found in Europe. Instead, in the Japanese case, individual candidates ran for office in multi-member electoral districts. In this hybrid system, each electoral district had between three and five representatives elected to the national assembly (Diet), but all candidates ran against one another, even if they were in the same political party. Votes were not transferable and there were no "party lists." Consequentially, each candidate had to develop one's own electoral machinery.

The result was that politicians became independent political entrepreneurs, each responsible to one's home electoral district rather than a particular party or ideology. Parties exercised far less control over their members' votes than their counterparts in European party machines. In fact,

---

[36] Exaptation is the idea that the function of a trait might shift during its evolutionary history; it originated with Charles Darwin (1859). A classic example is bird feathers, initially, bird feathers evolved for temperature regulation, but later were adapted for flight. For many years the phenomenon was labeled "preadaptation." However, that term suggests forethought, which is contrary to a basic principle of natural selection.

it has been (and continues to be) difficult to identify broad ideological similarities within parties in Japan. As noted earlier, it is more accurate to speak
of them (the LDP in particular) as coalitions of self-interested factions, allied
largely for the purpose of better catering to their constituents, than groupings
of ideologically motivated policy entrepreneurs. In this system participation
in a party coalition became more of a strategic calculation on the part of the
politician than a statement of ideological affinity (cf Scheiner 2005). Leadership of the party and government also changed hands frequently according
to the shifting winds of factional coalition arrangements. Thus oddly, while
the LDP has been in power for virtually all of the post-war years, it is difficult to say who has been in power in the LDP. Between 1945 and 2009 the
Prime Minister's office had changed hands 35 times. Ministers of Finance
tend to last for an even shorter length of time: Leadership of the Ministry of
Finance changed hands 53 times in the same period.[37]

Equality to Defend Democracy

American reformers also strongly believed that social and economic equality were essential components of a successful democratic society and that
Japan had turned to fascism in the 1930s in part because of extreme economic inequality (Milly 1999: 95–130).[38] United States economists and
treasury officials, who were studying the Japanese wholeheartedly, believed
that successful democracy depended on a more egalitarian society (Shinkawa
2007a). In order to achieve these goals, the Allies pushed a massive "land
reform" program that redistributed lands from the former great landholding
elite to the peasant farmers, who had worked the land for generations. In
keeping with Jeffersonian beliefs, they also believed that if citizens owned
their own land they would be more responsible voters. The occupation
forces also believed that a broad-based income tax system would help create
a more egalitarian society and give working people a direct stake in their
government, making them more interested in political affairs. "Ironically,"
as Margarita Estevez-Abe points out, "'democratic' taxation was implemented in a rather undemocratic way" (Estevez-Abe 2002: 165). Whereas
redistributive policies were developed in response to the growing power of

---

[37] Contrast this with Swedish parliamentary democracy where, for example, the Social
Democrats were in office continuously from 1936 to 1974 and had only three Prime Ministers and four Ministers of Finance during this entire period.

[38] Recent work by Toshiaki Tachibanaki and others demonstrates that Japan was indeed one
of the most unequal societies in the modernizing world at this time (Tachibanaki 2005:
70–85).

unions and leftist political parties, representing workers and/or the poor in the West, there was little indigenous pressure for such policies in Japan. As Milly notes, the Allies' progressive policies "gained less than solid support among the Japanese leadership and the general public" (Milly 1999: 129; see also Shinkawa 2007a: 77).

Post-War Goal #1 – Economic Growth

The Japanese hybrid was crafted to produce growth. To be sure, the leadership was concerned about the problem of poverty, which was widespread, but to them poverty was largely a product of low levels of economic development and not the product of another group having too much.[39] Economic growth, *not* redistribution, was the only real option available given this framing of the problem. But at the same time, as Milly shows, Japanese elites did not see a conflict between the goals of social equality and economic growth, instead they viewed these goals as tied together. The rub was that many of the poorest households in Japan were composed of rural farmers, small independent businessmen and their employees. At this time, more than 45 percent of all workers were employed in firms with fewer than 30 employees and these firms employed the lowest paid workers. The result was that the very basis of class politics motivating politicians and policymakers elsewhere was skewed in the Japanese case. Helping the poor survive effectively meant helping the "petite bourgeoisie." Consequentially, the LDP "articulated a vision for a conservative welfare state that gave priority to producer groups – including small scale producers – over labor groups" (Milly 1999: 176).

Although the key political issue facing Japanese politicians was *not* the conflict between economic or social classes, the very success of Japan's postwar economic development, which pushed resources toward the large export

[39] Ministry of Health and Welfare officials estimated that fully 45 percent of the population was living in poverty in the years immediately following the war. Twenty five percent were below a "physiological subsistence level" (Milly 1999:16). For example, Hirata Keiichiro, who held the positions of Tax Bureau Chief, Head of the National Tax Agency and Ministry of Finance Vice-Minister, said that at the time of the defeat "In collecting taxes from the poor, there were severe cases such as stories about chasing three chickens in for the levies on a farm household; that was certainly a pathetic time" (Ohtake 1991: 13). Moreover, they concluded that some parts of the economy, especially small businessmen and farmers, would be too difficult to effectively be caught in the tax net. The higher the tax rate imposed on these groups, the greater the incentive to avoid taxes. And given their economic position, they, like small businessmen and farmers in many countries, had plenty of opportunities to avoid paying these taxes.

oriented sectors of the economy, led to growing disparities between the
urban centers and the rural periphery. As in many countries, rural areas
suffered as economic rationalization spurred a massive movement of labor
away from agriculture and traditional industries toward the large manufacturing firms in the cities (Yoshikawa 1997, 184–85). But it is hard to
overemphasize the extent of this problem in the Japanese case. In 1945,
fifty-three percent of the population depended on agriculture for their living
in Japan; by 1970 this figure had been reduced to nineteen percent, which
was still many times higher than in Sweden or the United States. Unsurprisingly, it was often the relatively uneducated and the old that were left
behind. Of course, this was not just an economic and social problem, but a
political problem as well: The poorest districts in the country were depopu-
lating the quickest, but due to the electoral system, the poorest rural districts
generally have the most political weight. Unsurprisingly, then, tax policies
that increased the burden on these areas were anathema to politicians, while
public spending programs that focused public largess in their direction were
highly favored (DeWit and Steinmo 2002).[40]

The basic outlines of what was needed for successful economic development were well understood (heavy investment in steel, manufacturing, chemicals, infrastructure, etc.). As Figure 3.3 indicates, the Japanese workforce
changed remarkably quickly in the decades following the war. Manufacturing technologies had advanced significantly because of investments made
during World War II and these were also relatively stable during this period.
Japan also had geopolitical advantages at the time. Even though the country
had lost its war with the United States, the American authorities quickly
came to view Japan as their top strategic ally in Asia. American authorities
were deeply concerned with the spread of communism around the world
and, in particular, with the rise of Communist China (not to speak of the
experience of the Korean War). Several important policies followed from
this: First, many of the pre-war economic institutions, such as the famous
Zaibatsu, were allowed to rebuild and coordinate their economic activities
in ways wholly illegal in the United States. Although General McArthur, at
first wanted to break up the large integrated firms that dominated in the
pre-war era, the Allies quickly came to believe that these institutions could
be used in order to rebuild Japan quickly after the war – just as they had

---

[40] Travelers from crowded cities like Tokyo or Osaka are often surprised to find large but
deserted highways, bridges and tunnels in Japan's outlying areas. These facilities were built
not to alleviate any real traffic burden but to benefit Japan's powerful local construction
industry to secure employment in rural areas by using road-earmarked taxes. There may be
no better example of the producer bias of Japanese public policy.

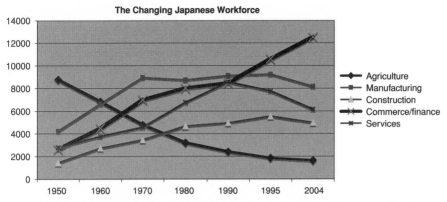

FIGURE 3.3. Economically Active Population: Japan (men) 1950 to 2004, (in thousands). *Source:* (Mitchell 2007) p. 107 table B1.

before the war.[41] Second, many of the same bureaucratic officials who had run the government during the war were allowed to retain their positions. Equally importantly, these bureaucrats were allowed to continue industrial policies, as they had done during wartime, in order that the Japanese economy could be quickly rebuilt. Finally, America pursued a highly discriminatory trade policy *in favor of* Japanese producers by opening itself up to Japanese exports while allowing the Japanese to protect themselves from American imports. None of these policies or concessions fit the American ideals of liberal capitalism or free markets, but apparently, fast economic reconstruction took priority over economic ideals.

The result was a unique hybrid in which a still very traditional and hierarchical Japanese society had highly egalitarian land policies and democratic political institutions imposed on it, at the same time that anti-liberal economic institutions were allowed to survive. The bureaucracy, the political system and the economic system were effectively merged in a type of symbiogenisis, that is, they produced a system of reciprocal helpfulness (Sapp 2003). As it turned out, this odd mix appeared to work quite well. The system was a particular fit, which had the result of making Japan highly successful and admired all over the world.

---

[41] Immediately after the war, the Zaibatsu were dismantled, but as the imputed threat of China grew, many were reconstructed. In the post-war years, the new integrated companies were now called *Keiretsu*. In some cases (e.g., Mitusbishi, Sumitomo) they retained the name of the original *Zaibatsu*.

TABLE 3.7. *Nominal GDP Growth Rates and Growth Rates in National Tax Revenues, Japan: Five Year Averages in Percent*

	GDP Growth Rate	Tax Revenue Growth
1952–55	11.43	10.89*
56–60	12.63	14.44
61–65	15.74	12.94
66–70	17.47	18.90
71–75	15.22	14.21
76–80	10.13	15.01
81–85	5.66	6.66
86	4.26	9.45

Note: * 1951–55.
Source: Ishi, Hiromitsu. 1990. "Taxation and public debt in a growing economy: The Japanese experience." *Hitotsubashi Journal of Economics* 31 (1):1–22, p. 6.

As is well known, the Japanese economy did indeed grow enormously during this period: Between 1960 and 1990 per capita GDP grew from just 5,000 USD to 22,000 USD. In the same years, the American figures were 12,500 to 26,000 USD. Importantly, so did government revenues – the automatic revenue growth generated by economic expansion allowed both the LDP and MoF to cut taxes for key constituencies and manipulate tax rates for industrial policy purposes with enormous success. As we can see in Table 3.7, the enormous expansion of the economy simultaneously increased government revenues making it possible for the bureaucracy to act as guardians of the fiscal budget while at the same time, servicing the electoral needs of LDP politicians.

It is also important to remember, however, that the security umbrella provided by the United States, in combination with the constitutional prohibition against building a strong military, allowed the Japanese to refrain from tax increases even as government spending grew. Whereas the United States was spending approximately 10 percent of its GDP on the military in the mid-1950s (down to 7.4 percent in 1965), Japan could devote less than 1 percent of its GDP per annum on defense (Saito 2000: 198–200).[42]

[42] I refrain from taking a position on the longstanding argument whether military spending provides economic incentives or not. My point here is that *absent* the need for revenue to finance military spending, the government was left in a better position to simply allow economic growth to bring in sufficient tax revenue (see Savage 2002).

Industrial (Not Social) Policy

Though there was a virtual national consensus on the necessity to increase standards of living rather than try to redistribute Japan's meager economic wealth in the early post-war years, the question of how to promote this growth remained. It is in this context that the elite bureaucracy took the role of managers of the economy, an adaptation that would come to have important consequences for the Japanese system. Japan had a long history of centralized economic development and now the needs of society were no less severe than they had been in earlier periods. Several important and highly elitist bureaucratic instruments were established in this period. The most important for our purposes was that of the Ministry of International Trade and Industry (MITI), which grew to take on the role of manager of Japanese industrial policy. MITI saw its role as that of promoting infant and/or strategic industries within the Japanese economy. The Ministry of Finance (MoF), in contrast, considered its role to be one of setting the broader context for economic growth and stability. Unsurprisingly, their policy positions often conflicted. MITI saw tax policy as a potent instrument for directing the economy through a variety of mechanisms, whereas MoF was more concerned with maintaining good financial balance.

By the mid 1960s, Japanese bureaucrats were beginning to look abroad for potential models for Japanese reform. As its success became clear, the argument that so much of national resources should be diverted to economic growth began to wane. Certainly economic growth was to remain a powerful goal, but "well being" was being put on the agenda as well. Once again, typical Anglo/European class politics were not a motivating force here. Instead, central bureaucrats began to change their attitudes as what was called "the old-people problem" (*rojin mondai*) came to view (Campbell, 1992: 104–128). Japanese views of community and family values traditionally held that older people should be taken care of by their families. The growing reality, however, was that these burdens were increasingly hard to bear and this posed significant challenges both for older Japanese citizens and their children. Over 60 percent of Japanese elderly lived with their children (compared to only twenty percent or less in the West), but as life expectancy lengthened, medical care became more sophisticated and more women began to join the workforce, the challenge of caring for the aged became more and more difficult. The modern market economy, while expanding wealth for the Japanese, was beginning to pull at the seams of society.

Campbell's comprehensive history of this policy domain demonstrates clearly that bureaucrats – not citizens' groups, party politicians, or unions – were the motivating force behind these changes. For example, the Welfare

Ministry adopted the goal of universal health insurance as early as 1955 and expanded the public contribution to the health insurance system in 1962, 1963, 1966, and 1967. LDP leaders also began to realize that population shifts would eventually lead to their demise unless they could begin to champion platforms that would gradually accommodate workers into its base of political support. Indeed, policy makers began to reconsider both how to open the policy-making process to include groups like labor and how to appropriately distribute the nation's growing wealth.

In direct response to this thinking the LDP adopted a "Labor Charter" in 1966, which advocated full employment, better working conditions, and enhanced social welfare (Garon and Mochizuki 1993: 160). Later, the LDP's "Report on the Circumstances of the LDP (1969)" encouraged the party to engage labor in more dialogue.[43] This seems to be a clear example of gradual adaptation on the part of the LDP to changes in its environment. The party had to change and adapt in order to survive. Curiously, the bureaucrats acted more promptly in adapting to this changing environment that did the politicians.

Despite the lack of strong political pressure for the expansion of the welfare state in Japan, there was growing interest in public welfare programs *inside* the bureaucracy and from some elements within the LDP. Why did they promote the expansion of welfare programs absent strong political pressures to do so? Kasza tells us . . . "bureaucrats and influential economists saw welfare problems as a structural inevitability during rapid growth. While heavy industry prospered, farmers, the self-employed and workers in small businesses and declining sectors would suffer growing inequality. The solution was welfare policy as a form of 'structural adjustment'" (Kasza 2006: 66).

With the exception of health insurance and unlike the more comprehensive social welfare systems being developed in most other countries at the time, the specific structure of social spending and tax policies in these years continued to target small producers, farmers, and the self-employed – *not* the unemployed, single mothers, or those otherwise left behind in the capitalist economy. In truth, these programs were subsidies to key elements of the LDP constituency. Certainly, one can argue that this was true in Sweden

---

[43] The Japan Socialist Party (JSP) experienced a decline in worker support because the Japanese market effectively contained conflict over economic issues within the private sector and narrowed the issues that might have been subject to partisan mobilization (Hiwatari 1989: 54); (Kume 1998a: 116). Also, the common company practice of addressing workers demands through various forms of worker participation in management helped diffuse many potential conflicts. (I thank Sara Kanoe for this observation.)

as well, but the key difference was institutional. Because labor was divided in Japan, a generalized workers' interest was not paramount in the construction of Japan's early welfare programs (Milly 1999: 177–78). But as growth stabilized and Japan increasingly saw itself as a rich country, many came to believe that they too could grow the kinds of welfare state programs found in Europe and America. Many believed that Japan was now "modern" enough to have a "modern welfare state." The LDP declared 1973 the "First year of Welfare" (*fukushi gannen*). Unfortunately, rather than create a coherent national social insurance system, clientelistic pressures worked to create a highly fragmented set of programs that could be managed and distributed for the political benefit of the LDP. Eventually, by the late 1980s there were literally thousands of programs at the national, prefectural and municipal levels of government established to service different groups in need (a.k.a. constituencies) (Campbell, 1992: 9). "Welfare bureaucrats and social policy experts," Shinkawa tells us, "held ideas of an integrated social security system, but obtained no opportunities to embody their ideas in a situation where politicians regarded social policy as nothing more than a measure of gaining support in elections. Politicians looked for prompt policy effects with no grand design of long-term welfare state building" (Shinkawa 2007a).

Although there was a broad consensus that old people should be taken care of by their family and, *if necessary*, the state, there was little political activity and certainly no consensus that Japan should develop the kinds of "welfare" programs targeted at economically vulnerable populations like single mothers or the chronically underemployed. "The essence of the consensus (mid-1970s) is that the welfare state, with 'high welfare and high state burden' as found in England, Sweden and the United States, is undesirable" writes Ezra Vogel in his book, *Japan as Number One* (Vogel 1979: 185). John Campbell agrees, "[Bureaucrats and media elites] argued that Japan should try to find its own path...the Japanese welfare society should be seen as part of the economic boom of the time, the spate of popular books and articles celebrating all aspects of "Japaneseness." While the West was seen as atomized, too individualistic and conflictual, Japan was idealized as a homogeneous and harmonious village, in which traditional community and corporate solidarity provide more 'real' welfare than can big government programs" (Campbell 1992: 220).

To sum up: Japan developed a highly fragmented system of policy programs to provide welfare services due to its political and institutional structure. Employers were given the main responsibility for these services in line with the culture of a "cradle to grave" relationship with the firm and matched it with the aim of preserving Japanese values. This worked well during the economic up-turn, but was put under significant pressure during times of downturn.

An Island Nation: The Oil Shock

One can scarcely have a conversation with a Japanese person without that person, eventually, bringing up the point that Japan is a small, resource poor country. This basic fact is imbedded in the national consciousness and an important part of national identity. When the Japanese bring up their geo-economic position, they are reminding themselves that they are profoundly vulnerable. As successful as Japan is, it does not have vast resources to fall back on. Just as it was emerging as a more self-confident nation, it was rudely reminded that even if it had become economically productive and successful, it could still be held hostage to global events: The quadrupling of the price of oil in 1973 was just such an event. The oil crisis dramatically altered the focus of Japanese politics. For one thing, it transformed budgetary politics from a positive-sum to a zero-sum game. As a result, the LDP could no longer rely on automatic revenue growth, generated by bracket creep and economic expansion, to fund public programs. At the same time, unions and big business interests were starting to bristle after years of footing the national bill for social and economic subsidies. It is one thing to subsidize others while rapidly becoming richer; it is quite another when subsidies force the payee to make sacrifices.

In response to this new political reality, big business and moderate labor unions became more critical of the expansion of a public welfare state (Kume 1998b: 190–5; Ito 1988: 59–66). The LDP also quickly changed its position. "Having just declared 1973 to be 'the first year of welfare' (*fukushi gannen*)... it announced a 'reconsideration of welfare' (*fukushi minaoshi ron*) and touted "Japanese-style welfare society" (*nihongate fukushi shakai*) in the late 1970s," which would "rely more upon family, community and corporate welfare than did the welfare state of the West" (Kasza 2006: 58: 5). Once again, we see an example of adaptation to a new environment. In the face of radical economic pressure big business, unions and many factions within the LDP changed strategies and, instead, claimed fealty to traditional Japanese values and retreated to the old Japanese model. Evolutionary adaptations are locally maximizing, *not* universally maximizing. In this case, as the economic pressures intensified, the system adapted to promixate environmental pressures by reverting to what was known rather than adding new functions and features.

By the mid-1970s, business interests began to fear that increased public sector growth would mean increased corporate taxes. Thus, big business became skeptical of public sector growth and demanded "administrative reform" and fiscal restraint (Ito 1988: 61–62). It is perhaps more surprising that Japanese unions did not actively support public welfare state.[44] We saw in the Swedish case how labor union elites came to favor economic rationalization policies *in exchange for* social welfare programs and active labor market policies that helped individual workers adjust in times of economic transition and hardship. In Japan, labor unions adopted very different policy goals because they had already achieved most of these benefits through their employers. "Core workers," at least, in the large successful firms were able to extract generous benefits (especially, guaranteed full employment, housing, health care, pensions, etc.) directly from companies, at least, in part, because unions were organized inside these companies.[45] The Japanese firm, in short, had already become the employee's welfare state. Workers, in the large export oriented firms at least, did not need and did not want an expanded public welfare state. Whereas Swedish unions were organized by craft, were nationally organized and had strong confederal leadership, Japanese worker interests were divided. In Sweden, the incentive for unions was to fight for the rights of all workers. In Japan, the incentive was to negotiate for the interests of their workers at the firm level (Ito 1988; Kume 1998a, 195).[46]

Another problem for advocates of a public welfare state was that Japanese workers employed in the large successful firms also paid higher taxes than their poorer cousins in the periphery. Eventually they came to resent this.

---

[44] The largest labor confederation, Sohyo, whose major member unions belonged to the public sector, advocated the welfare state and opposed the administrative reform of the 1980s. The second largest union confederation, Domei, whose leading unions were moderate ones in the private sector, did not oppose the idea of welfare state, but supported the administrative reform with the intention of undermining public-sector-centered Sohyo's influence. These unions, however, eventually came to realize the importance of more generalized public policies to protect workers' wages and working conditions but as we will see below, this was effectively too late. (I would like to thank Toshimitsu Shinkawa for pointing this out to me.)

[45] The T. J. Pempel argument that labor was left out of the decision making structure in Japan may appear to conflict with the analysis here. We do not, however, disagree. The point here is that labor unions in Japan did not play an active role in supporting the construction of a welfare state and were clearly hostile to tax increases. Had they been included in the decision making institutions more formally, we suggest that they would have been more likely to develop different preferences, just as Pempel suggests (Pempel and Tsunewaka 1979; Pempel 1978).

[46] For a similar logic see (Olson 1982).

Recall that the most significant redistributive policies funded by the Japanese state were directed at small business owners, farmers and rural workers who paid few if any taxes. The result was that Japanese unions came to see their interests in almost exactly the opposite way to Swedish, German, and even American unions. Whereas in other countries, unions saw public spending as a mechanism for increasing levels of consumption on the part of workers and the poor, Japanese unions saw public spending as subsidies to the unproductive but politically powerful rural and small business interests.[47]

Japan as Number 1[48]

The 1980s were good years for Japan. Not only were its companies outcompeting their rivals in a wide range of traditional manufacturing industries, but it was also coming to dominate and even control some of the world's most technologically sophisticated industries. The highly coordinated "Japanese model," it was widely believed, would become the model for the world.[49] Investors scoured the world looking for venues for their enormous economic largess,[50] buying such landmarks as the Empire State Building in New York, the Vail Ski Area in Colorado, and what to many seemed like half of the islands of Hawaii. There can be no doubt that at the height of the bubble many Japanese were delirious. To be sure economic

---

[47] In April 2003, the author was offered a short tour of the rural countryside in Kyusyu, the southernmost of the four major Japanese islands. On a crisp spring day, we drove into the mountains north of Nagasaki and, eventually, into beautiful and rich farmlands, which were being actively tended by small groups of Japanese workers. I asked my hosts where these workers came from and was told that they were the farmers themselves. It was typical the farmers would plant their own fields by hand and harvest them in this way as well. "Farm workers are too expensive," I was told. I also noticed a large number of truly beautiful and quite large homes in the area. These were splendid examples of Japanese architecture with elaborate tile roofs and large beautifully manicured gardens. When I asked who owned these beautiful estates, I was told, "Why, the farmers you see working the fields all around, of course." My colleague and guide scarcely even noticed the irony that in this region, farmers who would work their own tiny plots of land by hand would live in homes that were many times larger, more elaborately decorated and indeed more beautiful, than even a college professor.

[48] *Japan as Number 1* was the title of the book by Ezra Vogel in 1979. This book was one of the first to recognize Japan's unique economic model and to argue that it may prove superior to the American. Its subtitle was "Lessons for America" (Vogel 1979).

[49] There was a raft of books and articles published in the 1980s predicting the continued rise of the Japanese system and (often) the concomitant decline of America's neo-liberal model (see Morishima 1982; Thurow 1992; Borrus et al. 1982; Zysman 1983; Reich 1992; Thurow 1985).

[50] The real estate boom was particularly out of control. For example, it was widely reported that at the per square meter price of land in Tokyo, the property on which the Emperor's palace sits in central Tokyo was worth more than all the land in the state of California.

TABLE 3.8. *Rates of Growth in Real GDP Per Capita*

	1950–1973	1973–1992
Japan	8	3
U.S.A.	2.4	1.4
Sweden	3.1	1.2
OECD Avg.	3.4	1.6

Source: Maddison, Monitoring the World Economy, 1890–1992, pp. 62–63; cited in Kasza, Greg. 2004. "Japan's welfare policies in comparative perspective." Bloomington Indiana.

growth slowed somewhat from the frenzied 50s and 60s. But even including the difficult years following the oil crisis Japan continued to grow more than twice as fast as the US in the 1970s and 80s (see Table 3.8).

Remember, Japan was not just another economically successful country: To a much greater extent than any European Social Democracy, Japan offered an alternative vision of how a country could be successful in the international economy. While Sweden, or Germany for that matter, had been successful, few believed these models of "capitalism with a human face" could be more productive or innovative than the more liberal United States. Moreover, the Social Democratic states were not really alternative models of capitalism. To be sure, they had larger and more powerful unions, more generous social welfare systems and higher taxes, but in rather fundamental ways they were simply versions of the types of capitalism found in Britain and the United States. Japan, however, was different: Its ability to enter and conquer so many basic areas industry – from autos to robotics – was seen as an economic and ideational threat to the hegemony of the United States and its version of capitalism. Japan, moreover, was not bloated by a large welfare state: The country's national resources were devoted more exclusively to economic growth, productivity and increasing market share. More than a few American corporate executives, political elites and economists were frightened that the end of the twentieth century would be the beginning of a new era and although the twentieth century had been the American century, the twenty-first century would be Asian. In short, American style, neo-liberal capitalism was being *out-competed* by an Asian style, developmental state: Free markets could not compete with coordinated markets (Johnson 1982; Thurow 1980; Zysman 1983).

In other words, the hybrid which brought together a highly competitive industrial capitalism grafted onto a traditional society with its emphasis on deference to authority, respect for hierarchy and group solidarity appeared to have evolutionary step forward over the less well organized, expensive and undisciplined liberal systems of the Western capitalism. The truth is that this small, resource poor and densely populated island had been given enormous competitive advantages by its American benefactor. Not only did it have to spend very little on its own defense, but more importantly, its companies and indeed its political economy as a whole had been allowed to collude, while the Americans offered their market as fertilizer to Japan's economic growth machine. Unfortunately, for the Japanese at least, hybrids can be quite successful when conditions are favorable, but prove less adaptable to a rapidly changing ecology.

PART III

CHALLENGES IN A NEW CENTURY

In the last chapter we saw that, in the 1980s, Sweden began a period of change and transformation. These changes were, partly, in response to global competitive pressures and motivated by the dynamics of a mature welfare state. Sweden's position as a small open economy with a very large and expensive welfare state made the Swedish elite particularly sensitive to the currents of economic change taking place in the world economy at the same time that the huge size and generosity of its social welfare programs made it particularly sensitive to abuses of the welfare state. At the same time, due to changing social norms and lengthening life spans, Swedish society was rapidly aging. The demographic picture cast an even darker cloud over the future of the Swedish welfare state. I argued in the last chapter that the centralization of both economic and political power effectively facilitated the adaptive process helping this country to regain international competitiveness without undermining the foundational principles of their system. As we saw, by the beginning of the twenty-first century, Sweden had reformed a number of public institutions, invited hundreds of thousands of immigrants and their families into the country, regained competitive advantage in the world economy, balanced its budget and now faces the new century with a high degree of confidence. One might say that the economic crisis in Sweden offered an opportunity for the government to rethink and readjust political and economic structures so that it could regain economic stability while retaining the basic social democratic principles that underlie their system.

In Japan's case we see a quite different story. Japan also confronted an economic and demographic crisis at the end of the twentieth century. Unfortunately, this country has not yet been able to make the policy changes

TABLE 3.9. *Japan in the 1990s – the Lost Decade +*

	Per Capita GDP PPP, US$	Per Capita GDP, PPP Index (US = 100)	Public Debt (Outstanding Gov't Bonds, Trill. Yen)
1985	18,101	72.9	134.5
1990	22,332	80.3	166.3
1995	23,598	80.0	225.2
2000	25,140	73.9	392.4
2003/5	25,587*	73.2*	526.9^

Notes: * = 2003; ^ = 2005.
Sources: U.S. Department of Labor, Bureau of Labor Statistics. Office of Productivity and Technology, Washington, DC., July 26, 2004; Ministry of Finance. 2007. "Current Japanese Fiscal Conditions and Issues to be Considered." Tokyo: Ministry of Finance.

necessary to adapt to these mounting challenges. To be sure, several policies have been initiated.[51] But no one denies that these reforms are inadequate to deal with the looming demographic and economic crises facing Japan in the new millennium. As Table 3.9 demonstrates, the so called "Lost Decade" of the 1990s was difficult indeed: Economic growth stagnated, the while the population continued to age the tax system was wholly inadequate to deal with spending demands. Finally, the public's confidence in government plummeted and public debt soared to historic levels. No one can predict exactly how this or any other country will evolve in the future, but the view from here does indeed look problematic.

In 2009 a new government was elected to power in Japan and for the first time in post-war history, an alternative to the LDP controlled the majority in the lower house of the Japanese parliament. Enormous expectations have been placed on the new Democratic Party of Japan (DPJ) and its leader, Ichiro Hatoyama. Early indications suggest that the new leader and his government do want to genuinely change the patterns of Japanese politics. Some of these proposals will be discussed at the end of this chapter. But first we will explore the position Japan finds itself in today.

We saw above how Japanese society was essentially forced to adapt to liberal and egalitarian rules and institutions immediately after World War II. But we also have seen that Japan's social policy institutions did not grow in concert with the modernizing political economy. Clearly, over the years Japanese society and values "modernized" just as the economy also evolved. But still, by the last decade of the twentieth century, there can

---

[51] For example, the reforms in long-term care insurance and pension policies have been impressive (see Hieda 2010; Shinkawa 2007b).

be no doubt that Japan still remained a kind of a hybrid. This does not imply, however, that Japan had reached some kind of equilibrium. Quite the contrary, the Japanese political economy, just like every country, was replete with inconsistent institutions and consequent friction. In Japan's case, these have evoked three inter-related sources of continuing difficulties. First, notwithstanding its reputation as a "strong" government, with its powerful bureaucracy and activist industrial policy, policy making authority has, in fact, always been spread across a number of different institutions. As we previously saw, it was never true that the bureaucracy could dictate policy to the parliament, while at the same time the ruling political party (LDP) has never been a programmatic party. Policy has always been the result of a great number of compromises and, often, quite incoherent concessions between bureaucrats, local political leaders and powerful interest groups. In short, the Japanese state has never been as powerful as many have assumed.

Rather ironically, the *absence* of a comprehensive welfare state at the beginning of the economic crisis made it more difficult for the Japanese political economy to adjust. Contrary to the rather simple-minded argument that social programs somehow make the capitalist economy less flexible and efficient, in Japan's case, we see how *not having* well-developed public social programs has made economic adjustment and change more difficult. This is because companies ARE the welfare state in this case. As a consequence there has understandably been great reluctance to allow companies to fail or lay off masses of workers. Instead, huge amounts of monies have gone toward supporting and subsidizing these institutions, even those that were already highly inefficient before the crisis.

Japan's political and economic leadership grew increasingly attracted to neo-liberal ideas. As a result, it made a series of policy and economic changes that have not helped the system adapt well in the twenty-first century. Part of the problem, clearly, has been poor policy choices. Another part, certainly, has been the weakness of the central government when it comes to asking for sacrifices.

Finally, in my view at least, successive governments in the late 1990s and early twenty-first century pursued policies that they *thought* would help the country adapt to the new competitive pressures of a globalizing world. In fact, however, these policies did more to undermine the foundations of the system that they had build over the past 50 years. Partly because Japan lacks a strong state and partly because the liberal attitudes ideas about individual freedom have never been key to the system, the liberalizing reforms that have been instituted were insufficient to transform the system as a whole. Whereas Sweden seems to have managed to liberalize, while maintaining the core of what has made this country successful in the past, Japan has instituted reforms that seem to undermine key elements of their past success. The result is a system that continues to lie at a crossroad, unwilling or unable to decide which direction or path it will take: "a funny thing happened on Japan's way to the United States model:" Steven Vogel tells us in his outstanding volume, *Japan Remodeled*, "it never got there" (Vogel 2006: 3).

As we shall see, there have been a number of attempts to remodel the Japanese political economy and as Vogel points out, the Japanese have been more likely to "modify and reinforce existing institutions rather than abandon them" (Vogel 2006: 3). But whereas Vogel seems to see this as an example of "creative adaptation" in this analysis, we see more trouble ahead.[52] As we previously saw, growth and economic equality was widely seen as a foundation stone for Japanese post-war economic success. Trust in society and willingness to sacrifice the individual's short-term's interest in favor of the collective long-term interest worked well in Japan, in part, because everyone seemed to play by the same rules. Late in the twentieth century, these rules began to change.

After the Bubble Burst

By the late 1980s Japanese investors and politicians alike had become giddy with their success. Not only had Japan become a very rich society,[53] but now instead of copying the West, Japan had become a model for the world. Increasingly, people came to believe that you simply could not lose money investing there. Consequentially, prices spun into the stratosphere. The Nikkei 225 Stock index, for example, grew by nearly 300 percent in just five years (from 11,542 in December 1984 to 38,915 in December 1989). The real-estate market was particularly hot with housing values going up by more than 15 percent a year in many urban areas. It was widely said, for example, that the value of the Emperor's palace and grounds in central Tokyo was worth more (in per square meter price) than then entire state of California.[54] This was clearly absurd and it should have come as no surprise that eventually this bubble would burst. Of course it did. Between 1991 and 1994, the Tokyo stock market dropped in value by 560 trillion yen at the

---

[52] Vogel appears to move in this direction elsewhere (Vogel 1979: 34–5, 218).

[53] Per capita GDP grew from 36 percent of American in 1960 to 64 percent in 1970 to 72 percent in 1980.

[54] The commercial land price index for land in large cities increased from 38.4 in 1986 to 103.0 in 1989.

same time that the overall value of land in fell by 730 trillion yen (Fukukawa 1999: 5).[55]

In the first years after the collapse of the bubble economy most leaders believed that Japan's economic problems were temporary. In this view, there were no fundamental problems in the system. On the contrary, the Japanese system worked quite well. It simply had gotten ahead of itself. What was called for, then, was patience. Japan would ride out this storm and return to its ascendant position. The immediate response on the part of the government was first to reassure banks and investors that they would be protected via direct loans and guarantees, and second, to significantly increase spending on public works in order to protect jobs and insure continued employment.[56] Surely, most people (elites and citizens alike) understood that there were some problems in the system; too much waste in public works, too little competition in some sectors of the economy. But NOW was scarcely the time to radically change the system, they argued. Quite the contrary, there was a near national consensus that everything should be done to prevent the social dislocation and unemployment that massive bankruptcies would inevitably entail. Shinji Fukukawa represented this view quite well when he asked: "Now we must ask ourselves, is the Japanese system facing the scrap heap? Is the Western model superior?" Eventually, of course, he agreed, "the market framework will naturally become globalized in the information age. Even domestic rules such as competition, accounting, inspection and certification should be harmonized, since international standards would be beneficial for business operations." But, he, like many Japanese, continued to believe that "companies may operate with different strategies and cultural characteristics. Japan's corporate culture still has significant advantages in the age of the global economy" (Fukukawa 1999: 12).

Given that Japan never developed a classical welfare state and instead had its "welfare through work" model previously described, Japanese banks were "encouraged" to continue to support the firms that depended on them, even if they could not pay back their current loans. Given the close relationships between government officials and elites in the banking sector it is difficult to actually parse out exactly how this encouragement was accomplished, but there can be no doubt that banks held onto economically unproductive loans far longer than would have been possible in a

---

[55] The Nikkei plummeted to 15,951 in June 1992. The commercial land index noted above fell to 7.4 in March 1993 (Ito and Iwaisako 1995). The dollar to yen exchange rate fluctuated between approximately 120 to 130 yen to the dollar in 1991 and 1992.

[56] The government spent 41156 billion yen between 1990 and 92 on public work construction projects alone (Kasa 1999).

more traditional capitalist economy. According to Rina Fujii, unpaid liabilities totaled between 350 and 600 billion USD by the early 2000s.[57] "In most economies, creditor banks would have demanded payment and non-performing borrowers would have been declared insolvent, forcing them to close. In Japan, the banks shouldered their debts despite the probability that they would never be repaid." Why? "Social pressures discouraged causing bankruptcies and unemployment... Japanese corporate culture was famous for ensuring employment in the same firm from university graduation to retirement" (Fujii 2003: 1).

This was a period of enormous economic *and* political uncertainty in Japan, as indicated by a rapid turnover in governments. Between June 1989 and April 2001 Japan had ten different Prime Ministers and thirteen different governments.[58]

After years of consideration, it was decided to change the electoral system in 1994. The main idea was to usher in a more responsible politics. The most important feature of this reform was a change in the electoral system from the traditional Single Non-Transferable vote (SNTV) system to a modified and rather complex, electoral system that combines single member districts and a type of proportional representation. Limits were also put on campaign contributions and a series of legislative rule changes were introduced with the intention of strengthening the position of the Prime Minister.[59] The long-term effects of these reforms are certainly still in motion, but the short-term consequence was to cause several LDP factions split off from the main party and created new political organizations that have effectively pursued the same political strategies as the traditional LDP. Political authority, in short, became ever more uncertain.

It should not surprise us, therefore, that successive governments massively increased public infrastructure spending (a.k.a., public works). Once again, absent active labor market policies or even a public welfare state, the best way to keep people working was to build infrastructure – whether or not these highways, bridges and entertainment centers were actually needed. By

---

[57] By some accounts, non-performing loans accounted for 44 trillion yen or 10 percent of all outstanding loans already in 1992 (Huh and Kim 1994).
[58] Also an unfortunate number of scandals hit the media in which senior bureaucrats and politician were caught in a wide series of corruption scandals.
[59] For a discussion of these and their consequences see (Estevez-Abe 2008: 268–71). Estevez-Abe, almost presciently, argues that these reforms will eventually result in more programmatic party system. This is precisely what the newly elected DPJ has promised to offer, though whether they can deliver on this promise, given Japan's enormous fiscal and demographic difficulties, remains to be seen.

TABLE 3.10. *Public Fixed Investment Structure /*
GDP (%)

	1990	1997
Japan	6.6	7.8
USA	3.5	2.8
UK	3.2	1.6

Source: Kazatoshi, Kaza. 1999. "Economic Aspects of Public
Works in Japan." *Social Science Japan* (17): 15–19; Bank of
Japan. *Kokusai Hikaku Tokei* [International Comparative
Statistics].

the late 1990s, the Japanese government was spending nearly 7.8 percent
of GDP on public fixed investment, as Table 3.10 shows, more than in any
other advanced country.

The logic of such a massive spending program is clear (it appears that the
United States government will be pursuing something analogous beginning
in 2009). Unfortunately, spending on traditional make work projects does
very little to restructure the economy toward the future. "No one can doubt
that there has been lots of reform in Japan in the last decade." (Katz 2008:
10). But as Richard Katz points out, these reforms have too often been
misplaced and have effectively undermined many of Japan's most successful
sectors. He calls this "reversed Darwinism," (Ibid: 9) concluding that the
core problem was "that inferior companies are preserved because that's the
way to preserve the social safety net for core lifetime employees" (Ibid: 11–
12). While I agree with Katz's policy analysis, this observation reveals a
misunderstanding of evolutionary theory. Darwinism does not argue that
all adaptations or evolutionary changes are efficient or even likely to lead to
improved fitness.[60] Indeed, some mutations can easily result in the decline
of a population. The changes witnessed in Japan in the 1990s appear to be
excellent examples of this type of adaptive change.

Adopting the "Global Standard"

Eventually, the Japanese elite's confidence began to wane. It seemed that
no matter how much the government pumped into the private economy,
the economy simply continued to drag. By mid-decade, a more neo-liberal
argument began to take hold. Economic liberals saw Japan's economic trou-
bles not simply as the legacy of an inflated market, but instead rooted in

[60] Mayr 2001: 234–38.

the structure of the system itself. As Paul Krugman noted, "[f]ew Western commentators have resisted the temptation to turn Asia's economic woes into an occasion for moralizing on the region's past sins" (Krugman 1998). And the worst sin, of course, was for the government to intervene in the free market (McKenzie 1989). The famous business consultants, Michael Porter and Hirokata Takeuchi, articulated this view in *Foreign Affairs*: "What ails Japan runs deeper, has been brewing for decades and is rooted in the micro-economics of how Japan competes.... In Japan and elsewhere, it has been appealing for a variety of political and cultural reasons to believe that Japan had invented a new and intrinsically superior form of capitalism, one more controlled and egalitarian than the Anglo-Saxon version. This is simply not the case. The much-celebrated government model is wrong; in fact, it explains Japan's failures more than its successes" (Porter and Takeuchi 1999: 67).

The neo-liberal critique of the European high tax/large social welfare state simply did not apply to the Japanese case. Instead, they saw two basic problems: First, the state was too involved in the economy. And second, the system did not offer individuals sufficient incentives. If Japan were to regain economic competitiveness in the global economy, a steady stream of advisors from the United States argued, it would need to become a more flexible system that relied less on relationships, hierarchy and collective responsibility and rely more on individual creativity. The world economy had changed, they argued and Japan must change with it. "[The Japanese] economic and social model worked in an excellent way from 1960 until 1990," American economist and consultant to the Clinton administration, Nouriel Roubini, argued for example, "The old model worked so well for Japan that it became the 'growth model' followed by several East Asian countries. But this growth model does not seem to work in the 1990s" (Roubini 1996: 3). In other words, when you are playing "catch-up," and/or when the economic goals and targets are clear, a system that stresses cooperation, teamwork and co-operative management can be effective and efficient. However, when technological change is rapid and unpredictable, as in the 1990s, a coordinated system simply won't work anymore.

Structural reform was needed, this argument held and structural reform meant transforming Japanese government, corporations, banks, the tax system and, perhaps, even society itself. Remember, the mid-1990s was the heyday of the "Washington consensus," in which even Democratic Party consultants from the United States argued that the more freedom that existed, the more successful the economy would be. Indeed, some took the philosophical implications even further, arguing that we had reached "The End of History" with the evolution of capitalist democracy (Fukuyama 1992). If

Japan did not want to be left in the dustbin of history, it too had to embrace the future and allow individualism to blossom.

A Glass Half Empty

As Greg Noble points out, however, the kinds of radical liberal reforms imagined by the neo-liberals was never fully possible in Japan:

> The widespread reluctance of political, bureaucratic and corporate elites to countenance reforms that could increase unemployment fundamentally constrained neo-liberalism, impeding the development of a policy axis along which parties could clearly differentiate themselves and depriving voters of a clear choice of philosophies and policies (Otake 1994, 1999). This is a crucial insight, particularly for the period before late 1997, when few Japanese understood the depth of the country's structural ills and most clung to the illusion that stalling for time would allow companies gradually to outgrow their financial problems. It is also true that none of the three reformist prime ministers presented coherent, consistent and detailed philosophies of neo-liberalism and that each mixed neo-liberal economics with nationalism in a mixture more reminiscent of George W. Bush than the libertarian Cato Institute (Noble 2005: 2).

In fact, very much in line with Noble's argument, Vogel tells us that despite the apparent disarray in Japanese politics, various governments "embarked on a daunting array of reforms targeted at the micro institutions of the economy" (Vogel 2006: 78). Especially toward the end of the decade, numbers of policy innovations/reforms took place, effecting everything from the banking industry to corporate governance, accounting, and the labor market (Jackson 2003).

Of course, we cannot detail all of these changes here. Indeed, one of the things that is, perhaps, most interesting has been the "stealth" nature of many of these changes (Noble, 2005). For example, by many accounts Japan's very stable labor market has been a foundation of the entire model. Although it is difficult to specify an exact point of change or even to highlight the administrative rule changes that were the most influential, it is by now broadly understood that the traditional system of lifetime contracts is being progressively dismantled. Both because of regulatory reforms and new policies imposed by company leaders, the traditional Japanese labor market is eroding. Indeed, today few workers expect to work for the same firm their whole lives and, increasingly, people are being hired on temporary work contracts (*Paato Taimu*). As Table 3.11 shows, part-time and non-regular staff (people working on temporary work contracts) now account for approximately one third of the Japanese workforce.

TABLE 3.11. *The Changing Japanese Labor Market**

	1990	2000	2005
Percent full-time workers in share of size of labor force (1)(2)	54.6	53.6	51
Percent long-term contract workers as share of employees (regular staff)	80	74	67
Percent part-time workers (freeters and paato-taimu) workers in labor force (1)(2)	13.8	18.8	24.5
Percent non-regular staff (freeters and paato-taimu) workers as share of employee (1)(2)	20.1	25.9	32.6
Percent working for large companies (3)	24	24	24
Women working in share of labor force	40.6	40.6	41.3

Notes:

1) The data classified "Entrusted, Other" prior to Aug. 2001, except Aug. 2000 and Feb. 2001 ("Other (entrusted, etc)").
2) The data subdivided "contract employee or entrusted employee" and "Other" since Aug. 2001.
3) Rates are to the totals shown in breakdown of "Employee, excluding executive of company or corporation."
4) Employee in non-agricultural industry by number of persons engaged in enterprise that "persons 500 or more."
* I would like to acknowledge the assistance of Masato Furuichi in helping construct this data.
Source: "The Special Survey of the Labour Force" from 1984 to 2001, "Labour Force Survey (Detailed Tabulation)" since 2002.

    The incremental nature of these changes also makes it difficult to draw firm conclusions about the implications of the reforms. As Table 3.11 shows, the number of workers with the traditional lifetime worker contract has fallen from 80 percent to 67 percent of workers in the past 15 years. So, is the glass half empty, or is it in fact half full? Whereas Vogel argues, "taken together, these reforms represent a comprehensive program with the potential to transform Japan into a liberal market economy," he also tells the reader, somewhat contradictorily, "If we turn to the specifics, however, we find that the reforms have been designed more to preserve the essence of the Japanese model than to destroy it" (Vogel 2006: 78). But Vogel is not wrong in this contradiction, Japan's reforms have been largely incoherent: Employers began abandoning the traditional system which protected workers, but the government has done very little to take up this slack. Among other effects, one of the starkest is the enormous growth of homelessness in Japan. Considering its long reputation as an egalitarian society, it is shocking to see the thousands of middle age men living in cardboard boxes under bridges and in rail stations in almost every major city around the country (Gill 2001).

TABLE 3.12. *Social Spending in Japan, Percent GDP,*
1994, 1997

	1994/5	1996/7
TOTAL Social Protection of which:	12.6	13.5
Public Old Age Pensions	5.23	5.75
Sickness and Health	4.74	5.00
Survivor benefits	1.05	1.08
Invalidity benefits	0.34	0.34
Employment injury	0.21	0.21
Family benefits	0.33	0.38
Unemployment	0.40	0.44
Housing	0.03	0.03
Social Assistance and 'other'	0.30	0.28
Public Education (all levels)	3.60	3.50*

Note: * = year 2000.

Source: International Labor Organization (ILO), Social Security
Dept., March 2001; Snyder, Thomas D., Sally A. Dillow, and Charlene M. Hoffman. 2008. *Digest of Education Statistics 2007* (NCES
2008–022). Washington D.C.: National Center for Education Statistics, Institute of Education Sciences, U.S. Department of Education,
Table 405.

In the early 1990s, the neo-liberals had little direct effect, but over time
they become more influential both within the bureaucracy and amongst
some members of the LDP. Although in the traditional view the lifetime
job contract, high degree of collective responsibility and relatively flat wage
structures had been competitive advantages for the Japanese, in the new way
of thinking, this system was deeply problematic. A system in which management and workers stayed with the same companies their entire lives, and
salary and promotion was based almost exclusively on seniority and hierarchy, would necessarily undermine innovation and the development of the
entrepreneurial spirit that would be required in the globalized world economy. The simple truth is that employers *are* the social safety net in Japan:
When unemployment rises social welfare declines. Moreover, as Table 3.12
shows, though government social spending grew modestly in the late 1990s,
the lion's share of these small increases were taken up by spending on the
aged. If one takes out pensions and health care, the entire budget for social
spending in Japan was only 2.76 percent of GDP. It is also worth noting that
while the government increased spending on infrastructure by 2.2 percent
of GDP between 1990 and 1997, it cut spending on education from 3.6 to
3.5 percent of GDP in roughly the same period.

Tax Reform

A good example of the effects of reforms can be found in tax policy: As we saw earlier, Japan's system was a) nominally highly progressive; b) full of loopholes; c) heavy on companies; d) light on consumption; and e) insufficient to pay for Japan's quickly-aging society. The contraction of Japanese economy through the 1990s increased the pressure for more tax reductions. Though the "Laffer Curve" argument offered up in the Reagan administration in the United States was no longer taken very seriously by mainstream American economists, these arguments developed resonance in Japanese politics. The theory held that if the government cut taxes (especially on the wealthy) this would create greater incentives for these people to invest and, as a consequence, the economy would boom and tax revenues would return (Teles and Kenney 2006). There was also strong pressure from large export-oriented employers to cut income and profits taxes and replace these lost revenues with increases in consumption taxes.

Successive Japanese governments did cut income taxes beginning in 1995, embracing neo-liberal economic policy prescriptions, but unfortunately the strategy backfired. Instead of stimulating spending and boosting economic growth, citizens grew increasingly skeptical of government and their ability to manage the economy. Fearing that the government could not be trusted with their retirement funds, consumers did not respond as the economic models predicted and instead of using their tax cut gains in the market, they began saving more and spending less. Tax revenues continued to decline, the budget deficit soared and the economy slipped even further into recession.

The results were, then, not unlike the consequences of the 1981 tax cuts offered in the United States – the biggest budget deficits in the country's history. According to Professor Hiromitsu Ishi, the various tax cuts in the 1990s lost over 17 trillion Yen in revenues (128 billion USD) (Ishi 2002:2). The result was an explosion of debt. Between 1989 and 2003, government debt grew from 6.7 percent of total expenditures to 44.6 percent of total government spending. The approximately 450 trillion yen of total debt reached approximately 163 percent of GDP or eleven years worth of general account tax revenue in 2002 (Ministry of Finance 2003:10). By 2003, servicing the national debt alone consumed over 9 trillion yen or 11.1 percent of total government expenditure. Figure 3.4 illustrates the fiscal situation Japan entered in the 1990s. While most other countries were using the growth of the 1990s to pay down their public debts, in Japan public debt shot out of sight.

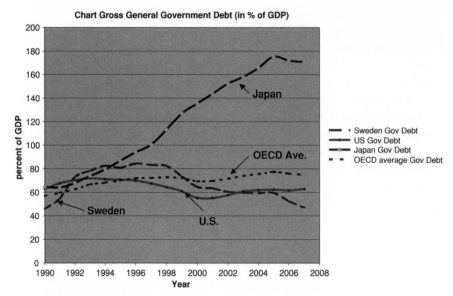

FIGURE 3.4. Gross Government Debt, Japan 1990–2008. *Source:* OECD. 2009. *OECD Factbook 2009: Economic, Environmental and Social Statistics.* Paris: OECD Publishing.

These tax cuts, combined with slow economic growth and Japan's aging society, meant it was ever more clear that Japan desperately needed a more secure and efficient revenue base. The income tax had become progressively more hollowed out and there was no enthusiasm in the government for increases, so the logical conclusion (which the Ministry of Finance had been pushing for now nearly twenty years) has been to continue pressure for increases in the consumption tax.[61]

The Koizumi Phenomenon

When Junichiro Koizumi (Japan's thirty-first post-war Prime Minister) was appointed Prime Minister in April 2001, the world was abuzz with excitement about this striking new leader. Not only did Koizumi look different,

---

[61] Interestingly, some Ministry of Finance elites also believed that consumption taxes would be *more* equitable than then current income tax system. This was because the extant income tax had become so riddled with exemptions for LDP constituents that it was far from the ideal income tax. Additionally, as Japan aged, the tax advantages offered seniors in the income tax would mean that the tax would become less and less equitable over time (as well as generate less and less income). See (Kawakami 2003).

but this motorcycle riding, opera loving, Japanese renegade gave hope to Japan and the world that *finally* someone could turn this country around. After more than a decade of economic stagnation and retreat, even the normally stoic Japanese citizens were anxious for change. "It seems the earth is shaking," said Mr. Koizumi, his flowery rhetoric getting the better of him, "The simmering magma is about to explode" (Economist 2001a). Koizumi appeared ready to offend powerful established interests, "an unheard of heresy in the LDP, which had prospered for nearly half a century precisely by protecting wealthy insider groups. He advocated the only real measure of serious financial reform that any of the candidates for the party leadership dared utter," reported the UPI. "All of a sudden, Japan's politics have become interesting. And the Japanese people have regained something they lost over the past year during sad, bad stewardship of Yoshiro Mori. Suddenly, they have regained the possibility of hope" (Sieff 2001).

Despite Kuizomi's political flair, popularity with the voters and reputation as a careful strategist and reformer, his government's performance was mixed.[62] Although his first several years in office appeared to be more show than substance, his reign was long by Japanese standards and several changes did take place. As Greg Noble, from the Institute of Social Science at the University of Tokyo argued, "more progress has been made in carrying out reforms than most observers acknowledge" (Noble 2006: 6). These included the relaxing of many of the regulatory barriers, the privatization of the Postal Savings Bank and the opening of competition in a number of sectors of the economy, perhaps most notably in telecommunications and insurance.[63]

Koizumi left his position as Prime minister in 2006, after five years in office and, in September 2008, declared his intention to retire from politics. Immense speculation had gone into his motive, but he simply argued that he was no longer interested. As if to demonstrate that things had not changed too much in Japanese politics, Koizumi chose his son to take his place and represent his district in the next election.

---

[62] Three years later, Mr. Koizumi suffered a humbling defeat at the polls and was barely able to hold onto the reigns of government (Economist 2004).

[63] In addition, the FILP program discussed above has been scaled back dramatically. Indeed, FILP funds contracted by 60 percent between 1995 and 2005 and, according to Noble, significant headway has been made toward cutting back on the *amakudari* system which, in the eyes of many, created too close a relationship between the regulator and the regulated.

Increasing Inequality

Since Koizumi resigned, Japan has seen a string of Prime Ministers, each promising "change" and "reform."[64] Until the 2009 election at least, these leaders were chosen precisely because they promised not to rock the LDP boat. Instead, they worked in the time-honored tradition of rebuilding the factions in the party and following short-term palliative policies in favor of their constituents. The problem with the LDP was, as many Liberal Democratic lawmakers themselves describe, that it was "frozen in mid-evolution, no longer its old self but unable to become something new" (Fackler 2008). Meanwhile, Japan's fiscal and demographic situation continued to deteriorate. At the same time, the policies pursued in the later 1990s and early 2000s brought about significant changes in the distribution of wealth in Japanese society. Many analysts believe that these many changes are responsible for a decline in the level of deference that Japanese citizens are willing to lend their leaders.

Though it is impossible to prove a causal relationship between the declining levels of public trust and economic policies and/or economic change in Japan, following the analysis of Tachibanaki, I submit that these changes are intimately connected.

The repeated tax cuts combined with consumption tax increased, unquestionably, contributed to the growing inequality in Japan during the 1990s. Since the reform of 1999, the Japanese income tax system has only four income tax brackets (10 percent, 20 percent, 30 percent, and 37 percent) and taxpayers were evenly lightened by 20 percent of the amount of an income tax by the "fixed rate tax cut." But upper income earners benefited far more than lower income class by tax cuts. Needless to say, consumption tax increase was a disadvantage for the poor. Additionally, as financial income was separated from income tax base and reduced rate was applied to taxpayers, the tax burden on high-income people was prominently eroded. As a result of these tax "reforms," even the nominal progressivity of the tax system was undermined. In other words, instead of making the system seem more fair, these reforms contributed to a widespread feeling that Japanese policy benefited those with power instead of the average citizen. As one high level official at the Ministry of Finance told me, "I think our system *should* be progressive. We need to think about

---

[64] Koizumi was followed as Prime Minister by Shinzō Abe (26 September 2006 – 26 September 2007), Yasuo Fukuda (26 September 2007 – 24 September 2008) and finally Taro Aso (September 24, 2008 – Sept 16, 2009).

TABLE 3.13. *Trust in Government, Japan*

Question	Answer	%	Year
Gov does not care what I think	Strongly agree or agree	74,8	2004
Mostly we can trust in gov	Strongly agree or agree	8,8	2004
Public service: Commitment to serve people	Very Somewhat committed	17,5	2004
Public service: Correcting own mistakes	Very Somewhat likely	22,9	2004
How much confidence in Parliament	A great deal or some confidence	4	1998
Politician has not much impact	Strongly agree or agree	73,4	1996
Elections make Gov pay attention	Strongly agree or agree	58,7	1996
Politicians keep promises	Strongly agree or agree	14,1	1996
Civil servants can be trusted	Strongly agree or agree	18,7	1996

Source: International Social Survey Program.

what kind of society we want to build – not just about cutting people's taxes."[65]

Declining Trust

Public trust in government had been declining for some time in Japan. The Japanese once looked to their leaders and believed that these elites used their powers in the interest of the whole society. Thus, when asked to sacrifice on behalf building a stronger nation whether as workers or consumers, Japanese citizens were willing to do their share (Garon 1997). The enormous economic growth the system provided seemed to justify their confidence, but over the past two decades average Japanese citizens have become ever more skeptical. Repeated financial scandals on the part of politicians and top bureaucratic officials, as well as public policies that have dramatically increased inequality, have worked to convince citizens that the politically powerful no longer care what average people think or want (see Table 3.13).

We saw in the previous chapter that distrust of politicians has increased in Sweden in recent years as well. However, we also saw that there is a fund of confidence in the system as a whole and a continued willingness to pay taxes in favor of this system, despite its high costs. As Rothstein has argued, it is precisely because citizens feel that the system is "fair" that they are willing to support it to the extent that they do (Rothstein 2005). Japan it appears, has

[65] Anonymous. Interview with author, Ministry of Finance, Tokyo May 22, 2002.

fallen into a trap where citizens do not believe the government acts in their interest and, therefore, threatens to punish any politician who dares talk of raising their taxes. Consequently, the government has insufficient revenue to even meet current obligations, no less increase spending on programs that would benefit the middle classes. This, in turn, leads citizens to believe that the government does not do much for them and so the cycle goes around.

Reforms Not Taken

One of the difficulties of writing a comparative analysis like the present one is not only that outcomes differ, but there are even variations in what was and was what not attempted. In the previous chapter, we ended describing a set of reforms the Swedes pursued which used market forces to improve social welfare services. Allowing for the development of private health care services and even more surprisingly, the development of privately run schools funded by vouchers seemed, at first, to be incongruent with the traditional welfare state. But as we saw, the Social Democrats disagree, arguing that the purpose of these programs is to provide services to citizens. If these services can be made more efficient with the introduction of market competition, then they serve even Social Democratic goals.

In the Japanese case, neo-liberal reforms appear to have directed more toward creating competition in the private sector. Thus, inequality and the feelings of individual insecurity have increased remarkably in recent years. Whereas in the high growth years (male) workers could reasonably expect that once they had a job, they would keep that job their entire life and that they and their family could reasonably expect that they would "be taken care of" by the company that they worked for. Neo-liberalism meant risk. Absent a developed welfare state, however, this meant that risk would be borne by the individual and his own family. Similarly, throughout the post-war years, Japanese families were called upon restrain consumption in favor of national savings (Akaishi and Steinmo 2006; Garon 2006b; Horioka 2006). They apparently believed that their national leaders also sacrificed on the nation's behalf. By the beginning of the new century, as inequalities grew and as the scandals mounted, it was increasingly hard to believe that the sacrifices demanded by economic changes were being equally shared.

Indeed there has been a growing sense in Japanese society, especially among younger people, that the political leadership is out of touch with their needs and desires. Once again, instead of adapting public policies in accord with the evolving social values, in particular attitudes toward women and families, both public and private policies looked backward and tried to "protect" traditional values. The result has been increased friction between the political and social systems.

Gender Inequality

In Japan, as in many countries, recent years have witnessed a change in attitudes toward women's role in society, particularly among the young. In some respects, public policies were also changed to reflect these changing norms. For example, in 2000 the Women's Equality Act was passed, making it illegal to discriminate against women in the workplace and requiring employers to offer some basic maternity benefits. Still, it would be a mistake to assume that women in Japan had become empowered by these rule changes. There has been change, no doubt. There is real substance behind the fact that women feel discriminated against in the workplace (several looked at me with surprise when I asked if they felt fairly treated in their jobs.) For a Westerner, it is surprising that still today, it is often expected that when a woman marries she will quit her job and become a "housewife" (*okusan*). Obviously, many women chafe against this system and are frustrated that, as one professional woman told me, "in Japan we have a cement ceiling." Many women feel that they are not treated well in the labor market. For example, a female professor told me, "When I ask for my legal maternity leave benefits, the dean called this to the attention of the entire faculty and informed them that I was asking for 'special treatment.'" In the private sector the situation is even more difficult, though an individual woman may be willing to devote 60 to 70 hours a week to a job, as is common for "salarymen" in Japan, the male dominated system of interpersonal relations and after hours socializing makes it difficult for women to compete effectively – even if they devote their lives to their job.

Japanese women are discriminated against in the job market far more explicitly and completely than in either Sweden or the United States. As we saw in the last chapter, though Japanese women are active in the labor market, they are paid significantly less than their male counterparts. Indeed, the "gender gap" (the difference between male and female wages) is 31.6 percent in Japan, as compared to 14.8 percent in the US and 4.1 percent in Sweden (see Table 2.8 in previous chapter).

There are several explanations for this gender wage gap: Women are much more likely to work part-time in Japan than most other countries and are much more likely to leave full time work once they are married, even if they have not yet had children. Women tend to work in professions that pay less and only rarely continue working after they are married. The Japanese tax system discriminates against two earner couples combining their income and taxing the second income at the top marginal tax rate of the larger income. On the other hand, the second income earner (almost always the woman) is allowed to earn a relatively small income without paying any taxes on that income. Finally, as long as the wife does not earn over a set income limit, the husband's salary is increased to help him support his wife.

Given these structural facts, many women choose to exit the labor market as soon as they can. This fact, of course, justifies the gender based employment system on the part of employers in Japan. "Women leave after five or six years of working anyway," I was told by several people (men and women). These structures and behaviors are the context in which young women today make life choices. It may be quite rational in the Japanese case, for women to say and genuinely believe, that their lives will be better off if they can just "find a rich man to marry."

We saw early in this chapter that Japan's economic institutions were adapted to a traditional society. One of the tenets of this society was that women should be responsible for the care of the elderly, especially their husband's parents. While attitudes have changed somewhat in recent years, there is no doubt that these ideas are still quite potent in Japan today. During the extreme high growth years in which Japan could borrow technology from abroad and still grow enormously, the second-class position of women in Japanese society was less of an *economic* problem. The situation is quite different today, however, where the productive capacity of educated women could well help Japan compete in the global economy. Still, Japanese political leaders have done very little to empower and even less to support women's ability to succeed or even stay in the labor market. The result? The lowest birth rate in the modern world is a demographic time bomb that will make the housing bubble look inconsequential.[66]

The Aging Society vs. a Homogenous Nation

In the last chapter we saw that Sweden also faces very significant demographic problems as it enters the new millennium and that Swedish governments have attempted to address these challenges though a combination of

---

[66] The newly elected DPJ government promised voters in its 2009 electoral campaign that it would introduce policies to make it easier to balance a job and family. They also proposed a child allowance of 26,000 yen (approx 250 USD) per child.

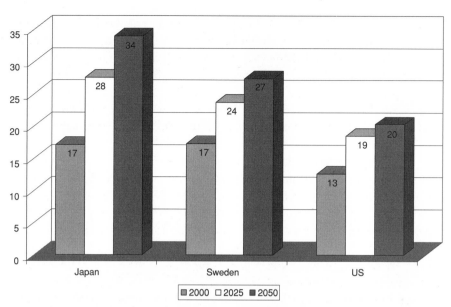

FIGURE 3.5. Percent of Population over 65 Projected to 2050. *Source:* U.S. Census Bureau, International Data Base. Retrieved from http://www.census.gov/ipc/www/idb/.

(1) fiscal policy changes designed to make the fiscal system more sustainable into the next decades, (2) women, child and family-friendly policies that are intended to encourage Swedish families to have more children and (3) an opening of immigration. Japan faces a far more serious demographic and fiscal crisis than Sweden today. It is fair to say that this is because they have been unable to make any of the hard policy choices necessary to engage this demographic challenge.

One such problem is Japan's aging population. Figure 3.5 shows population aging in each of our three countries. As we can see, Japan demographic crisis is by far the most severe with over 34% of the population expected to 65 years old or older by 2050. Of course one way to deal with this demographic crisis is to encourage immigration. However, as I noted earlier, one of the strong positions of the Japanese Right is its desire to keep Japan ethnically pure. The problem is that these views are also prominent in the LDP. The idea that Japan should be open to a variety of ideas and cultures is an exceptionally difficult issue for a society that has prided itself on its cultural homogeneity and group consciousness. While many in the bureaucratic elite are acutely aware of the need to bring in immigrants to help address the "aging society problem," politicians and voters are far more hostile. In 2005, immigrants make up approximately 1.5 percent of the population. More importantly, though a limited amount of foreign workers are tolerated in the country, especially health care workers, Japanese law remains extremely restrictive against individuals who wish to migrate there (Kashiwazaki and Akaha 2006).

I was told in several different interviews by a significant number of bureaucratic and academic elites in Japan that they felt that the demographic crisis that is looming over Japan's head is by far the country's largest policy challenge. In each case, when asked why this problem is so difficult to solve, I was given some version the following answer: "We know we must do something, but it is very difficult. There is no political consensus."

Immigration continues to be highly controversial, indeed. In 2006, the government tightened immigration policy, making it more difficult to gain permanent residence in the country. Former Prime Minister, Junichiro Koizumi, stated in 2005, "If [the foreign labor] exceeds a certain level, it is bound to cause a clash. It is necessary to consider measures to prevent it and then admit foreign workers as necessary. Just because there is a labor shortage does not mean we should readily allow [foreign workers] to come in" (Kashiwazaki and Akaha 2006).

In sum, Japan possesses not only the largest budget deficit in the advanced world, but also the most dismal fiscal future. Two basic facts are in collision: First, over the years this country has built a remarkably inefficient tax system and despite its huge national debt (which is currently equal to eleven years of tax revenue), it seems politically incapable of either reducing public spending or increasing tax revenue. Second, Japanese society is aging faster than any other country in the world at the same time that it is facing negative population growth. This means that with each year a smaller and smaller number of working age people are supporting a larger and larger number of people on retirement. One can say this about most advanced countries, but nowhere is this problem more severe than in Japan.

Regime Change?

On August 30, 2009, Japanese voters decisively turned against the ruling Liberal Democratic Party in an historic election that, for the first time in post-war Japanese history, gave a clear majority to a non-LDP Prime Minister. The LDP and its coalition partner, Komeito Party, was reduced to only 140 seats while the new Democratic Party of Japan (DPJ) more than doubled the number of seats they held in the Lower House of the Diet to 308.[67] Many

---

[67] Before the election, LPD had 331 seats and the DPJ held only 126.

have interpreted the election simply as a repudiation of the LDP's handling of the Japanese economy, but the analysis here suggests that there is more to this election. I submit that this electoral route was instead the consequence of the increasingly intense frictions in the society and economy between the socially traditionalist ruling elite, the neo-liberal economic policies introduced by successive governments and the emerging socially more progressive values in society (particularly among the young and in the major cities).

Prime Minister Ichiro Hatoyama and the DPJ clearly promised "regime change," and while at the time of this writing (November 2009), the government is far too young to be evaluated on its accomplishments, it is quite interesting to see that they have already committed themselves to a series of institutional reforms that may indeed lead to longer term change in Japanese society. We cannot know what this government will actually be able to accomplish during its tenure, but it appears that they do not intend to simply graft American neo-liberal policies onto the Japanese system. Certainly, many Japanese elites understand this point.

Professor Naohiko Jinno, former Dean of the prestigious Faculty of Economics at the University of Tokyo and the head of the central government's Local Finance Commission, wrote the following with two colleagues for the National Governor's Association:

We are in the midst of an historical crisis, as we move from an industrial society centered on heavy industry to a postindustrial society centered on knowledge. This shift involves rethinking the role of the state... Yet rather than build a big state, it is best to be strategic and stress social services over simply redistributing money... One can heavily deregulate labour markets in the pursuit of economic growth as is the case in the United States. But that strategy entails the enormous costs of escalating income inequality and poverty. It also risks further undermining trust in government as the fiscal balance worsens and hopes for sustained growth are dashed (Jinno 2009: 4)

Equally, important will be the issue question of how, or whether, the new government is able to reform the policy making process. As Andrew DeWit pointed out just after the election, "one of the most important items to keep our eyes on in Japan is the new Hatoyama government's ongoing organizational changes and how they play out." Certainly, the DPJ promised reforms in this area. "One of the main points that distinguished the LDP and DPJ election campaigns were proposals for the governance of policy making. The LDP was, almost by default, committed to the status quo... The DPJ, on the other hand, offered thoroughgoing reform of how and where decisions are made" (DeWit 2009: 14).

The new government did indeed promise to invest in in its people to work towards a more developed welfare state. For example they proposed to finance child payments to families and also made somewhat more vague promises to subsidize day care centers that will aid women who would like to work even after they have children. According to the DPJ party program, "In preparation for the era of fewer children and an aging population, we shall dispel citizen's apprehension about the future by building a social security system based on universality, individuality and support for independence" (Democratic Party of Japan 2009). Hatoyama has also implied that they will "root out waste," break down the "construction state" and replace it with a more developed social welfare programs (DeWit 2009).[68]

Unfortunately, however, the Democratic Party has not shown the courage to confront Japan's fundamental fiscal dilemma. During the election, Hatoyama's spending promises were calculated to be over 7 trillion yen (almost 70 billion USD). More disappointingly, the new government has promised that they would not raise taxes. Instead, they've made promises to cut gas taxes and increase support for rural farmers (Tabuchi 2009). This does not sound like "regime change."

Conclusion

The current [Japanese] model does not represent a stable equilibrium ... but rather is a matrix of institutions undergoing a continuous evolution." (*Vogel 2006: 218*).

In the preceding pages, I have tried to outline an evolutionary narrative that helps us make sense of the Japanese hybrid. As such, it provides an example of the fact that not all evolutionary adaptations are efficient and not all evolution is progressive. As Mayr notes, "most evolutionary changes are dictated by the need to cope with current temporary changes of the physical or biotic environment. Hence, considering also the enormous frequency of extinction and the occurrence of regressive, it is inevitable that one must reject the notion of universal progress in evolution" (Mayr 2001: 235).

It should also be clear that this is far from a "path dependent" story, even while the legacies of the past play heavily. First and most obviously, many of the formal institutions that are at the core of this story were literally brought in from the outside. We saw how these institutions shaped and were shaped by the peculiar setting into which they were placed and how this process itself was framed inside an evolving world economy. More recently, we have seen how the system became destabilized and, eventually, fell into a long period of what might be called "decreasing returns," or "negative symbiosis" in

---

[68] According to the IMF budget deficit will reach 240 percent by April 2010.

evolutionary terminology. This shift from positive to negative cycles was neither predictable nor predetermined. At the same time, we saw how the Japanese adapted to the extraordinary changes brought by Commodore Perry, as well as to the occupation and new institutions imposed by the American forces at the end of World War II. They were as successful, in no small part, because they were able to fuse existing institutions and norms with those brought in from the outside.

The original hybrid model of large export oriented capitalism grafted to a more traditional and hierarchical society is currently undergoing a particularly rapid stage of change. This is, as Vogel implies, because the friction within the matrix of institutions has grown especially intense in recent years. Globalization and the competitive pressures it implies are certainly part of this story. During the growth years, successful Japanese firms did so well that they could *both* provide social welfare benefits for their employees and effectively subsidize the large unproductive and inefficient sectors of the economy. Today, however, when these companies are under much greater economic stress, they are asking the government to pick up some of their social welfare costs, on the one hand and redistribute the tax burden toward the smaller firms and their employees, on the other. The political fact is that those who have been subsidized so long strongly oppose to any moves that would force them to be more competitive. They are poor, they argue and just like the government that can't make tough choices because it is so far in debt, so, too, the small businessman and farmer can't afford to restructure because he is already losing money.

Ironically, "globalization" presents Japan with far greater challenges than it does Sweden, despite the fact that Sweden has the largest welfare state and the heaviest tax burden of any country in the world, while Japan has low taxes and tiny welfare state. I do not mean to suggest that Japan could turn its fortunes around simply by increasing taxes and building a more comprehensive welfare state (though both are clearly needed). Rather, in my view, Japan faces a deeper set of problems: First, there is the deep mistrust of the political and economic leadership in this country that has clearly been exacerbated by the policies of recent governments. Second, the fusion of Japan's traditional hierarchical social norms and its liberal, political and economic institutions remains awkward and unresolved.

Japan's current challenges are clearly not the same as the profoundly destabilizing effects of the destruction at war's end. Perhaps the Japanese will once again find the means to build on their strengths and adapt to their future. But in my view, Japan will have difficulty if it continues to attempt to copy foreign policies and ideas and directly import them into their own system. It is specifically a mistake for a country as developed and independent as Japan to be a copy of either American neo-liberalism or Swedish social democracy. We saw in the last chapter how Sweden has grafted liberal ideas into its universalist system. The question remains whether Japan can find a way to adapt without undermining the foundations of what has made this system work so well in the past.

"Do you know the famous joke about elephants? OK, one day there was a conference of all authors who wrote books about elephants get together, from each country. The first author appeared, she was an American author. The title of the book is "How to Make Money by Feeding Elephants in the Backyard" backyard is American, make money is American. Secondly there is the British author, this book's title is "How to Look for Elephants in the Darkest Africa." Thirdly the French, "How to Cook Elephants." Fourthly, Italy "How to Make Love with Elephants" and fifthly German: Germany has five volumes and 20 appendices, title is "A Short Explanation about Elephants". Lastly, Japanese, the Japanese offer two books; first title is "A Misunderstanding between Japanese and Elephants", second title is, "How Do Elephants See Us Japanese". This story shows how we write and see ourselves as Japanese. We write such kind of books." (From interview with author, S. Morinobu, May 24, 2002.)

4

The United States

Strong Nation – Weak State

The United States of America is the richest and most powerful nation on earth. It is, by definition, unique. Indeed, the study of American politics is generally considered to be so special that it warrants its own sub-field in most political science departments. Those who *do* try to compare America typically write about what is called "American Exceptionalism."[1] Of course this makes eminent sense, America is the dominant military and economic power in the world and it has used this power to shape the world around it. Even in the midst of one of the worst economic crises in history, America produces approximately 25 percent of the world gross product. No other country has the influence (for good or ill) as does the United States.

I argue below that America's particular political and economic systems are themselves products of its unique political origins and geographic position. But unlike some students of American exceptionalism, I do not believe that America's pilgrim origins defined its specific path. Instead, I try to weave an evolutionary narrative that shows how the initial conditions and timing of American democracy have interacted over time with this country's resource wealth, fragmented political institutions and historical experience. In other words, while it is true that we can draw a line back through history and sketch the developmental pattern, this does not mean that there was any kind of determinacy in the particular outcomes we find today. Indeed, I believe that the conflicting pressures or forces embedded in America's beliefs and structures make it extraordinarily difficult for either the citizens, or the political elite, to have a clear eyed picture of what this nation has developed into in the twenty-first century. Thus, for example, it is commonly believed that the United States has a free market economy and a small welfare state,

[1] The most famous of these writings are (Hartz 1983; Lipset 1996; King 1974).

whereas in fact, the United States has a remarkably extensive social welfare state, extraordinarily detailed governmental regulation of the private
economy and a remarkably interventionist tax system.

I submit that the disjuncture between Americans' beliefs about the nature
of their political economy and political system, on the one side, and the
realities, on the other, create a situation in which Americans have grown
increasingly skeptical of government at the same time that they try to use
government to help solve their private ills. The result is an increasingly
incoherent policy system and consequentially an increasingly frustrated and
alienated nation.

In the first section of this chapter I will examine the structure of the American system in some detail. The emphasis will be on the unexpected extent to
which government intervenes in the economy and society and the surprising
size of its welfare state. Next we will explore the evolution of this system over
time. In this narrative we will begin further back in time than we did in earlier chapters for the simple reason that the American model began to emerge
earlier than either the Japanese or the Swedish systems. In this case we see a
kind of institutional *allopatry*:[2] The idea of limited government, which for
obvious reasons confronted significant resistance in Europe, found fertile
soil in the American frontier and was rather quickly institutionalized into
a new kind of political system. Importantly, America's democratic political
institutions were established *before* mass democracy, and were intentionally
designed to limit the political power of its own political elites. This system
not only survived, it thrived. Like the rabbit in Australia, or even the Kudzu
in the American Southeast, this foreign system was enormously successful at
exploiting its new environment. To be sure, the new Americans were hugely
advantaged by the massive resource wealth found in the new continent.
But, it is equally obvious that the weaknesses of America's political institutions facilitated the evolution of its dynamic and entrepreneurial economic
culture. Just as in the other countries studied in this book, the political system and the economic systems have *co-evolved*. In America's case we have
developed a *strong nation and a weak state*.

Of course, the system did not stand still. Though initially designed to
prevent a strong central government, American institutions were forced to
adapt to an increasingly complex world as well as to the demands of its

---

[2] Allopatry refers to a form of speciation in which a sub-population moves into a new ecological
niche. Over time, the different ecological contexts allow for different evolutionary adaptations
that can eventually lead to quite different evolutionary patterns. Darwin on the Galapagos
Islands most famously observed this.

citizens. This adaptive process has not always been smooth or coherent. I argue that the fragmented structure of American political institutions was eventually adapted (more precisely exapted)[3] to new functions. Remarkably, American political institutions have increasingly become *more* fragmented as the system tried to deal with increased complexity. The result has become a system in which government intervenes in society and economy extensively, but the state is weak.

In the last section of this chapter we will explore how the American system is evolving in the context of increasingly anti-state attitudes and increasingly fragmented institutions that have emerged over the past 30 years. Thus, Americans see a system that allows very narrow private sector actors to wield substantial influence over public decision makers and biases the system in favor of quite specific benefits and specific interests. I will argue that the increasing frustration and disappointment Americans have with their political system has made it even more difficult for political leadership to ask for sacrifice and/or impose short-term costs. While there is widespread agreement that difficult choices are necessary as we enter the twenty-first century, both the incentives facing political leaders and a culture apparently addicted to affluence makes sacrifice something that everyone else should do.

The election of the massively popular Barack Obama in 2008 and the subsequent disappointment with his administration's inability to bring about the kinds of change that his election promised is the most recent example of the consequences of this system. Neither American political institutions, nor American ideology are well suited to a time when decisive governmental action is required. The result instead will be a further layering of incoherent and inconsistent policies on an already incoherent welfare state. While private interests attempt to influence public policy-making in their favor in all polities, the United States stands out for the degree to which the political system is specifically open to this kind of influence. There are, for example, more than 26,000 registered lobbyists in Washington, D.C. alone, whose sole job is to extract benefits for the tens of thousands of interest groups who pay their salaries. No other democratic political system in the world has anything like this number of lobbyists for the simple reason that no other

---

[3] Exaptation, once again, is the process in which a function or trait can take on other functions. The classic example of this in biology is bird feathers, which were originally developed for warmth but were later adapted for flight. This process is widely understood to be a main contributor to the imperfect design of most of the biological world. It also contributes substantial complexity. Thelen and Streeck call this process *layering*. The prime example of this in their book, *Continuity and Change*, comes from the analysis of the evolution of Congress by Erik Schickler, (Streeck and Thelen 2005: 23), (see Schickler 2001).

political system is as open to and so deeply penetrated by narrow specific interests (or factions) as the American pluralist system (Dahl 1967; Polsby 1964).[4]

PART I

AMERICA'S "HIDDEN" WELFARE STATE

A growing number of scholars have begun to demonstrate that the United States spends at least as much, and perhaps more, on social welfare (i.e., child care, health care, foster care, elderly care, etc.) as most other rich countries. Contrary to many people's expectations, the key difference between the US and other countries is not the level of social welfare provided in society, but rather how social welfare benefits are provided and how they are financed. Chris Howard has nicely captured this system with the phrase "The Hidden Welfare State" (Howard 1997, 2003; see also Hacker 2002). The United States government is intimately involved in subsidizing these private welfare efforts in a number of ways, but *indirect* (tax) financing and subsidies appear to be the preferred methods in the US. In fact, as Howard points out, when we take all the indirect subsidies into account, "[t]he American welfare state is not unusually small. It compares favorably with some of the largest welfare states in the world. Its size has been measured incorrectly by many people and organizations for a long time." Thus, "[t]hose analysts who spend a lot of time and energy explaining why the American welfare state is so small should reconsider their initial premises" (Howard 2007: 25).

Combining public expenditure and private expenditures by companies (which are, once again, subsidized through the tax system) reveals that the US is by no means a laggard as it is often thought. In fact, if we combine both public and private social expenditures (See Table 4.1), we find that total per capita social expenditures in the United States are *higher* than in Sweden. Of course, one needs to be careful in interpreting this data. Most importantly, per capita expenditures in the US are high in large measure because per capita incomes are high. Still, the United States clearly does spend enormously on social welfare benefits to its citizens.

America's Unique Tax System

One of the reasons public policy in the United States *appears* to be so different from other countries is that the tax system is used more extensively

---

4 Lobbying in the European Union has increased dramatically in recent years. In 2000 there were 2,600 registered "interest groups" in Brussels.

TABLE 4.1. *Per Capita Net Social Expenditures in Japan, Sweden, and the United States in 2001 (US Dollars and PPPs)*

	Japan	Sweden	USA
Gross Government Social Expenditure	4,951	9,549	5,544
Direct and Indirect Taxes on Expenditures	214	1,932	353
Tax Breaks for Social Purposes	294	0	742
Net Government Social Expenditure	4,978	7,618	5,968
Net Mandatory Private Social Expenditure	214	109	141
Total Publicly Mandated Social Expenditure	5,192	7,699	6,074
Net Private Social Expenditure	937	707	3,178
Total Public and Private Social Expenditure	5,914	8,325	8,652
Percent of Group Mean			
Gross Government Expenditures	70.5%	136.1%	79.0%
Net Public Expenditures	78.0%	115.7%	91.3%
Net Total Public and Private Expenditures	76.4%	107.5%	111.7%

Source: Calculated from data originally presented in Adema, Willem, and Maxime Ladaique. 2005. "Net Social Expenditure, 2005 Edition: More Comprehensive Measures of Social Support." In *OECD Social Employment and Migration Working Papers*, No. 29. Paris: OECD Publishing; World Bank. 2007. World development indicators (CD-ROM). Washington D.C.: World Bank; Jordan, Jason E. 2006. Who is in? Who is out?: Inclusion and exclusion in Western welfare states. Ph.D. Dissertation, Department of Political Science, University of Colorado at Boulder, Boulder, p. 56.

as an instrument of public policy, rather than a means of direct public "on budget" spending. Simply put, the United States is unique in the extent to which it attempts to regulate, reward, subsidize and manipulate private decision making through its tax system. Clearly, every advanced country uses its tax system to effect private decision-making (King 1984; Steinmo 1986; OECD 1984), but the United States stands out for the enormous number and extraordinary level of detail of these tax manipulations. For reasons we will explore below, American policy makers increasingly appear to prefer spending money on social and economic objectives via the tax system instead of spending money directly out of the budget. In 2002, tax expenditures in the United States accounted for over 913 billion dollars in federal government outlays. This was equivalent to 50.29 percent of direct federal government expenditures (Noto 2004: Table 1). Federal income tax expenditures alone amount to approximately 8.76 percent of GDP in 2002. It is interesting to consider that if the USA actually collected this revenue, it would be close to average within the OECD at about 36 percent of GDP.

Jacob Hacker describes the American "welfare regime" as *The Divided Welfare State*. "The dramatic rise of the American state in the twentieth century did not displace the role of the private sector in providing social welfare goods and services," he tells us. "To the contrary," he argues, "via regulatory and tax policy, with incentives and restrictions, through the omissions and commissions of public programs, and by oversight and by design, American government contributed to the construction of a sphere of private social benefits far larger than any other affluent democracy" (Hacker 2002: 276). The result is that middle-class Americans increasingly feel that government spends money on "other people" even when the majority of public spending goes directly toward benefits for the middle class.

It is important to understand that tax expenditures *are* government spending. Instead of collecting money from taxpayers and then spending the money directly, tax expenditures allow companies and individuals to avoid paying their statutory taxes *if* they fulfill very specific requirements laid out in the tax code (e.g., make certain types of investments, purchase specific types of goods, or provide specific types of benefits for their employees). The reality is that the supposedly 'free market' United States of America has a tax code that is so littered with specific rules, regulations, complications and exceptions that it would boggle the mind of even the most anti-market socialist bureaucrat (King 1984; Witte 1983; OECD 1984; Howard 2003; Cowie 1993). As we see in Table 4.2, the US government spends a great deal of money in virtually every category of public effort through these tax expenditures. In some cases, tax expenditure spending is greater than the total on budget expenditure.[5] For example, according to the Congressional Research Service, U.S. Federal government tax expenditure outlays in "Education, Training, Employment and Social Services" are 143 percent greater than traditional on budget public expenditures ($100,900 million in T.E.s vs. $70,544 in direct outlays).

The choice to subsidize social welfare through the tax system rather than through direct public expenditures has significant implications for the distribution of benefits. For example, instead of subsidizing childcare programs for all citizens, the United States offers child care tax credits to families. This credit certainly is a great help to the middle class families who largely benefit from it, but is insufficient to finance the total costs of childcare for those who are most in need of this aid. Similarly, rather than provide health insurance for all citizens through a mandated state program, in the US *some* employees *may* exempt the costs of *some* parts of their health insurance from their

---

[5] The Congressional Research Service estimated that the Federal government lost over 1.024 trillion dollars in tax expenditures in FY 2002. This was equivalent to 50.96 percent of total federal expenditures (Noto 2004).

TABLE 4.2. *Revenue Loss from Tax Expenditures in the United States by Expenditure Category, 2002*

Category	Budget Function	TE (millions)	Outlays (millions)	TE as % Outlays (millions)	TE + Outlays (millions)	TE as % of GDP
Defense	Category Total	$2,540	$348,555	0.73%	$351,095	0.02%
Human Resources	Education, Training, Employment, and Social Services	100,900	70,544	143.0	171,444	.97
	Health	151,850	196,545	77.2	348,395	1.46
	Income Security	179,983	312,511	57.5	492,494	1.73
	Social Security	24,980	456,413	5.4	481,393	.24
	Veterans' Benefits and Services	3,370	50,984	6.71	54,354	.03
	Category Total	461,083	1,086,997	42.2	1,548,080	4.42
Physical Resources	Energy	4,320	483	894.4	4,803	.04
	Natural Resources and Environment	1,810	29,454	6.5	31,264	.02
	Commerce and Housing Credit	315,030	385	818.26	315,415	3.02
	Transportation	3,040	61,862	4.9	64,902	.03
	Community and Regional Development	1,050	12,991	8.3	14,041	.01
	Category Total	325,250	105,175	309.2	430,425	3.12
Interest	Category Total	510	170,951	0.3	171,461	0.00
Other	International Affairs	23,430	22,357	104.8	45,787	.22
	General Science, Space and Technology	12,220	20,772	58.3	32,992	.12
	Agriculture	1,840	22,188	8.3	24,028	.02
	General Assistance	86,810	17,385	499.3	104,195	.83
	Category Total	124,300	82,702	150.3	207,002	1.19
TOTAL	Category Total	913,683	1,816,737	50.3	2,730,420	8.76

Source: Noto, Nonna. 2004. "Tax expenditures compared with outlays by budget function: Fact sheet." In *CRS Report for Congress.* Washington, DC: Congressional Research Service.

income for tax purposes and/or *may* be able to take advantage of other tax deductions *if* their health care costs exceed *certain* limitations under *certain* circumstances *and if* they meet specific income limitations.[6] This description sounds complicated, but in fact it simplifies the reality quite substantially. Ironically, because it is so complicated, it is also expensive. First, the complications allow for many to cheat. Second, it takes a lot of bureaucrats to monitor a system that is this complicated. Consequentially, the system reduces the amount of money collected in general revenues *and* undermines public support for the expansion of universal programs precisely because it is so complicated and so patently unfair (Hacker 2002; Witte 1983).

Targeting

Contrary to the image of being a social welfare "laggard," the United States actually spends comparatively large amounts on programs targeted directly on specific groups – including the poor. The problem is, as Jason Jordan has demonstrated, that these target programs do not alleviate poverty, are hugely expensive to administer and even create "poverty traps," making it even more difficult for individuals on these programs to ascend into the middle classes (Jordan 2006b).

Even while the American welfare state is intentionally targeted, it is not the case that the majority of public benefits go to the poorest citizens. In fact, the poorest 20 percent of American citizens benefit from only 33.6 percent of non-pension transfers (this figure includes the Earned Income Tax Credit). In the United States – as in most countries – the major recipient of public transfers is the middle class. But once again, since they receive so much of that benefit through the tax system (i.e., the benefit is that they pay lower taxes than they would if they didn't get x, y, and z tax expenditures), only very rarely do they feel that they benefit from government social spending (Forster and d'Ercole 2005: Table A5).

A good example of the problems with the American system of targeting is seen in our National Health Insurance (NHI) programs. Many Americans believe the United States does not have a National Health Insurance System This is, of course, quite wrong. In fact, the U.S. has two:[7] Both Medicare and Medicaid are national health insurance systems. These programs cover nearly 30 percent of American citizens and account for over 50 percent of total health care spending in the United States. The issue is that these

---

[6] The tax reform of 2010 will certainly further complicate this scenario.
[7] Actually three if you count the Veteran's Health Administration.

TABLE 4.3. *Population Coverage of Public and Private Health Insurance in 2005*

	Public (%)	Private (%)
Germany	89.6	10.2
Japan	100.0*	0.0
Sweden	100.0	0.0
United States**	27.3 (Medicare 13.7) (Medicaid 13.0) (Military health care 3.8)	68.5

Note: Health care coverage refers to percent of population eligible for health care goods and services under public or private programs; * Japan: data is for 2004; ** United States: categories are not mutually exclusive, people can be covered by more than one type of health insurance during the year.

Source: OECD. 2007. "Health Data"; U.S. Census Bureau. 2007. "Income, Poverty and Health Insurance Coverage in the United States: 2006." Washington, DC: U.S. Government Printing Office, p. 58, Table C-1.

programs are not *comprehensive* systems like the NHI programs found in most other countries.

The somewhat surprising fact is that the United States government spends approximately as much as most other rich countries in **public** health care. In 2004, US public health care expenditures were 6.8 percent of GDP. The OECD average was 6.4 percent. The key difference is that in almost all other countries this public expense covers most of their populations, though the American public health system covers only 27 percent of the population, as illustrated in Table 4.3. When we add total public and private health care expenditures together (see Figure 4.1), we see that America spends over twice as much per person on health care than most other OECD countries. Sadly, however, this enormous expense does not result in better health for the American population, as shown in Table 4.4

Because American social welfare spending is targeted on particular groups and because the benefits are subsidized indirectly through the tax system, most beneficiaries of public welfare spending do not see themselves as beneficiaries. For example, when a family gets a tax deduction for health care expenditures, this tax break reduces their overall tax burden, but they *do not* see this as a grant from the government to help them finance their health care. In countries with directly financed public health care services, the sense of benefit is quite different.

In sum, the image of the United States as an inactive state in which the market is allowed to determine social outcomes is simply false. Much of the

TABLE 4.4. *Health Care Outcome Indicators in Germany, Japan, Sweden, and United States, 2004*

	Life Expectancy (year)	Infant Mortality ((per 1000 live births)	Maternal Mortality (per 1000 live births)	Perceived Health Status (%) *1	Potential Years of Life Lost *2
Germany	78.6	4.1	5.2	72.6 (in 2003)	3360
Japan	82.1	2.8	4.4	38.7	2757
Sweden	80.6	3.1	2.0	72.4	2825 (in 2002)
US	77.8	6.8	13.1	88.6	4934

Note: 1. Percentage of the population aged 15 years old or more who report their health to be "good" or "better"; 2. under 70 year-old (years / 100.000 pop.). Potential Years of Life Lost (PYLL) is a summary measure of premature mortality, which provides an explicit way of weighting deaths occurring at younger ages, which are, a priori, preventable. The calculation of PYLL involves summing up deaths occurring at each age and multiplying this with the number of remaining years to live up to a selected age limit.
Source: OECD. 2007. "Health Data."

social welfare system is delivered through the tax code and private social benefits. The consequences are: (1) the upper and middle classes are the major beneficiaries of the social welfare spending and (2) most people (even recipients) do not *perceive* that they benefit from public social welfare.

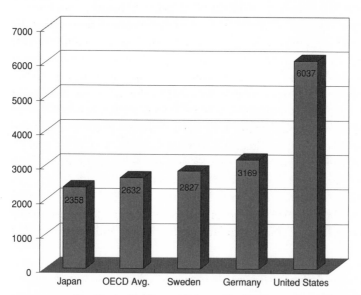

FIGURE 4.1. Per Capita Public and Private Health Expenditures in 2004 (US $, PPP).
Source: OECD, Health Data, 2007.

We noted in Chapter 2 that even the term "social welfare" has a different meaning in countries like Sweden, precisely because the benefits for these programs are so widely distributed. In the United States, a "welfare" program or policy implies a program specifically designed and targeted on the very poor. Although, for example, Social Security (Old Age Security and Disability Insurance – OASDI) is clearly a social welfare program in that it takes income from one group of citizens and redistributes it to another, Americans do not believe that Social Security is a form of welfare. In sum, although most people don't see it this way, the United States has an extensive and expensive social welfare state. But instead of providing benefits through direct public spending, it spends huge sums through the tax code: Instead of spreading social benefits widely it targets them on specific groups – and largely through the back door. As we shall see, this system has significant consequences for how Americans view their welfare state.

The Free Market?

The USA has perhaps the most flexible and dynamic economy in the world. It generates enormous wealth and rewards the most successful "winners" lavishly while it allows "losers" to fall very low indeed. Peter Hall and David Soskice describe the United States as a "Liberal Market Economy" (LME). Thinking about the American political economy in this way is quite useful because it gets us away from the idea that this is somehow a free market. By Liberal Market Economy, they suggest a system where there is relatively little *explicit coordination* of the private sector activities either by private sector actors or by public officials (Hall and Soskice 2001: 96). In principle, neither the government (as in Japan) nor the main banks should act as coaches, or even quarterbacks, in the national economy. The government should instead act as an umpire, ensuring that the basic rules of the game are followed and contracts are adhered to. In the idealized version of this system, at least, it is illegitimate for government to intervene in ways that might advantage or disadvantage specific actors in the private economy.

In fact there is a fair distance between reality and ideal in this regard.[8] The state is in fact deeply involved in private economic decision-making, especially through government regulation, the courts, and the tax code.[9]

---

[8] See (Bruszt and McDermott 2008) for an interesting discussion of regulatory regimes and a specific critique of the banal notion that "free markets" will create the best development incentives in poor nations.

[9] Measuring and comparing regulatory burdens across countries is extremely complicated and difficult. Most studies that have tried to do so have had strong ideological perspectives and,

We will discuss many of the ways that the government intervenes in the American economy, but there can be no gainsaying that private firms have more flexibility and freedom of action than do similar firms in other rich democratic countries. A simple example is illustrative: If employers wish to get rid of an employee, they can simply fire that person on the spot. No warning is legally required, no severance pay, no retirement, no sick leave, not even any reasoning is legally required. Indeed, it is *legal* for an employer to terminate the employment of a worker (even one who has been with the firm for many years) on the grounds that the employer is dissatisfied with the employee, or even because the employee is ill.[10] It is even quite common to change the locks on the office when an employee is fired in this way.

In many ways one can say that most private sector employees in America are temporary workers.[11] As Pontusson notes, "the United States stands out as the country in which employers enjoy the most unrestricted regulatory environment" with the lowest levels of employment protection and the shortest employment tenure in the OECD (Pontusson 2005: 119–20).

We saw in Chapter 3 that the huge integrated conglomerate *zaibatsu* in Japan provided significant coordinating functions within the private economy. In the United States these private coordinative institutions and practices are illegal. Beginning in the early twentieth century, the Federal government *did* begin to actively intervene in the economy but largely with the intention of preventing cooperation and coordination among private sector actors.

for example, count the overall tax burden on the economy as a regulatory burden *without* attempting to evaluate the specific regulatory effects of taxes in any particular state. For a good survey of analyses of regulatory burdens (see Hopkin and Blyth 2006). Having said this, it still seems clear that business in the United States have fewer controls placed on their behavior through direct policy or legislative action, BUT the regulatory burden placed on them through the judicial system is very high by international standards (see Nivola 1997).

[10] It is, however, illegal to terminate an employee due to their race, gender or sexual orientation, or because they have become pregnant. If the worker has become injured on the job, termination rules are more complicated and may vary by state. The employee has a right to collect his or her earnings on work performed up to the moment of termination. If the employee is terminated for "no fault of their own" they may be eligible for government provided unemployment benefits. (See U.S. Department of Labor, http://www.dol.gov/dol/topic/termination/index.htm)

[11] Technically, this is called "at will" employment. Some employees, however, have collective agreements or individual contracts with their employers in the United States. But, less than 15 percent of employees in the United States were covered by collective bargaining agreements in 2000. While government does enforce legally binding contracts, the state (ideally) plays no role in sanctioning, encouraging, and facilitating these private contracts between private individuals. See (Davidsson 2007) for an overview of the development of temporary work contracts in the early twenty-first century.

The early Progressive Era moves to break up emerging monopolies and oligopolies were later followed by New Deal policies designed to specifically prohibit collusion between finance and industry.[12] Whereas in most other, less "liberal," political economies governments have encouraged the concentration of capital and market power, one of the most important regulatory functions of American public policy has been to prevent the concentration of capital and market power. At least in the ideal, government's role is to protect *the market* and not the actors in the market.

It would be profoundly naïve to assume that government has consistently followed the principle of building and defending a free market, however. The reality has been a complex mix of interventions that protect and/or subsidize particular private sector actors and activities.[13] Additionally, in recent years, there have been an enormous number of specific and highly detailed regulations and incentives that are designed to prohibit specific practices (e.g., racial discrimination), encourage other activities (e.g., employee health and safety or environmental protection), or subsidize yet other practices (e.g., employer provided health insurance, pensions, or child care). The problem, however, is that these rules, regulations and incentives are rarely considered or structured in any kind of coherent or comprehensive fashion. Instead, they are generally meant to address very specific issues and/or aid narrow constituencies. Frank Dobbin offers the following example: "Instead of setting a single standard of pensions for instance, Congress, under the guise of maximizing employer freedom in the design of pension programs, wrote a 300-page manual of Byzantine regulations... The ambiguity and complexity of federal regulations causes employers to hire specialists to make sense of the law and devise local compliance solutions" (Dobbin 2002: 71). Dobbin goes on to argue that this private pension industry then becomes a powerful political force demanding the extension of subsidies for private sector solutions and against comprehensive or coordinated public programs to deal with these public problems. "What makes America exceptional here is not its refusal to pay for social protections... What makes the American state exceptional is the fact that it makes benefits nominally private

---

[12] Hofstadter offers a good overview of these policies and the motives behind them (Hofstadter 1963). Kolko, however, offers a cautionary note demonstrating that many of these so-called market oriented reforms were in fact pushed by domestic producers who used the reforms to build barriers to entry (Kolko 1967).

[13] David Vogel has written extensively on the structure and character of American regulation and how the patterns differ from other countries see for example, (Vogel 1986, 1995, 1996). For an insightful comparison of difference between Swedish and American approaches to environmental protection see (Lindquist 1980).

rather than public" (ibid). Some will find these assertions surprising and even controversial.

Next, we will explore the evolution of this political economy over time. In this historical narrative we will step back further than we did in earlier chapters for the simple reason that the American model began to emerge earlier than either the Japanese or Swedish systems.

In the last section of this chapter we will explore how the American system is evolving in the context of the twin forces of globalization and demographic change. It is very important to understand that the *perception* of the United States as a free market system is also key to understanding its evolutionary path.

PART II

THE EVOLUTION OF THE AMERICAN MODEL

"The chief circumstance which has favored the establishment and maintenance of a democratic system in the United States is the nature of the territory that the Americans inhabit. Their ancestors gave them the love of equality and of freedom; but God Himself gave them the means of remaining equal and free by placing them upon a boundless continent." Alexis De Tocqueville.

No one intentionally designed America's political economy or its welfare state. Instead, they evolved through the layering of many different governmental functions and tasks onto old ones through a political system that is specifically designed to limit the use of public authority in a society where people have grown increasingly skeptical and even hostile to government itself. There is, moreover, no single causal factor that can be isolated and examined independently from which it emerged and no singular reason that will explain why the US has gone down this path. Indeed, there are virtually limitless numbers of alternative possibilities and paths that could have been taken in this particular species of democratic capitalism. But having said this, I do not mean to suggest that we cannot offer explanations for how and why this system developed. Quite to the contrary, I will do precisely this here. We must recognize, however, that we are trying to explain a singular outcome. There really are no other countries that are just like the United States of America.

Three initial conditions stand out as critical factors for America's unique evolutionary path. First, when the early colonies agreed to their founding institutions they were fundamentally divided over the question of what kind of society they wanted to build. The result was the founding of a unique political system that divided and fragmented public authority, on the one hand, and unified and expanded the nation, on the other. They built a strong nation with a weak state. Second, the enormous resources of North America facilitated the development of a uniquely individualistic and egalitarian ideology as the United States spread across the continent. Third, though the fundamental equality of all men was a key principle of the country's founding institutions and ideology, the reality was that systematic discrimination and disenfranchisement against specific racial groups was legal and common practice for most of the country's history.

These factors, it must be noted, are not *in*dependent variables. They are instead interdependent traits that have woven together and intersected with American history and experience. Once again, just as each of the countries explored in this book is unique, the key factors that help explain each of these nations' developmental path are unique. No other advancing nation had access to, or the advantages of, the enormous and rich resources found on the vast North American continent as it was developing its nationhood. No other successful democracy relies on political institutions specifically designed to fragment political power in anything like the U.S. Constitution. Finally, no other nation has been so proud of its democratic institutions while so obviously violating the fundamental principle of equality before the law. These are more akin to genetic traits conditioning how the US has coped and adapted to the challenges it has faced over the course of its evolution.

In previous chapters, I began the historical narrative in the early or midtwentieth century. Undoubtedly, there will be those who would argue that to understand the evolution of these political economies I should have started earlier. Perhaps this is correct. But I believe that it also makes sense to begin these narratives with the period when we see the formation of the modern democratic institutions that govern these countries today. To find this period for the USA, however, we need to go back much earlier than is the case for Sweden and Japan.

A System of Checks and Balances in the Land of Milk and Honey

The early timing of "democratization"[14] in America is itself a hugely important fact for understanding the subsequent evolution of the American state. In the middle of the 1700s, ideas about limited government, and

[14] Desmond King argues that we cannot call the United States democratic until it passed the Civil Rights Act in 1965 (King 1995b). While I am quite sympathetic to this argument, I will continue to use the term "democratic" to describe American political institutions even in the earlier periods, if for no better reason than I lack a better term.

democratic authority, were spreading in Europe and America alike. But, in the American context, these ideas found very fertile soil. The result, as we shall see, was that as these ideas were transplanted and eventually institutionalized into the American context, they took on a life of their own. They subsequently changed the world.

Of course the story is well known: The young elites in America were angry that they were shut out of from authority by the English aristocracy and thus demanded equal representation. At the same time they were fearful of democratic governance and the potential rule of the mob. Consequentially, America's founding document which eventually emerged after the revolution was set up to prevent majorities from dominating the political system. While many had warmed to the idea of a republican system in which citizens should be able to check the power of their governors, most were still deeply afraid of the democratic impulses that were emerging after the Revolutionary War of the 1770s. To be sure, there was considerable disagreement over the merits of democracy as a principle in the first place, but by the late 1700s many had come to truly believe in republican institutions. The challenge was how to get the institutions to control themselves. The brilliant solution was to accept the principle that all men (or at least all propertied, white men) did have a proper and legitimate role in governance, but also to insist that the potential power of this democratic body should be severely checked. Thus, a series of institutional barriers to democratic governance were put into place, including the rule that any law passed by the democratic legislature must also be approved by a body of appointed elites selected from the various states (they called it a Senate) and must also be agreed to by an executive (called a President) who was to be selected by another group of elites (the Electoral College). Even these institutional barriers to popular democracy proved insufficient to mollify the fears of many. Before the entire document was agreed to, ten amendments were added which further, and rather fundamentally, constrained and limited the scope, power and realm of the new national "democratic" government.

Of course most readers will know this story – even if it is not the conventional high school version of the origins of American democracy. I elaborate it here to emphasize the point that the foundations of America's governing institutions were explicitly anti-popular government. To be sure, the designers of the Swedish and Japanese constitutions also concerned themselves with the problem of how to limit the abuse of power, but they were less afraid of the people than were the fathers of the American Republic.

Given the intentional inefficiencies designed into the American political system, one might wonder how this system survived in the first place.

Addressing this question brings us to the heart of our argument about the co-evolution of political and economic systems. The American constitution was designed to prevent one faction or group (including a majority) from dominating and imposing its will on other groups. It was also clear, however, that these ex-colonies had several interests in common. Joining into a common economic market could provide advantages for both commodity producers and emergent manufacturers, for example. But it was the desire to have a united front facing both east and west that ultimately proved to be the most important factor shaping the future American polity. Already before the Constitution was signed, disagreements over the control of the newly available lands west of the Appalachian Mountains emerged. Who should control and benefit from these enormously rich resources? How should boundaries be drawn? What should be done about the Native Americans that currently lived to the west? Should slaves be used to exploit this wealth or not?

The convergence of these questions evoked a remarkable and unique answer: *Build a strong nation, but a weak state.* The phenomenal wealth, both within and at the borders of the new American nation, allowed for an institutional compromise that explicitly limited the authority of government over its citizens but simultaneously facilitated the expansion of that nation across the continent. Thus, simultaneous with the Constitutional Agreement came the Northwest Ordinance[15] that specified how the newly acquired lands would be divided and developed. The implication of this profoundly democratic and egalitarian act can scarcely be over-estimated for the future development of the American polity.[16] They were to build what Jefferson called "An Empire of Liberty."[17]

---

[15] The Northwest Ordinance was passed in a series of steps between 1784 and 1787. Each of these steps laid out the rules for bringing in new lands into the United States and then specified the rules for land ownership, town development and ultimately colonization of the enormous resources. The July 13, 1878 measure specified that slavery would not be legal North of the Ohio River. Though no direct connection can be proved, this measure was passed in Congress the day before the Constitutional Convention passed the highly controversial "three-fifths compromise," which counted slaves as three fifths of a person (despite the "all men are created equal" rhetoric) for representation purposes in the House of Representatives (see Countryman 1985: 181–92, 191).

[16] One of the most important parts of this act was to establish a fixed percentage of the new lands must be laid aside for education. It was clearly understood that new immigrants would arrive and they and/or their children should be educated (see Hirshland and Steinmo 2003). Thomas Jefferson drew out the original map of the new territories and was influential in the development of these new democratic principles.

[17] A brief comparison with the Latin American states to the south is instructive here. At the time of their independence these countries had great resources at their disposal as well. But instead of opening these resources to the immigrant and/or the mobile, elites in these nations

It would be a fundamental misunderstanding of the argument of this book to conclude that America developed differently simply because its unique political institutions were established in the eighteenth century, not later or earlier. This is not the point. The point is, rather, that political institutions *only* operate in a context and that they co-evolve with that context. Here, this context happens to be the eighteenth century, and this had a huge impact on the co-evolution of the American political system and the economic system. Nature and nurture are thus inextricable intertwined in this evolution: The remarkable expansion of the United States across the richest land mass in the known world shaped both the ideas and beliefs of the American people, and consequentially, the institutions as they grew and adapted to the realities of modern and increasingly complex governance. By dividing and fragmenting power in Washington, the Constitution made it more difficult for those with power to control and dominate the new western lands as they became available for exploitation.

The importance of America's geographical inheritance was great: The sheer size of the western lands that progressively became available to the new Americans was overwhelming. The less than four million people who lived in the thirteen states east of the Appalachian Mountains in the 1780s could have no idea of how far the continent expanded, but by 1784, they had already claimed the land Northwest of the Ohio River, effectively expanding the new nation by over 260,000 square miles. In 1803 Jefferson secured the Louisiana Purchase and expanded the size of the country another 828,000 square miles. The entire population of the United States at that time was approximately 5.5 million people, and expansion did not stop there. By mid-century the country had managed to purchase or conquer the entire continent (over three million square miles). These lands needed people. Both domestic growth and immigration led to an historic expansion of the American population. Table 4.5 shows both the enormous land wealth in nineteenth century America AND the fact that the population nearly doubled every twenty years – from just over seven million in 1810 to over 92 million a hundred years later.

The physical expansion and population explosion of the United States had multiple consequences. First, and most obviously, it brought to a head the embedded conflicts between the fundamentally different worldviews of

divided the spoils amongst themselves rather than allowing those with no power or influence access to these lands. Consequentially, their attempt to build strong states undermined the evolution of strong nations. For a similar argument, see (Centeno 2002), although Centeno's argument is that ultimately this solution undermined the longer-term legitimacy and capacity of these states.

TABLE 4.5. *United States Population, Area Measurements, and Density: 1790–2000*

		Land Area		Density	
	Total Population	Square Kilometers	Square Miles	Per Capita Hectare	Per Capita Acre
1790	3929214	2239692	864746	57	141
1810	7239881	4355935	1681828	60	149
1830	12866020	4531107	1749462	35	87
1850	23191876	7614709	2940042	33	81
1870	38558371	9170426	3540705	24	59
1890	62979766	9170426	3540705	15	36
1910	92228496	9186847	3547045	10	25
1930	123202624	9198665	3551608	7	18
1950	151325798	9200214	3552206	6	15
1970	203302031	9160454	3536855	5	11
1990	248718302	9159116	3536278	4	9
2000	281424603	9161966	3537438	3	8

Source: U.S. Census Bureau, Statistical Abstract of the United States. Retrieved from http://www.census.gov/compendia/statab/tables/08s0001.pdf.

elites in the North and the South. Eventually the conflict over what kind of nation the United States would become resulted in the bloody Civil War of 1861 to 1865 (Moore 1966), in which the commercial economy and its more individualistic/egalitarian ideology defeated the hierarchical and profoundly inegalitarian South. Thus, as this American polity continued to expand, it was a particular vision or version that dominated in national politics. Unlike the potentially wealthy countries south of the United States, then, the enormous resources of this young nation would not be reserved for the extant political and economic elite. Instead, even the new immigrant who could neither read nor speak English had access to land and resources unimaginable in their homelands and unattainable to their brothers and cousins who had the misfortune to take the boat to South America rather than the North.

One can scarcely overemphasize the scale of America's wealth or the implications of having these resources available to individuals with little money and no political clout. Figure 4.2 below shows America's share of world production of most of the important natural resources essential for industrial take off in the early twentieth century. The USA was the number one largest producer of each one of these basic minerals, with the sole exception of Gold (Transvaal was number one, the US was number two

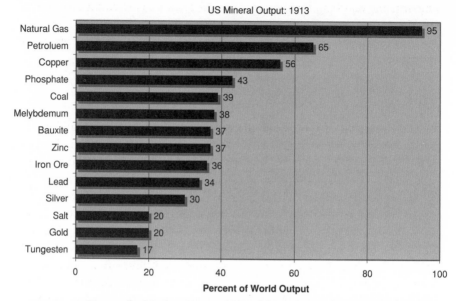

FIGURE 4.2. Geography Matters: Resource Wealth in America, 1913. *Source:* (David and Wright 1997) using data from: *Minerals Yearbook*; *The Mineral Industry–Its Statistics, Technology and Trade* (supplement to *Engineering and Mining Journal*); American Petroleum Institute, *Basic Petroleum Data Book*, Vol. X (September 1990); National Coal Association, *International Coal*; COE/EIA, *Annual Prospects for World Coal Trade* (1991).

in 1913). Though the "American Dream" was absolutely not available to everyone (Limerick 1987), the fact is that it was available to many and they could easily allow themselves to believe that it was available to anyone who worked for it. America grew rich and with it so did most of its people.

Two things are important to understand here. First, whereas the resources were available to the majority of Americans, they were not available to everyone. Second, although this was not the experience of all, this did not prevent the creation of a fundamental generalized public philosophy: "I made it from nothing, therefore anyone who works hard can make it from nothing." The corollary of course, is, "Those who are poor for one reason or another did not work hard enough and therefore deserve their fate." Truly the reality and the ideology conflicted (Huntington 1982; Smith 1993), but either because of raw racism, ignorance, or a combination of both, the cognitive dissonance that this fact might have evoked rarely emerged – at least not until the Civil Rights movement and television brought it into American homes. In short, the initial conditions of this country, with huge amounts of wealth and resources, allowed for a specific culture to evolve. Within this culture lay a particular understanding of the individual. Everybody can make his own fortune – and therefore everyone *should* make his own fortune.

The Emergence of a Modern/Active State

By the beginning of the twentieth century, demands for more authoritative government were increasing in America, as in Europe. The industrial revolution was by now in full swing on both sides of the Atlantic, and increasingly Americans, like Europeans, demanded that the state intervene in the economy on their behalf. Despite the mythology created around the American dream, the reality was that a working class was developing, and they too wanted a share of the profits generated by American capitalism. The union movement in the United States lagged behind Europe because of the vast wealth of the nation, the steady streams of immigrants anxious to take almost any job, and the fact of racial discrimination. As a result, class identity and strong union movements were retarded in America (Hattam 1993). But in America, as elsewhere, the evolution of modern capitalism brought with it the demands for a more active government.

Those who believe that American's have always held an anti-state ideology have not studied this era of American politics. This was a time of enormous activism and demand for the authoritative use of state power. However, the way in which the United States adapted to these pressures was unique. Because democratic institutions were already in place, the inequalities of early capitalism could not evoke a demand for the right to vote. Societal dissatisfaction thus had to find alternative modes of expression. In fact, middle class democratic reformers saw the party system in place in most of the country as an obstacle to fair and effective government (Bruenker 1985; Hofstadter 1963). Rather than try to centralize power in order to make government more effective and efficient in the context of the growing demands of a modernizing political economy, reformers attempted to depoliticize American political institutions. Several reforms initiated in these years proved to have profound and largely unintended consequences for the evolution of the American polity.

Early industrialization in America, along with the enormous economic opportunities offered by the shear wealth and size of the young nation, also allowed successful industrialists to amass huge wealth. Since the early days of the republic, there had been a powerful strand of ideology that resisted the development of an American aristocracy. Thus, the growth of families such as the Rockefellers evoked considerable cynicism and skepticism. In later developing countries, like Sweden and Japan, a major problem facing the country was how to concentrate enough resources and build enterprises big enough so that they could effectively compete with the Americans and the British. In the US the problem was how to prevent specific interests or individuals from concentrating too much wealth and thereby dominating the economy and polity. There was plenty of wealth in the West. The trick was to make sure that everyone would have access to it.

Thus, at virtually the same historical moment, while Japanese, Germans, Swedes, and many others were building stronger and stronger linkages between the most important actors in the economy (i.e., finance, industrial enterprises, and even sometimes labor unions) progressives in America demanded and eventually won a set of anti-trust laws which were specifically designed to break up economic concentration.

First, by the end of the nineteenth century all states had implemented the so-called "Australian Ballot" that allowed voters to vote in secret and to mark the individual candidate of their choice on their ballot. The purpose of such a ballot, from the democratic reformers point of view, was to allow voters to cast their preference away from the watching eye of local and/or party elites. It certainly had this effect. But it also made it much more difficult to organize and maintain strong political parties (Shalev and Walter 1980; Skowronek 1982).

Next, democratic reformers further decentralized power in Washington, DC, on the one hand, and attempted to break up strong political parties at the state and local levels around the nation, on the other (Gerring 1998; Dodd 1981). Political demands for a fairer distribution of income and wealth, better regulation of the private economy, and pressures for public spending and programs to benefit specific groups, interests and regions required a transformation of the old "parties and courts" system of governance that had functioned up to that point (Skowronek 1982). In order to actually govern – given the increased complexity of the task and size of the young nation – Congress created what came to be known as the *committee system* (Polsby 1968). This system evolved in the face of pressures for government to function better as it became more and more complex. But while it certainly allowed the system to handle greater complexity, its effects went well beyond this alone.

It is hard to over-estimate the effects of the creation of the committee system for the future evolution of the American polity. In the early twentieth century all developing countries were facing substantial difficulties in addressing the increasing complex problematic of governance. We saw how in Sweden this problem was eventually addressed through a set of institutions that facilitated compromise between the leading figures in the business community and labor. In Japan, the solution was more draconian and was to centralize authority and power into the hands of increasingly dictatorial leaders. The US lacked the small size, cultural homogeneity and economic concentration of Sweden, but its already long democratic traditions and constitutional separation of powers undermined those who would centralize power.[18] Absent centralized power, the problem became: How could the Congress exercise its constitutional duty to make law? The answer was to decentralize authority for specific arenas of policy to particular committees. This "committee system" thus subdivided authority for national policy between different functional units and gave power to specific congressmen over these functional domains. Reasonably, if you were from an agricultural district, you would likely serve in one of the agriculture committees. Without explicitly intending it, then, the new system of governance that was emerging turned authority for regulatory policies in America to the very interests that were about to be regulated (Kolko 1967).

In the early decades of the twentieth century, then, the United States was developing the model in which the increasing complexity of governance was addressed by dividing authority.

The successes of the Progressive administrative reformers were scattered and incomplete, and their partial successes combined with the weakening of party competition in the early twentieth-century United States to exacerbate tendencies toward dispersion of political authority within the American state structure as a whole. Conflicts increased among presidents and congressional coalitions, and the various levels of government in the federal system became more decoupled from one another. (Weir and Skocpol 1985: 135)

The unintended consequence of this decision making model was to create a policy structure that targets benefits and has difficulty distributing costs (McConnell 1966).

Building America's Welfare State

Of course, American government *did* grow. Over the next decades, in Europe and America, public authority extended into virtually every aspect of private

---

[18] The most serious episode in this direction occurred under the famous leadership of the Speak of the House Joe Cannon. In his tenure as Speaker he worked to concentrate authority in the House in his hands and was finally rebuked in 1910 when the power of the Speaker was significantly cut back.

commerce and life. Crucially, however, this authority has been extended through the back door. When new responsibilities have been taken, they have rarely been embraced. As we shall see, the consequence was that as the American welfare state and tax system evolved, it became ever more ad hoc, uncoordinated, and inefficient. The result was *not* that the American welfare state remained small. Instead, it grew into one of the largest, most extensive and expensive welfare states in the world, as the previous section of this chapter has already made clear. But because it mostly targeted benefits toward specific groups and used the tax system as a primary tool for delivering public goods, it became what Christopher Howard calls a "hidden" welfare state. The effect was to build a welfare state that does not provide much actual welfare, a tax system that is highly inefficient and is widely perceived to be unfair and, ultimately, a public that increasingly distrusts its government.

If Franklin Delano Roosevelt is the father of the modern American welfare state, then the Great Depression is its mother. The collapse of the stock market, the rise of mass unemployment, and the loss of millions of Americans' life savings to an insolvent banking industry during the 1930s gave lie to the myth that government should stay out of the economy. Interestingly, Roosevelt was not elected on an activist program. As Leuchtenburg notes, at the time of the 1932 elections, "[n]ational Democratic party leaders criticized Hoover not because he had done too little, but because he had done too much. The main criticism they leveled at Hoover was that he was a profligate spender" (Leuchtenburg 1963: 3). But quickly after the election, very quickly in fact, Roosevelt and his administration embarked upon an historic number of major policy initiatives that were meant to realign the relationship between the private sector and the state. On March 4, 1933, President Roosevelt declared in his first *State of the Union* speech, "[t]his Nation asks for action and asks for action now." Describing the state of the Union, Roosevelt declared, "[t]he people of the United States have not failed. In their need they have registered a mandate that they want direct, vigorous action." And as economic historians, Atack and Passel, simply state, "[t]hey got it. Within days the scope of government was suddenly and dramatically expanded" (Atack and Passell 1994: 665). By June 16, 1933, the administration introduced twelve major programs that would change the face of American government.[19] It is important to appreciate the extent

---

[19] March 9, The Emergency Banking Relief Act; March 31, Civilian Conservation Corps Reforestation Act; May 12, Federal Emergency Relief Act; May 12, Agriculture Adjustment

to which the first 100 days of Roosevelt's administration changed America's political economy. The twelve programs proposed to deeply intervene into the private market in ways that exceeded the proposals made by Swedish Social Democratic elites at the time (Steinmo 1993: 85–91; Swenson 2002: 5–7).

It took the huge social and economic dislocations created by the depression – a serious shock to the American political system and a critical juncture in its evolution – to defeat the idea that government should stand back and let the market decide who wins and who loses. Whatever resistance to active government may have existed in the country before the early thirties was now overwhelmed by the persuasive powers of a popular and dynamic President and the clear demands from the people to get government working for the people (Leuchtenburg 1963).

However, the way in which the system adapted to this shock was conditioned by the factors we have detailed thus far. Despite Roosevelt's best intentions, the American system of checks and balances was specifically designed to make it difficult to translate the majority will into public policies – as would have likely occurred in the other countries in this study. Roosevelt's historic battle with the Supreme Court and his ultimately successful threat to pack the court with those who supported his policies is a useful illustration here. Eventually the president was able to pass a series of legislative initiatives that expanded government authority and developed a set of programs that are today the keystones of not only the welfare state, but more broadly of the modern capitalist political economy in the United States. But it is sometimes less well appreciated, however, how *narrow* his legislative victories were in Congress, even while his party dominated both houses of Congress and at a time of such obvious crisis.

Moreover, the president's successes also had an important unintended consequence of making further changes along these lines more difficult. The great irony of Roosevelt's sweeping electoral victories in 1932, 1936, and 1940 was that they served to ensconce racist Southern Democrats (*Dixiecrats*), with no serious interest in reform, into senior positions of power in the U.S. Congress. Recall that early in the century Congress chose to decentralized authority for specific policy arenas through a committee

Act; May 18, Tennessee Valley Authority; May 27, Federal Securities Act; June 6, National Employment Act; June 13, Home Owner Refinancing Act; June 16, Banking Act of 1933 (Glass-Steagall); June 16, Farmers Credit Act; June 16, Emergency Railroad Transportation Act; June 16, National Industrial Recovery Act (see, Atack and Passell 1994: Table 23.2 for a list and descriptions).

system. The purpose of these reforms was to make Congress a more effective decision making body and to decentralize power. One of the ancillary reforms that evolved in this context was the tradition of allowing the most senior member of the majority party to serve as chairman of the committee. Committee chairmanship became a prized and powerful position because committee chairs had the power to control the committee agenda and effectively decide which bills would be considered and which would not.

This system worked to the advantage of Southern Democrats because one of the key legacies of the Civil War was that most of the South became a one party system. For decades after the war, former confederate states voted virtually exclusively against Lincoln's Republican Party, thereby allowing local (Democrat) elites and party bosses to dominate southern politics. This system was sustained and reinforced by the economic and social hierarchies from the pre-war era long after slavery had been abolished. Thus, even while the Democratic Party of FDR in the North took aim at the economic injustices created by advancing capitalism, the Southern Democratic Party used its power to protect the economic and social inequalities that were left over from a neo-feudal world. The irony was that because of the seniority rule and the committee system used in the U.S. Congress, the very elections that swept Roosevelt into power also yielded power to a racist white elite in Washington, DC. Remember, in the United States, Congress writes law – not the President. These Southern Democrats were not necessarily opposed to economically progressive or redistributive policies, but as a rule they opposed programs and policies that might upset social hierarchies and balances of power in the districts they represented.[20]

Here again we see the way in which America's uniquely fragmented political institutions structured the evolutionary path of American social policy. Roosevelt and his team of advisors clearly wished to introduce broad and comprehensive policy solutions to deal with America's economic ills (Derthick 1979). But Congress had other ideas. Certainly, several hugely important and major policies and programs were introduced, but in almost all cases these programs became littered with special provisions, exemptions, and exceptions that targeted particular interest groups or communities who

---

[20] FDR's impressive electoral victory in 1936 was most considered a national mandate for continued progressive reform. The rub was that this election even further entrenched Southern Democrats in position of power in Congress. For example, Robert Doughton of North Carolina headed the House Ways and Means Committee. Senator Byron "Pat" Harrison of Mississippi chaired the Senate Finance Committee. William Bankhead of Alabama was the majority leader of the House of Representatives and Joseph Robinson of Arkansas lead the Senate (see Patterson 1967).

were either favored or specifically *dis*favored by powerful men in Congress. Roosevelt, who was by most accounts the most popular president in modern American history (and the only President to win four national elections) eventually came into significant conflict with the leadership of his own party over taxing and spending policies. Indeed, Roosevelt felt compelled to veto 372 bills sent to him by Congress. This is more than any other President in American history. Perhaps even more significantly, however, he had nine of these vetoes overridden, even though his own party controlled both the House and the Senate. Again, in any other democratic political system a conflict of this magnitude between the legislature and the chief executive would have brought a collapse of government and new elections. In the American case, due to the institutionalized checks and balances of the Madisonian system, in combination with the committee-based decision making system, the government was left intact, while Roosevelt's victories worked to further empower his enemies.

The Social Security Act of 1935 is a case in point. Though originally intended as a comprehensive social welfare measure designed to address the sources of poverty across the nation, what eventually passed was a limited and hesitant program that covered only a minority of American workers. Robert Lieberman describes it as a "race-laden institutional bargain" (Lieberman 2002: 113). The original proposal would have been a fully national social insurance system for all workers with financial support for state public assistant programs, such as mother's pensions. However, "this package – inclusive, national social policy – proved unacceptable to the Southern Congressional leaders" and was limited in such ways that excluded three fifths of the African American workforce from social protection (Lieberman 2002: 114).[21]

Tax policy in this era provides another powerful illustration of these dynamics. In the first years of his administration, Roosevelt's activism on the spending side of the budget was not matched by an activist tax policy. Roosevelt chose to avoid using the tax system in an all out assault on the inequitable distribution of wealth in his country, even while he became increasingly frustrated with what he called the "Economic Royalists." As Stein noted: "Roosevelt and the business community were suspicious of each other but still recognized that they needed each other" (Stein 1969: 75). But as the spending demands grew, so did the need for revenue. There was a broad consensus that increases in taxes were necessary – or at least that budget deficits needed to be limited. Congress eventually agreed to expand

[21] See also (King 1995a: 10, 14, 180–81).

the tax base by bringing more and more individuals into the system. But the increase in the tax burden also increased the incentives (and political rewards politicians could benefit from) for letting specific groups and individuals out of the system. The 1938 tax bill was just one example: It consisted of over 224 pages mostly devoted to special amendments offered to politicians' most favored clients.

As the revenue needs of World War II continued to mount, the administration attempted to reintroduce the idea of a national sales tax (now called a *"National Spendings Tax"*). Once again, Congress would not go along for fear of undermining local revenue authorities. What they could agree to, however, was steep increases in tax rates – to be coupled with deep reductions for their supporters. Revenues did increase, but so did the complexity of the tax code. The abuses of the system became so gross that Roosevelt vetoed the 1943 tax bill that he labeled "not a tax bill, but a tax relief bill." However, the Democrats in Congress overrode the first presidential veto of a revenue bill almost immediately (Steinmo 1993: 103).

World War II also marked a new era for American foreign politics. Although warfare had long been essential to the American state,[22] it was not until World War II that America built a standing army. During this war the United States underwent massive mobilization of available national resources to fight with the allies against Germany and Japan. It was a mobilization of resources far greater than all the ones in the entire previous history of the United States. After the war, the world was left with two superpowers. This fact had enormous implications for the future evolution of the American polity. Not only would the military spending dominate the treasury for many years while the defense industry become central parts of American politics,[23] but, more importantly, America came to embrace the notion of America as the protector of the free world.

In sum, the state evolved as a result of a crisis, which put considerable pressure for state action. However, the way in which the state responded – and thereby evolved – was heavily constrained by its political institutions, which had themselves developed in order to solve other problems.

An Activist State Settles in

Like the other countries in this study, World War II had a tremendous impact on the American political economy. As with Sweden, the United

---

[22] Indeed American history is one of numerous military adventures ever since King Philips war against the Indians in 1675.
[23] Military spending *rose* from 7.4 percent of GDP in 1951 to 14.2 percent of GDP in 1954. In 1959 military spending still consumed 10 percent of American GDP.

States received huge economic benefits from the conflict. The enormous fiscal and economic challenges of the war also brought the American federal government into an even more powerful position *vis-à-vis* the American economy.[24] After the attack on Pearl Harbor especially, few dared argue that the market should simply be left to its own devices. Instead, there was a national consensus that America should mobilize its resources so that it could fight and win the war. To be sure, there was considerable disagreement over exactly how interventionist the state should be, but there was little doubt, even from the business community, that government should and could help stimulate, regulate and even coordinate the private sector. As Blyth notes, "businessmen ran the new institutions of war management, and despite deep political conflicts over such institutions, the founding and staffing of these wartime agencies both helped to legitimate these new institutions and to establish a pattern of business-government cooperation that was to have far-reaching consequences in the postwar period" (Blyth 2002: 79).

The understanding that government can and should play an active role in regulating the economy and redistributing income and wealth in society was deeply embedded by the end of World War II. Although there were huge disagreements over the extent of that regulation and redistribution, there was virtually no argument over the basic principles. The lesson learned from the Great Depression was that capitalism was too volatile to be left alone. Remember, even capitalists lost enormous sums in this era. At that time, no one aside from the still truly marginal neo-liberals, like Fredrik von Hayek, believed that government should fundamentally roll back. Instead, the general consensus, even among conservative elites and economists, was that government intervention in the economy was a positive force. Even progressive taxation that imposed much heavier burdens on companies and rich individuals than on the poor was, by now, widely accepted (Slemrod 1995). Clearly, many argued that government regulation was too burdensome, and others argued that tax rates were too high, but no one took serious the idea that America would be better off with a "free market" (Blyth 2006; Skocpol and Ikenberry 1983; Stein 1969; Weir 1989).

A People of Plenty

The 1950s were also very good times for America. Now clearly the dominant system in the world, the country experienced a strong and steady expansion

---

[24] For a fascinating analysis of the politics of revenue raising during World War II, see (Jones 1990).

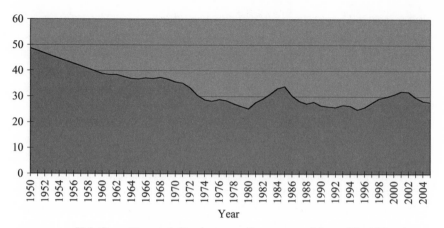

FIGURE 4.3. U.S. Gross Domestic Products as a Percentage of Gross World Products, 1950–2005. *Note:* 1. The data of 1951–1954 and 1956–1959 are missing. 2. Since many countries have no data on 1950 and 1955, the data before 1960 and after 1960 are not comparable. *Source:* 1950 and 1955: Author's calculation based on World Bank. 1984. *World tables: From the data files of the World Bank, the third edition.* Baltimore: Johns Hopkins University Press; 1960–2005: World Bank. 2007. *World development indicators* (CD-ROM). Washington, DC: World Bank.

of jobs and sustained growth. Real incomes grew rapidly for the middle class while the share of national income and wealth of the richest Americans dropped dramatically and stayed relatively low throughout this period.[25] As Figure 4.3 shows, the United States accounted for nearly 50 percent of the world domestic product.

In this period of seemingly unbridled affluence, the United States continued to see itself as the most egalitarian and open society in the world. America was certainly advantaged by its powerful economic position after the war, but also by its increasingly well educated workforce and huge public investments in education and scientific research.[26] Although progressive intellectuals and reformers argued for the construction of a more comprehensive social welfare system and more coherent tax policies similar to those being developed in Europe (e.g., national health insurance plans and broad based national consumption taxes) to go hand in hand with this new prosperity, with a Republican president in the White House and the continued

[25] The share of national income taken by the top 1 percent dropped from over 19 percent in the late 1920s to approximately 8 percent in the 1950s to the early 1970s (see Piketty and Saez 2007: 146).

[26] For a broad overview of the history of American education policy (see Hirshland and Steinmo 2003).

dominance of Southern elites in Congress, there was little chance of the American welfare state being made either more comprehensive or coherent (Stein 1969: 181). There was instead, a steady, though piecemeal, expansion of individual programs and tax relief for particular constituencies who could gain the ear of powerful committee chairmen.

Social Security, for example, was extended to ever broader constituencies, even while they had often not paid into the system (Derthick 1979). At the same time, the "automatic" revenue windfall that was generated through economic growth and bracket creep allowed Congress to dole out tax benefits to a dizzying array of constituents. Interestingly, Congress appeared less willing to introduce across the board tax reductions than to use the tax system to reward particular groups and interests. Surprisingly, the top personal income tax rate in the United States remained over 80 percent throughout the 1950s. On the other hand, specific tax expenditures (e.g., loopholes) were given away literally by the hundreds. John Witte described the 1951 Tax Revenue Act as, "A veritable landslide of special interest provisions were enacted aiding a wide range of groups foreshadowing a pattern that would emerge in all subsequent revenue bills, tax increases in one form or another were compensated for by conferring benefits in another" (Witte 1985: 142).

Americans had grown understandably proud of their country and confident in their future. The National Opinion Research Center (NORC) study conducted for Gabriel Almond and Sidney Verba's seminal study, *Civic Culture*, found that an overwhelming 85 percent of Americans were aware of the government's impact on their lives and 76 percent of these viewed this impact as positive. Indeed, when asked what made them most proud of their country, 85 percent said "the government" or some other "political institution." Steven Bennett summarized the evidence about American attitudes toward government in these years in the following way: "Most Americans expected to be treated fairly by government agencies, and roughly four fifths believed that their views would be given at least some attention by a government office. Most Americans also viewed their fellow humans as altruistic, which undoubtedly buttressed rosy views of government and public officials" (Bennett 2001: 55). Similarly, Herbert McClosky's 1958 study, "Political Beliefs and Attitudes," found that roughly 90 percent of Americans "usually have confidence that government will do what is right" (McClosky, 1964: 320, cited in Bennett: 50).[27]

---

[27] It should be noted that these early public opinion studies have subsequently been criticized for over-representing well-educated, white and middle class citizens' views. Clearly, survey

This was also reflected in America's expansive foreign policy and military force, which became one of the means to maintain this superiority and the ideas carrying it. Although America had historically spent little on defense in peacetime, after World War II, the military was now becoming institutionalized in the American society. As President Dwight Eisenhower said in his Farewell Address in 1961[28]:

America is today the strongest, the most influential and the most productive nation in the world [...] A vital element in keeping the peace is our military establishment. Our arms must be mighty, ready for instant action, so that no potential aggressor may be tempted to risk his own destruction [...] This conjunction of an immense military establishment and a large arms industry is new in the American experience. The total influence – economic, political, even spiritual – is felt in every city, every statehouse, every office of the federal government. We recognize the imperative need for this development. Yet we must not fail to comprehend its grave implications. Our toil, resources and livelihood are all involved; so is the very structure of our society.

Defense and security was thus becoming a part of American politics in order to safe guard the *strong nation*. As Eisenhower also pointed out in his famous farewell address, there were powerful political and economic interests, which stood to gain from America's extension of American power. But equally, the national identity was increasingly wrapped into the idea that Americans now had a responsibility to protect, defend, and even promote their model around the world.

Big Government – Weak State

Thus by the 1960s the United States had developed a profound sense of its superiority. This vision embraced the idea that America was a land of freedom, justice and equal opportunity. This identity, however, eventually created enormous friction with the realities of American social inequality, in particular with respect to the position of African Americans. While

---

data and techniques have improved over the decades. Nonetheless, these data *are* important because they reflected the middle class view that America was a fair and just society and that the political institutions played a positive role in this system. It was precisely because these beliefs were so strongly held that the revelations of the social, economic and racial inequalities in America in the 1960s proved so emotionally devastating and politically powerful.

[28] The speech can be found in its full length at http://eisenhower.archives.gov/All_About_Ike/Speeches/Farewell_Address.pdf.

many might acknowledge that racial discrimination existed, the fact was that most middle class Americans did not themselves experience the consequences of the structural inequalities in their daily lives (Dudziak 2000).[29] But the spread of a new technology– the television – was about to change this and indeed change American politics in quite unpredictable ways. The TV brought both *The Adventures of Ozzie and Harriet* and politics directly into America's family rooms with serious consequences for the system itself.

The infamous Senator Joseph McCarthy was the first political leader to successfully use the TV to press a political agenda in the 1950s, but it did not take long for other politicians and activists to master this medium. The young and telegenic Senator John Kennedy used the television particularly effectively. It allowed him to beat Richard Nixon in the 1960 election, who most commentators agreed had the better of their radio exchanges but came off far worse in pictures. Kennedy called out to the best in his fellow Americans, imploring them to "[a]sk not what your country can do for you. Ask what you can do for your country." But he also used this new medium to bring the realities of the appalling poverty and gross racial discrimination into the living rooms of middle class Americans who, up to that point, had formed an highly idealized "Beaver Cleaver" vision of their nation's progress.[30] Many people who were coming of age at that time can still remember the images of poor Appalachian families shoeless and dressed in rags and later the images of police dogs attacking unarmed protesters in Montgomery who were simply asking for equal rights under the law.[31]

Kennedy's assassination in November 1963 clearly contributed to the sense that something was wrong in the country. But instead of defeating a hopeful America, it galvanized the country around the idea that this rich and powerful nation should not allow for the kind of poverty, discrimination,

---

[29] Dudziak provides a rich and fascinating account of the ways in which America's racial structure interacted with domestic and international politics during the Cold War, showing how American ideals were both repressed and instruments of political advantage for America's Civil Rights movement.

[30] Steven Teles' insightful analysis of the evolution of welfare policies in the United States, shows that in the early 1960s a clear majority of Americans supported increased spending on welfare, with over 60 percent believing that America spends "too little," and less than 10 percent believing that America spends "too much" on welfare. By 1977, these figures had been essentially reversed. (see Teles 1996: 44).

[31] For an excellent examination of the ways in which public opinion and racial attitudes were shaped in this era, see (Lee 2002).

and injustice that was becoming increasingly obvious. The result was a massive electoral landslide to the Left in the 1964 election.[32] Virtually everyone believed at that time that this election offered a mandate for comprehensive reform. Instead of piecemeal and underfinanced welfare programs that had been built up to that point, the construction of a much more equal and complete social welfare system could begin.[33] Unfortunately, these expectations were not fulfilled. Certainly, many very important pieces of legislation were passed in the months following the election in a general assault on poverty and inequality in America. The *War on Poverty* introduced Medicare, Medicaid, and a variety of programs intended to offer help for the poor in America. But once again, the fragmentation of political authority in the U.S. limited their effects. Many believed, for example, that the United States would now introduce a comprehensive national health insurance program, but as Theodore Marmor has shown, the best-intentioned and well thought out plans still had to make it through Congress (Marmor and Marmor 1973). Here the lobbyists for the medical industry who were against what they termed "socialized medicine," found support from the Southern Democrats who *still* controlled the most important committees. The result: Instead of a comprehensive plan, a limited and targeted program that focused on the most needy (the aged and the very poor) was passed. This program (*Medicare/Medicaid*) certainly helped many of the most medically needy, but it also fuelled the fires of medical inflation and undercut the political drive for a more cogent response to America's medical problems (Hacker 2002; Watts and Steinmo 1995).

Other major pieces of Johnson's *Great Society* programs met similar fates, although in many of these cases, the problems were more in the implementation of the programs. In order to get the plans through Congress, they were set up to provide incentives for state and local authorities to bring them into being. This meant, of course, that there was a huge diversity in the effects of these programs, depending on which state and/or local authority chose to take them on (King 1995b). In many cases (like the Civil Rights Act) they were not implemented at all, until the Supreme Court intervened and National Guard troops were sent in to impose the will of the Court.[34]

---

[32] President Johnson took 61.2 percent of the popular vote against Goldwater's 38 percent. Johnson also won 486 out of 538 possible electoral votes. The Democrats also won a 2/3rd majority of the seats in both the House and the Senate.

[33] Seventy-one new liberal freshmen Democrats were brought in along with President Johnson who promised to fulfill Kennedy's vision.

[34] See also (King and Smith 2005).

Though the progressive reformers during both the Roosevelt and Johnson administrations hoped to build comprehensive social welfare systems not unlike those being developed in Europe, the realities of the American legislative process prohibited this option. Race and racial prejudice played a powerful role as well. Although much of middle class America was inspired by Martin Luther King's "I have a Dream" speech and likely felt sympathetic to the basic principles of the Civil Rights movement, these emotions were very clearly not universal. To many, integration and equal rights was perceived as a threat to what they saw as an essentially zero sum game. When the national government forced integration of the schools it did not provide new resources to expand these same schools. Similarly, when the Courts demanded bussing of white students into black schools, they did not provide resources to improve these schools either. In short, precisely because the American state distributes public benefits in both meager and narrow ways (this includes education), it was perhaps understandable for those who have benefits to want to protect them. Race played an increasingly powerful role in these debates.

Perhaps it is worth taking a brief moment here to take stock of where we are in this narrative. At this point we are in a critical juncture in American political history. We see building friction within society and between local and national institutions, as well as between social values dominant in different parts of the nation. Once again, it is often the friction between sub-systems that explains evolutionary change. In this case, the progressive idealism of American ideology has, once again, been beaten back by the narrow interests of a small and unrepresentative group of congressmen (and perhaps some of the constituents that they represent). In my view this is a very important moment in American history. America has made its second major effort toward constructing comprehensive social welfare policies and twice failed. It is essential to understand that if the United States had had parliamentary political institutions or, for that matter, another decision making system that better translated the majority's preference into public policy, there can be little doubt that this country would have had a comprehensive national health care system by the mid-1960s. But it is not just National Health Insurance that failed in the era. The ambitions of reformers in the Roosevelt, Kennedy and Johnson administrations were consistently hobbled by the reality of the old adage "In America, all politics is local." What this really means is not that local politics is more important than national politics, but rather that all national politicians represent local constituencies. The consequence is that in order to get national legislation through the Congress, local interests have to be served.

The multiple obstacles to the growth of central government did not stop the growth of government. Instead, the expansion in the size and range of competencies of the government had to be wheedled through the legislative process or legal system by invoking a language of "rights." In what Paul Pierson and Skocpol call "The Great Transformation," public authority expanded enormously in these decades. Not only did government non-defense spending nearly double between 1959 and 1975, but probably more importantly, the national government extended itself in innumerable ways into society via intricate regulations, grants, mandates, and incentives.

> Whichever instrument one examines, the broad story is the same. After 1960 there was a very sharp expansion in the domestic policy role of the national government... [by the mid-70s] one could see a new national state in the United States. This new state had far greater spending capacity, regulatory reach, responsibility for a range of social rights, and ability to structure incentives through the tax code than the state that preceded it." (Pierson and Skocpol 2007: 31)

Through these mechanisms, reformers were often able to achieve part of their goals. Thus, for example, it would have been clearly preferable to reformers to have universal programs, but the American system of checks and balances proved too great an obstacle. Even this system, however, could not block the demands for equal rights, smaller more focused spending programs, or tax cuts for powerful clients. The social welfare agenda was thus transformed from a broad progressive agenda to a "me too" clamber for particularized benefits, public subsides and tax breaks. As Theda Skocpol points out, the expansion of public authority and particularly the structure of particularized benefits quickly evoked an "advocacy explosion" (Skocpol 2007). What this effectively meant was that activists came to understand that they could achieve many of their policy goals by championing the narrow interests of specific groups. Once again, the United States system was not well suited for those who pushed for general policies directed at the public interest. But the American system, both through the increasingly fragmented political structure and through the increasingly impatient courts, proved to be very receptive to those who demanded special treatment and/or particularized benefits.

No one, including the activists who used the system to extract specific benefits for constituents or clients, felt that this was the best way to make policy. But if this was the only way to make policy, it was certainly better than nothing.

Between 1964 and 1976, trust in government declined by 46 percent points (Alford 2001: 44). Certainly, Watergate and the failure of the

Vietnam War played hugely important roles. But in my view, so did the government's apparent inability to deliver on its promises. Government authority and influence over people's lives grew substantially in the 1960s and 1970s in the United States, as in Europe, but the programs and policies that were passed in these years were not the kind of large, comprehensive, or universalist programs, which would clearly and openly benefit average citizens. Instead, in order to get through the Congressional labyrinth, policies had to be targeted on narrow constituencies and generally delivered and financed indirectly. America's *War on Poverty* provides a good example of the consequences: Instead of winning this war, the federal government created a maze of complicated regulations and rules defining who should get government help and under exactly what conditions thus creating an administrative nightmare for both those who had to administer it and for those who were supposedly the recipients. Worse yet, in attempts to constrain spending and insure that only the "deserving poor" received public help, social help programs were targeted on single mothers and ended up contributing to the break up of families. Similarly, the desire to constrain costs and focus benefits also resulted in a system where each dollar a recipient might earn in a job could cost them more than a dollar in lost social welfare benefits. The result? Incentives to cheat the system and/or not seek work grew. Also, the number of people in poverty grew from about 25 million in 1970 to 35 million by 1985. In short, poverty won the war.

To sum up, in the later half of the twentieth century the American political system was forced to adapt to a very new environmental context than that of the nineteenth century. The frontier was now closed and instead of being a distant nation somewhat outside the intense conflicts of the warring European states, America was now at the center of the world. Absent the ever-expanding western frontier, Americans were forced to confront the inconsistencies in their own ideologies. National political institutions adapted by creating a committee system by layering or exapting new functions onto old rules. The national government grew in power and importance and ultimately this led to a confrontation between national ideals and local politics as never before. America was evolving toward a more complex and more integrated society, but as we shall see, this process was neither easy nor comfortable.

A Crisis of Confidence

We saw in earlier chapters how the energy crisis of the mid-1970s led to a series of economic problems in rich countries. In Sweden, the Social

Democrats lost their control of the government for the first time since 1932 and in Japan the fiscal problems effectively halted their plans to build Western style social programs. The United States was nominally in a better position to deal with the quadrupling of the price of oil than other countries for the simple reason that it was the third largest oil producer in the world at that time and depended on imported oil for only 28 percent of its total consumption. The problem for America was not that it was so dependent on imported oil, but rather that it had become addicted to extraordinary high levels of consumption. With less than 5 percent of the world's population, the US consumed 31 percent of the world's energy in 1972 (Energy Information Administration 1998: Tables 5.1 and E1).

Jimmy Carter won the election in 1976 by running *against* Washington rather than for it. (He would not be the last President to follow this strategy.) He came to office in a period of great political and economic distress. The American economy was suffering what was then called "stagflation," with interest rates running into the double digits, high unemployment and the worst recession since World War II. He also came to office in a period of growing distrust of government. Both the Vietnam War and the scandal of Watergate had broken American's confidence in their government.

Still, during his four years in office he introduced an enormous array of legislation addressing problems as diverse as environmental protection, worker health and safety, housing reform, tax reform, and energy savings. Unfortunately, in response to the apparent abuse of power by Nixon, the US Congress reasserted itself as the prime decision maker. To accomplish this task, given the enormous complexity of governance by the 1970s, Congress further decentralized policy authority to its committees and new subcommittees in what was called the "Subcommittee Bill of Rights." The result was that policy making became even more unwieldy.

The new policy process is characterized by a proliferation of overlapping and competing policy subsystems, with legislative proposals spewing forth from hundreds of subsystems in an often conflicting and contradictory fashion. Because so many congressional actors have some degree of significant authority, the role of the central leaders is extremely difficult. (Dodd and Richard 1979: 154)

The floor of the sausage factory, so to speak, was becoming even messier. The consequence was that no matter how well thought-out, or well designed the Carter administration's policies were, Congress wrote its own laws. And as power was ever further distributed across the 538 members of the House and the Senate, the final policy outcomes became less and less coherent. By

1978 only one in four Americans believed that government could be trusted to do the right thing most of the time (Alford 2001: 30).

On July 15, 1979, President Carter went before the American public in a special televised address to the nation and announced quite frankly:

I want to talk to you right now about a fundamental threat to American democracy.

I do not mean our political and civil liberties. They will endure. And I do not refer to the outward strength of America, a nation that is at peace tonight everywhere in the world, with unmatched economic power and military might.

The threat is nearly invisible in ordinary ways.

It is a crisis of confidence.

It is a crisis that strikes at the very heart and soul and spirit of our national will. We can see this crisis in the growing doubt about the meaning of our own lives and in the loss of a unity of purpose for our nation.

The erosion of our confidence in the future is threatening to destroy the social and the political fabric of America.

Perhaps Carter was just unlucky, or perhaps he was just too honest. In this televised talk and a series of other presentations to the American people he tried, vainly it turned out, to convince them that they needed to adjust to the reality that America consumed too much (oil in particular) and lived beyond their means.

Quite simply, Americans did not want to hear it.

"Government is the Problem, Not the Solution" Ronald Reagan[35]

The next President of the United States promised a new day in America. His campaign ran straight against the dour pessimism of the Carter administration and forecast a New Dawn. Ronald Reagan fundamentally understood America's growing cynicism. He also understood that many of the targeted programs that had squeaked their way through the legislative labyrinth in the past twenty years created a great deal of frustration and resentment among white working class Americans. In a system where benefits are meager and targeted, it is easy to perceive inequity and inequality. When one adds racial distrust and prejudice, as Reagan did, it should be no

[35] The full quote is "[In this present crisis], government is not the solution to our problem; government is the problem." Inaugural Address, January 20, 1981, at http://reagan.utexas.edu/archives/speeches/1981/12081a.htm.

surprise that the squeezed lower classes could easily be brought against the state.[36]

For the first time in American history *in*equality was growing in America, but what made it far worse was that now it was the white working class that was feeling the squeeze. Traditionally the Democratic Party represented the white working poor, but increasingly these constituents came to believe that this party represented the demands of special interests with whom they had very little in common. Increasingly, this group that came to be know as "Reagan Democrats" came to believe that even though they paid taxes, public spending increasingly went to benefit someone else.

Reagan fundamentally understood this frustration and seized on a new strategy: Instead of promising to make government better, Reagan promised to get rid of it. Government, he argued, was not the solution: It was the problem. America is a great country and a corrupt government could not make it better, he implored. He did not say it, but what he meant was "Ask not what the government can do for us. Ask what we can do for ourselves."[37]

Reagan thus launched a two-pronged attack against "welfare" on the one hand, and high taxes on the other. He rather successfully played on the fears and insecurities of white Americans, implicitly claiming that the reason that their taxes had grown so much in recent years was that a wasteful government was dolling out too much money on an undeserving (and largely black) lower class. He was especially fond of telling a fictional story of a Cadillac driving "Welfare Queen" who had up to 80 different names, 12 social security cards, and 30 addresses in South Chicago and "bilked the government out of $150,000."[38] These themes clearly hit a powerful chord, especially among working class whites (Teles 1996: 48). Reagan avoided attacking programs targeted at the middle class, such as tax subsidies for homeowners, and instead focused on programs aimed primarily at aiding the lowest income brackets. [39] Also untouched by the budget were entitlement

---

[36] See (Mendelberg 2001) for a sophisticated and comprehensive treatment of the use of race and racial images in recent American political history.

[37] Linda E. Demkovich, "How Reagan Would Turn the Welfare System Back to the States." *National Journal* 12 (October 25, 1980), 1809.

[38] Reagan told this story in many occasions over the years and the story (which he claimed to be true) was never verified. He changed the details over the years as well (see Washington Monthly 2003; Ford 2008).

[39] His Omnibus Budget Reconciliation Act (OBRA) consolidated 57 means-tested social spending programs into 7 block grants, and coupled this with a 12 percent, $50 billion reduction in social spending by 1984.

programs widely enjoyed by middle-class voters, such as Social Security, Medicare, and Supplemental Security Insurance?[40]

Reagan's most important legacy, however, was not on the spending side of the budget. Instead, he helped build a new economic philosophy. Taking up the logic of an economist to whom he had recently been introduced, Arthur Laffer, Reagan advanced the then counterintuitive argument – although it is now often seen as accepted wisdom – that cutting taxes would actually stimulate growth and therefore increase revenues taken in by the state. Following this logic, Reagan introduced the most sweeping tax cuts in American history. The problem, however, was that Democrats controlled the House and the Senate and they were not inclined to offer the President such a potent legislative victory, particularly after having so successfully beaten Carter's policy initiatives.

Reagan and his advisors, principally Ed Meese, James Baker, and David Stockman decided to make a strategic gamble: Knowing that Congress would find it difficult to say no to special tax cuts benefiting particular interest groups, the administration effectively declared a free for all. Since interest groups like tax gifts, why not make this tax bill a giant Christmas tree?

The logic was simple. In order to pass a huge tax rate cut, the administration offered to add literally hundreds of tax expenditures to the bill to "sweeten" the package (Stockman 1986: 44). What started out as a side deal here and a side deal there, however, ended up becoming an avalanche. Some, no doubt genuinely, believed that cutting taxes would actually be good for the economy, but only the hopelessly naive believed that this was good tax policy. "The hogs were really feeding," a congressional staffer recounted to this author. "The greed level, the level of opportunism, was just out of control," reported another Congress watcher (Grieder 1981:5). But, as Witte correctly points out, "It should be remembered that this bill was unique only because it was extreme, not because it established new trends in tax legislation" (Witte 1985: 235). By the time they were through, Congress passed and Reagan signed a 25 percent, across the board tax rate cut and hundreds upon hundreds of special tax expenditures (appropriately called

---

[40] Funding for Aid to Families with Dependent Children (AFDC) fell 17.4 percent; Food Stamps payments shrank by 14.3 percent; federal outlays for the Social Security Block Grant (SSBG) were rolled back 23.5 percent. Second, OBRA more indirectly reduced the size of these programs by tightening their eligibility requirements. As a result, enrollment numbers plummeted. Unemployment insurance recipients were forced off the rolls while 400,000 people were dropped from AFDC, and one million no longer qualified for Food Stamps.

"loopholes" in this context) to particular clients. The *Economic Recovery Tax Act* reduced government revenues by over $750 billion over the next five years.

The immediate consequence of the 1981 tax reform was the massive increase in the public deficit. But in my view, the longer run effects were more consequential. First, "Reaganomics" became the new philosophy for the Republican Party. Instead of trying to make government better, the philosophy essentially holds, hand cuff it and make it less dangerous. Government cannot be made to behave well, it seems, so better to "starve the beast." The second major consequence of Reagan's time in office was to reinforce cynicism among the American public. "As the fiscal crisis worsened, and the political conflict intensified," David Stockman, Reagan's budget director admitted, "we have increasingly resorted to squaring the circle with accounting gimmicks, half-truths and downright dishonesty in our budget numbers, debate and advocacy" (NYT, June 28, 1985: 30).

Perhaps that was Reagan's plan all along. Not only could deficits "starve the beast," but the gimmicks and dishonesty of this administration would make it ever more difficult to rebuild confidence in American *government*.

President Jimmy Carter warned in his famous Crisis of Confidence speech in 1979:

We are at a turning point in our history. There are two paths to choose. One is a path I've warned about tonight, the path that leads to fragmentation and self-interest. Down that road lies a mistaken idea of freedom, the right to grasp for ourselves some advantage over others. That path would be one of constant conflict between narrow interests ending in chaos and immobility.

By the mid-1980s, the American tax system had become so littered with tax expenditures and loopholes that not even staunch progressives could defend it any longer. What Carter had once called, "a swamp of unfairness," had by now become even worse. By 1986 the federal government lost more revenue in special tax breaks than it collected with the Federal Income Tax (Witte 1983). It was in this context that the Reagan administration pressed the historic Tax Reform Act of 1986, which pushed down tax rates on top earners to 35 percent (a 50 percent reduction from where they had been when Reagan entered office in 1981) in exchange for the revenue gains made by closing many of the most egregious loopholes – many which had been introduced in 1981.

The new tax plan fit Reagan's general philosophy – cut back on government and let the market work. By now the economy was returning to health, helped in no small part by the huge stimulus created by the deficit

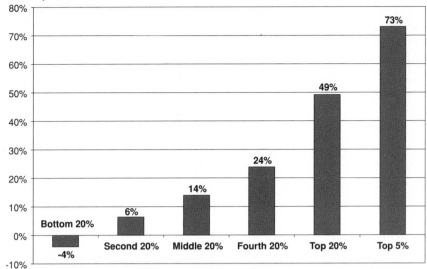

FIGURE 4.4. Drifting Apart: Change in Family Income in the United States, 1979–2008. *Source:* Calculated on the basis of data from U.S. Census Bureau, Historical Income Tables, Table F-3 [Available from http://www.census.gov/hhes/www/income/histinc/incfamdet.html].

spending incurred during the first five years of the administration's term. This economic boom, along with a series of deregulations in banking and commerce, contributed enormously to the steep rise in wealth of America's richest individuals and families.

It is impossible to know whether the young entrepreneurs who were busily creating and inventing the new information technologies base on the microchip would have been less eager or less successful had they faced higher tax rates. But it is clear that many entrepreneurs became enormously wealthy in these years. By the end of the decade several things were apparent: The American economy had improved markedly in the past ten years, inequality was rising and large swaths of American citizens had lost their faith in their public institutions. Figure 4.4 tells part of this story. The top was getting a disproportionate share of the American pie.

The Evolving World Economy

Whether they needed the incentives or not, American entrepreneurs were both eager and very well placed to take advantage of the new technologies that were increasingly coming on line as a product of the exploding world of computing technology. America, once again, was a less regulated economy than the others we study here, but it was equally important that the massive domestic market in the United States gave American inventors a broad and rich market to produce for. While Europeans were still trying to work out the details of the emerging European Union, America had a domestic market of over 250 million consumers. At the same time, successive presidents used America's enormous political and economic clout to push for free trade agreements around the globe. Many American firms saw fantastic opportunities in investing in lower cost localities: Others saw opportunities in exporting to new markets. Free trade was both embedded in American ideology, and also likely to serve the interests of many of the most powerful interest groups in Washington.

"The Era of Big Government is Over"

When Bill and Hillary Clinton moved into the White House in early January 1993, many hoped that the anti-government philosophy of Ronald Reagan had played itself out. Clinton promised change toward a kinder more forgiving nation. America, he claimed, was founded on the principles of equal opportunity and government could and should play an active role in insuring this opportunity. To this end, he proposed to overhaul America's inefficient and unjust welfare state. Specifically, his administration would introduce a National Health Insurance plan as well as a fundamental reform of the AFDC (a.k.a., welfare) program, which would convert this targeted system with a comprehensive set of social welfare services, child care programs, and active labor market policies.[41]

With over 30 million Americans without health insurance and tens of millions more who were seriously worried about losing their insurance, even the middle class felt a clear need for reform. Poll after poll indicated that between 70 percent and 82 percent of the American public favored NHI (Roper, 1994). Bill Clinton had also made National Health Insurance a keystone of his electoral campaigns. Finally, as Clinton's "The Era of Big Government is over" comment indicates, even the provider community appeared to concede that health reform was not only politically inevitable, but also morally and economically necessary.

---

[41] For an excellent discussion of what went wrong with Clinton's welfare proposals see (Teles 1996: 147–66). For an explanation of the failure of the health care plan see (Watts and Steinmo 1995).

Even the American Medical Association softened its longstanding hostility to a national plan.

> A long-term crying need has developed into a national moral imperative and now into a pragmatic necessity as well...An aura of inevitability is upon us. It is no longer acceptable morally, ethically, or economically for so many of our people to be medically uninsured or seriously underinsured. We can solve this problem. We have the knowledge and resources, the skills, the time, and the moral prescience. (Journal of the American Medical Association, May 15, 1991)

Of course, we all know that the Clinton health care plan failed. While many have blamed the political strategy chosen by President Clinton and his wife, Hillary, for the plans failure, in my view the explanation is far more obvious. Once again, the game of politics in America is institutionally rigged against those who would use government – for good or evil. James Madison's system of checks and balances, the very size and diversity of the nation, the Progressive reforms which undermined strong and programmatic political parties and the many generations of congressional reforms have all worked to fragment political power in America to an ever greater extent. As we saw above, this fragmentation of political power, which had become more severe in the past twenty years, offered the opponents of reform huge opportunities to undermine Clinton's popular plan. It is important also to remember that Clinton's bill needed support from *more than* 50 percent of the members of the House and 60 percent of the members of the Senate. Congressional rules (i.e., institutions) in force in 1994 allowed a minority to block legislation as long as they could control just 40 out of 100 votes in the Senate. *No other modern democratic system in the world requires support of 60 percent of legislators to pass government's public policies.*

Second, despite the fact that the 1990s were marked by the highest level of public support for government intervention (Peterson, 1993: 406–7), the debt reaching over $3,000,000,000,000 facing American taxpayers (most of which has been accumulated since Reagan's tax cuts) made government *financing* of health care reform exceptionally unlikely indeed.[42]

The increasing fragmentation of power in Congress continued to the point where congressional representatives had become independent policy entrepreneurs. This meant money. Between January 1, 1993 and July 31, 1994, candidates for the House and Senate received $38 million in campaign contributions from the health and insurance industries alone. The

---

[42] Each comprehensive reform that was floated in Congress in 1994 crashed at the door of Robert Reischauer, director of the CBO, who was continually forced to give reformers the bad news: Comprehensive and universal coverage will cost money – at least in the short run.

TABLE 4.6. *America's Trust in Government*

Date of Poll	Q1 Government is Run for a Few Big Interests	Q1 Gov't is Run for All the People	Q2 Gov't Wastes a Lot	Q2 Gov't Wastes Some	Q2 Gov't Wastes Little
March, 1993	68%	23%	75%	22%	3%
Jan. 1994			83%	16%	1%

Note:
Q. 1) Do you think government is pretty much run by a few big interests looking out for themselves or that it is run for the benefit of all the people?
Q. 2) Do you think the people in government waste a lot of money we pay in taxes, waste some
of it, or don't waste very much of it?
Source: Roper, Organization. 1994. "A polling review of the great debate: The public decides on
health care." *The public Perspective* 5 (6):28.

AMA[43] had the single most generous Political Action Committee in the
country.[44]

In the end, Clinton's failure to bring about health care reform worked to
further reaffirm American's skepticism about politics. Once again, the failure of American political institutions to address the polity's problems – even
when there had been clear public will for action – worked to undermine the
public's faith in its governmental institutions. Given the disjuncture between
political promises and policies delivered, it perhaps makes sense that citizens
feel that government is hostage to special interests. As Hibbing and Theis-
Morse argue in the conclusion of their volume, *What is it about Government
that American's Dislike?*, distrust of government is also a problem of pro-
cedural justice. "The preference for people-power is merely a manifestation
of the public's aversion to being taken advantage of by special interests and
self-interested politicians" (Hibbing and Theiss-Morse 2001: 250).

Clearly, the relationship between attitudes and policies is both interdependent and iterative. By the 1990s, citizens had increasingly come to believe

---

[43] The AMA has contributed over $16.8 million to Congressional campaign coffers. The
American Dental Association contributed over $7 million and the National Association
of Life Underwriters contributed over $8.3 million in the same period. All together the
fifteen largest health and insurance PAC contributed over $60 million between 1980 and
1994.

[44] Unsurprisingly, powerful interests particularly favored members who were in particularly
pivotal positions. Interestingly, Jim Cooper, one of the key players whose "bi-partisan"
plan did much to take the wind out of the Clinton plan's sails in August 1994, was
the single largest recipient of health and insurance company money. He received over
$668,000 in contributions from the medical and insurance industry in less than two
years.

that the system did not work.[45] The problem was yet again exacerbated by the election of a President who promised a broad social agenda. As political analyst Stuart Rothenberg said the day after the November election, "Voters expected change. They believed they had voted for change. A year and a half later, they think they got more of the same" (Thomma 1994:8a). Public opinion polls confirm what many observers have noted: "In general, do you approve or disapprove of the job Congress is doing in handling the issue of health care reform?" 26 percent approve, 65 percent disapprove, and 9 percent don't know (Roper 1994: 27).

In sum, the massive campaign run against the Clinton health reform plan was a campaign against government generally. And, given the repeated inability of this government to act on the will of the people, this theme fell on receptive ears. The opponents, we should remember, were very careful not to argue against any health care reform. They instead argued that they supported reform, it was just that *this* reform was not the right one. The following dialogue was broadcast in yearlong advertising campaign financed by the American Hospital Association:[46]

LOUISE: This plan forces us to buy our insurance through these new mandatory Government health alliances.
HARRY: Run by tens of thousands of new bureaucrats.
LOUISE: Another billion dollar bureaucracy.

The failure of the Clinton's health care plan proved to be yet another example of government promising what it could not deliver. If America could not pass a national health care plan when it had this level of support from the public and with both House and Senate in the hands of the Democrats, when would it be able to pass any kind of comprehensive reform of a system that was clearly dysfunctional? The failure of health care reform had direct implications for Clinton's plans to reform "welfare as we know it."

What was bad for the American welfare state, however, was good for the Republican Party. It has been quite common in American electoral history for the President's party to lose seats in the interim elections between national electoral bouts. But 1994 was a rout of the Democratic Party. Building on the "Southern Strategy" initiated by Ronald Reagan, the Republican

[45] In early September 81 percent said they believed that Congress would be unable to agree on a health care plan.
[46] The association spent over $14 million on adds like these to defeat the bill. (Goldsteen et al. 2001: 1326). It was estimated that a total of $60 was spent in advertising to defeat the bill (ibid).

Party finally moved the South into their side of the isle.[47] For the first time since 1954 Republicans controlled both the House and the Senate. They seized the agenda, introducing what they called the "*Contract With America.*" This contract featured prominently, "The Personal Responsibility Act," which laid out a new round of spending cuts for welfare programs, set tougher program eligibility requirements, restricted welfare enrollment to two years, and gave further responsibility to states (Republican National Party 1994). When Republicans seized both Congressional chambers in the 1994 elections, it seemed that their contract and its welfare provisions had been given the full force of a public mandate by a more conservative America.

In the end, Clinton was forced to concede ideological ground and sign the 1996 Personal Responsibility and Work Opportunity Reconciliation Act (PRWORA), terminating AFDC and replacing it with the Temporary Assistance for Needy Families (TANF) block grant. After 61 years and under two democratic administrations, the New Deal fell victim to the New Way.

Tax Cut ... Not Spend

It is in the context of growing citizen frustration with public authority that the Republican Party build on Reagan's basic insight: Cutting taxes is the best way to deal with public problems.[48] Even poverty, they came to believe, was best addressed through the tax code. Recall that President Clinton's second major promise for his administration was to reform the welfare system. Many people had to agree that this system made poverty worse rather than better because the targeted and under funded system created poverty traps, broke up families and built incentives for recipients to cheat and/or not work. But rather than increase spending, or building a more comprehensive system which would expand government, *The Earned Income Tax Credit* (EITC) tried to give tax incentives for people to go to work. The EITC grew out of the idea for a *Negative Income Tax* that became an unsuccessful element of both the Nixon and Johnson Administrations. The notion of an EITC was initially designed to prevent taxing of working

---

[47] The historically "Yellow Dog Democrat" Southerner switched parties in droves. In the 1994 election 65 percent of Southern voters voted for Republican members of Congress. Also, a new force was emerging in electoral politics – the organized Christian Conservative. Seventy six percent of white "born again" Christians voted Republican in 1994.

[48] For a full discussion of the history of the EITC see (Meyer and Holtz-Eakin 2001).

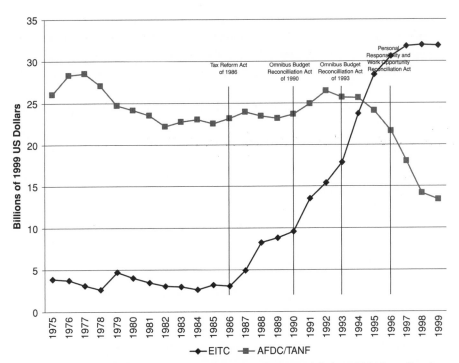

FIGURE 4.5. Changing Strategies: The History of TANF and the EITC (Spending in 1999 U.S. dollars). *Source:* Author's calculations based on data made available from Scholz, John Karl, and Kara Levine. 2000. "The Evolution of Income Support Policy in Recent Decades."

individuals into poverty by offsetting the burdens of social security taxes for working families.

During the 1990s, the EITC grew to become the most significant anti-poverty program in the United States. Clinton expanded the EITC as a means of increasing income support for the poor and offsetting the substantial cuts in more traditional welfare requirements demanded by the Republican majority in Congress. Not only did this system hide social spending from the direct budget, but it was also defended as a system that improved work incentives. The expansion of the EITC corresponded with a dramatic drop in other funding for other anti-poverty efforts. Funding of the government's major anti-poverty program, TANF, formerly known as AFDC, fell dramatically from levels approaching $30 billion in 1977 to less than $15 billion in 1999. Reductions in AFDC/TANF spending has also been followed by stricter eligibility requirements and work requirements.

The narrative above has emphasized the ways institutions, ideas and historical context co-evolve with one another over time. There are no "independent variables" here. American national institutions were indeed designed to limit public authority and there is no denying that they have had this effect (Steinmo 1995). But we have also seen how these institutions adapted to new demands. Ironically, precisely because the U.S. already had democratic institutions, reformers took a quite different path than those followed by their counter-parts in Europe. Instead of further centralizing power with the idea of harnessing power in pursuit of the public interest, they chose to divide and fragment it even more. Thus new demands on national government gave rise to a new policy-making environment that yielded enormous power to committee chairs, and thereby special interests and lobbies. A twist of history exacerbated this problem by lending Southern political elites extraordinary influence as America constructed its welfare state.

The result has been the evolution of a hyper-pluralistic decision making system in which public power has increasingly catered to the powerful but often failed to address the general interest. America's egalitarian idealism has been the primary victim. Unsurprisingly, the public's mistrust of government has grown. This system was neither designed nor intended – not even by the architects of the young republic. Instead it evolved along an understandable (in retrospect) but unpredictable path. The new century will bring with it new challenges and the United States will continue to evolve in unpredictable ways. Perhaps the new President Obama will indeed change the course of America's future.

PART III

CHALLENGES AT CENTURY'S END

"Democracy made this promise, but the riches of North America fulfilled it; and our democratic system, which, like other systems, can survive only when its ideals are realized, survived because an economic surplus was available to pay democracy's promissory notes." (Potter 1954: 93)

But what happens when the surplus is no longer shared?

Looking back from the perspective of the end of the first decade of the twenty-first century, one could be forgiven for romanticizing the last decade of the twentieth. To be sure, America faced problems, but at least this was a decade of growing prosperity, balanced budgets and increased wealth. Once we take off our rose-colored glasses, however, a slightly different picture emerges. In this picture we see an enormous expansion of wealth *for some* and stagnating incomes for many. Looking even more closely, we find a remarkable expansion in private consumption subsidized by cheap goods from Asia and cheap labor from Latin America. The rich got super rich, but the changing distribution of wealth did not stop there. Between the mid-1980s and mid-2000s, even middle class Americans drove ever-larger SUVs, ate out in better and better restaurants, and sent their kids to more and more expensive schools.

Bill Clinton did not cause this change of fortunes in the American story. It seems very fair to say that he fought desperately against it. He and his advisors focused on creating a universal health insurance system precisely because they understood that inequalities in access to and use of healthcare is one of greatest producers of inequality in America. But, as we previously saw, his proposal failed. The next President, George W. Bush, promised to be a "uniter, not a divider." Also promising a new kind of "compassionate conservatism," Bush Jr. suggested that he would bring America back to an older era when politics was not so intense. "He would overhaul Medicare, Social Security and public education; cut taxes; reinvigorate the military; restore civility to the political system; and help the poor with tax credits for health insurance, assistance buying homes and charitable-giving incentives" (Milbank 2004).

One can never know what might have happened. Politics and history is laden with contingency. Evolution is not predictable. Certainly, American politics would have taken a different route had Vice President Al Gore been selected by the Supreme Court to be America's forty-third president. At any rate, there can be no doubt that the catastrophic events of September 11, 2001 altered Bush's presidency. His domestic agenda was overtaken by an even more ambitious international agenda. But the reader should not be surprised that one of Bush's domestic policy goals was executed: Tax cuts. Perhaps one should also not be surprised that these tax cuts followed a pattern becoming ever more common in America: They increased inequality.

In 2001 Bush, Jr. realized his major campaign goal with the Economic Growth and Tax Relief Reconciliation Act (*EGTRRA*). The Bush tax cut follows the pattern of the earlier Reagan tax cuts by making extremely large tax cuts for the wealthiest Americans. As Larry Bartels notes in his fascinating analysis, *"Homer Gets a Tax Cut"*:

the most significant domestic policy initiative of the past decade has been a massive government-engineered transfer of additional wealth from the lower and middle classes to the rich in the form of substantial reductions in federal income taxes. Congress passed, and President Bush signed, two of the largest tax cuts in history in 2001 and 2003. One accounting put the total cost to the federal Treasury of those cuts from 2001 through 2013 at $4.6 *trillion* – more than twice the federal government's total annual budget at the time the measures were adopted.[49] (Bartels 2007: 162–63)

Many have criticized Bush Jr.'s administration for following a policy of tax cuts during an era of increased expenditures and war. But perhaps what is most surprising about these tax cuts is, as Bartels points out, that Americans overwhelmingly supported these tax cuts *even when they would not benefit from them.*

This fact reveals a new and troubling feature of the American political economy in modern times. Although America stood out in the world's imagination and in its own self-conception as the land of freedom and equal opportunity, increasingly it appears that Americans are settling on a belief of free markets and special opportunities. Not only has America moved from being the most egalitarian country in the advanced world to the most unequal country in the advanced world. But it also increasingly appears to be a country that accepts inequality as natural, or even good. Instead of striving to achieve a world in which everyone is well off, America seems willing to abandon this goal in favor of a world of *have and have-nots*. Immigration is key to this strategy, but its foundations are also embedded in the structure of the system itself.

America's peculiar social welfare has distributive consequences. Table 4.7 shows what many analysts have long noted: America is the richest country in the world, and also one of the most unequal.

Average per capita income is almost 30 percent higher in the United States (almost $10,000 *per person*) than in the other very rich countries in this study – yet many of its people do not seem to benefit from this wealth. The US ranks seventeenth in the UN's Human Poverty Index, largely because the poor are so very poor in this country. America has the "highest level of inequality by far," because, as Brandolini and Smeeding observe, "the United States differs, above all, in the relative disadvantage of its poorest residents" (Brandolini and Smeeding 2006: 23). Curiously, what many would see as an irony (poverty amidst wealth) others argue is precisely that which makes America so strong and competitive. America is evolving into

---

[49] The $4.6 trillion figure is for both tax cuts combined, and includes additional interest payments stemming from the resulting increase in the federal budget deficit; in addition, it assumes that a variety of nominally temporary rate reductions and credits will subsequently be made permanent (Friedman et al. 2003).

TABLE 4.7. *Human Development Index, 2003*

Country	GDP Per Capita	Population Below 50% of Median Income (%)	Human Poverty Index Rank	Income/ Consumption of the Poorest 10%	Ratio of Richest 10% and Poorest 10%	Gini Index
USA	$ 37,562	17	17	1.9	15.9	40,8
Sweden	$ 26,750	6,5	1	3.6	6.2	25
Japan	$ 27,967	11,8	12	4.8	4.5	24.9
Germany	$ 27,756	8,3	6	3.2	6.9	28.3

Source: (World Bank 2005a, 2005b) Various tables.

a country in which a guiding principle seems to be that inequality is *good* for the economy. Recently, many American leaders seem to have taken this logic one step further to argue that the greater the inequality, the better off the American economy.

As David Leonhardt observed, "[r]eal median family income more than doubled from the late 1940s to the late 1970s. It has risen less than 25 percent in the three decades since. Statistics like these are now so familiar as to be almost mind-numbing. But the larger point is still crucial: The modern U.S. economy distributes the fruits of its growth to a relatively narrow slice of the population" (Leonhardt 2008).[50]

Another major (and growing) source of inequality in the U.S. is *education.* As the United States enters the twenty-first century, where international competition for jobs is increasing, the education of significant shares of America's young is grossly inadequate. According to a recent report, *"Leaving Boys Behind: Public High School Graduation Rates,"* 72 percent of all American high school age girls and 65 percent of high school age boys graduate. The numbers are worse for minorities: 59 percent of African American girls and only 48 percent of African American boys earn high school diplomas today (Lewin 2006). Variations by state tell yet another story. While 90.3 percent of ninth grade students attending public high schools in New Jersey graduate four years later, only 48.3 percent graduate in South Carolina (NCHEMS 2000). In New York City, only 33 percent of African American

[50] Piketty and Saez report that the income share of the top 10 percent of income earners has increased in the last decade to the highest level for which we have records. Whereas the top decile had approximately 30 percent of income in the mid-1930s (it dropped to 20 percent after World War II), by 2000, it had increased to more than 35 percent of national income (see Piketty and Saez 2007: 159).

TABLE 4.8. *Measures of Inequality*

	Year	Poorest 10%	Poorest 20%	Richest 20%	Richest 10%	Richest 10% to Poorest 10%	Richest 20% to Poorest 20%	Gini Index
Norway	2000	3.9	9.6	37.2	23.4	6.1	3.9	25.8
Australia	1994	2.0	5.9	41.3	25.4	12.5	7.0	35.2
Canada	1998	2.5	7.0	40.4	25.0	10.1	5.8	33.1
Sweden	2000	3.6	9.1	36.6	22.2	6.2	4.0	25.0
USA	2000	1.9	5.4	45.8	29.9	15.9	8.4	40.8
Japan	1993	4.8	10.6	35.7	21.7	4.5	3.4	24.9
Denmark	1997	2.6	8.3	35.8	21.3	8.1	4.3	24.7
UK	1999	2.1	6.1	44.0	28.5	13.8	7.2	36.0
France	1995	2.8	7.2	40.2	25.1	9.1	5.6	32.7
Germany	2000	3.2	8.5	36.9	22.1	6.9	4.3	28.3

Note: Countries listed by their Human Development Index Rank.

a. Data show the ratio of the income or consumption share of the richest group to that of the poorest.

b. Results may differ from ratios calculated using the income or consumption shares in columns 2–5.

Source: World Bank. April, 2005. "Correspondence on income distribution data." Washington, DC: World Bank.

boys and 30 percent of Hispanic boys graduate from high school (Lewin 2006).

Americans and Attitudes Toward Government
From "Ask Not…" to "What Do I Get Out of This?"

The commonplace explanation for America's low levels of public spending and taxation is that Americans simply dislike or fear government. This *'American Exceptionalism"* argument has a long and venerable pedigree (Hartz 1983; King 1974; Lipset 1996). There are various versions of this argument, but the basic outlines can be easily summarized: America is a land of immigrants, most or many of which came here to escape oppressive regimes. Thus they came here with a basic antipathy for government and have passed this antipathy down from generation to generation. In other words, as Anthony King succinctly put it, "The state plays a more limited role in America than anywhere else because Americans more than any other people, want it to play a limited role" (King 1973: 418).

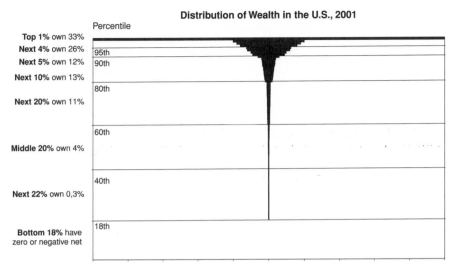

Distribution of Wealth in the U.S., 2001

Percentile

Top 1% own 33%
Next 4% own 26% — 95th
Next 5% own 12% — 90th
Next 10% own 13%
— 80th
Next 20% own 11%
— 60th
Middle 20% own 4%
— 40th
Next 22% own 0,3%
Bottom 18% have zero or negative net — 18th

FIGURE 4.6. The Distribution of Wealth in the United States, 2001. *Source:* Adapted from Wolff, Edward D. 2004. "Changes in Household Wealth in the 1980s and 1990s in the U.S." In *Economics Working Paper.* Annandale-on-Hudson, NY: The Levy Economics Institute.

There are, however, at least two major problems with this argument. First, the American government, was *not* appreciably smaller than European governments in terms of taxation or spending until the 1960s. Second, people distrust their governments *more* today than they have in the past and yet neither taxes nor spending have declined appreciably. What has happened over the past several decades has been that public expectations have been inflated by a series of politicians who promised to help America live up to its dreams, only to have these promises dashed against the shoals of Congress. Instead of passing policies that help bring about more equality and opportunity, the political system increasingly doles out benefits to ever more particularized constituencies.[51]

Americans were often told that raising inequality was inevitable in the era of global competition. Perhaps they had come to accept and even believe this argument. Perhaps they simply had lost faith in their government's ability to do much about their declining fortunes. Perhaps, however, we are at a new critical juncture and America's path is about to change?

[51] See (McCarty et al. 2006) for an excellent analysis of the interaction between policy outcomes (mostly economic) and increasingly polarized and frustrated public attitudes. It is interesting to note that Americans tend to *believe* that they live in a comparatively equal society – despite the strong evidence that this is no longer the case (Förster and d'Ercole 2005).

Conclusion

We began this chapter examining the structure of the American social welfare state and tax system. I have tried to show that America was once a
country that had strongly egalitarian values and a political economy that
offered enormous opportunities to virtually all (white) individuals and families. It was thought of as a land of freedom and equal opportunity, not only
by the outside world, but also by the residents themselves. There was always
a dark lie that this myth covered up, but nonetheless it was a powerful sym-
bol and organizing principle for the country as a whole. This system worked
quite well and was able to sustain itself in large measure because of the
enormous physical wealth of this country. Literally millions of acres of land
were given away to anyone who had the fortitude to take it. The fragmentation of political power worked well in preventing elites from appropriating
America's wealth and using it for their own private gain, as was the norm
across the rest of the Western hemisphere.

But as the frontier closed down and the demands on government increased
throughout the twentieth century, the fragmentation of political power
proved less efficacious. As demands increased, frictions between conflicting
political institutions, on the one side, and quite different social/political systems, on the other, became even more intractable. Governance itself became
more complex and consequently power was further fragmented and divided.
The result has been to create a political system that divides public decisions
so that elected officials can take maximum credit for the minimum amount
of spending. The metaphors of "bringing home the bacon" and Congress as
a "sausage factory" are apt indeed. It should be no wonder, then, that Americans increasingly distrust their political leaders and distrust their ability to
do the right things.

However, the inefficiencies of the U.S. system are not the product of the
personalities it picks to hold public office, but are a result of the particular
evolution of the system itself. The liberal ideals and democratic institutions
that were brought over to the North American continent by the European
immigrants were planted in fabulously fertile soil. And so, this nation and its
people expanded enormously as its people became richer and richer. In some
sense the system itself became addicted to growth (and consumption). American political institutions adapted to the changing society and new layers of
responsibility placed upon them, but there continues to be great friction, for
these institutions were not designed to be effective or easy to manipulate.

There is no doubt that the American system of fragmented authority and
limited public power worked quite well in the context of an expanding nation

with seemingly unbounded resources. Just as there can be no gainsaying that the American economy thrived – even while it failed to meet some of its philosophical goals. In the process of expansion and growth, the country developed a remarkably dynamic economic system and individualistic public philosophy. These ideas and institutions were reinforced by the sad legacy of slavery: Instead of building public policies that might work to further the American dream of equality for all, public policies remained targeted and rewarded special interests while eschewing collective responsibility, at least in domestic affairs.

The result is that the American welfare state has become increasingly large, inefficient and unpopular.

The new President has promised change and has convinced Congress to borrow over a trillion dollars to subsidize failing banks and industries, invest in infrastructure projects and give the middle class yet another tax break. These policies may all be necessary given the current economic crisis, but it seems highly unlikely that there will be any significant changes in the direction of building a more comprehensive and/or coherent system. Candidate Obama was careful not to promise a universal health care system and has been clear that the public benefits targeting the middle classes will remain. At this exact moment in history, it appears likely that the Democrats in Congress may be able to bring some kind of health reform bill to the President for his signature.... But if they do, it is even more likely that what he eventually signs will be a far cry from a simplified, public system (or option) that helps control costs and rationalize the system. Whatever his intentions, moreover, we can be certain that Congress will insure that programs and tax breaks benefiting the largest and most well organized constituencies will continue, even while the beneficiaries rail against the welfare state.

It may well be that the new President is able to galvanize the obvious discontent Americans have developed for their system into a new kind of political will. I must say: I certainly hope so. But the narrative we have followed so far, unfortunately breeds skepticism. Perhaps the good news from this perspective is that evolution is truly unpredictable. In short, we will see.

5

"And Yet It Moves"*

In this book I have tried to present two interrelated arguments: First, contrary to the convergence theses that were so popular only a few years ago, advanced capitalist welfare states are not locked into a "race to the bottom." Instead, different countries are moving in quite different directions, even as we move into an increasingly interdependent and globalized world. Second, history can be understood as an evolutionary process. The simple reason that different countries are moving in different directions is that they are in fact quite different *systems* adapting in an evolving environment.

In the following pages I will treat each of these arguments separately. First, we will explore the policy implications of the three narratives presented in this book. We will then explore in greater depth my argument that history is an evolutionary process.

THE END OF NEO-LIBERALISM?

In the early years of the twenty-first century, America and its particular form of neo-liberal economics, was ascendant. Communism was dead and American economic growth outpaced virtually all other industrial countries. The only countries that seem to be doing better were countries like Ireland, which had adopted even more radical forms of neo-liberalism than America. The

---

* Legend has it that Galileo uttered the phrase "And yet it moves" after being forced to recant his theories in his famous Abjuration in 1633. In the Inquisition, Galileo was made to deny his scientific research and admit that the earth was stationary and the sun revolved around the earth. There is in fact no proof that he actually uttered this phrase, but it has come to stand for the idea that conventional wisdom can be wrong – no matter how powerfully it is held. Forced to kneel before the Holy judges he declared his errors and accepted the fact that the earth is the center of the universe.

"Washington Consensus" had taken over all the major international financial institutions in the world and conservative or center-right governments were winning elections around the globe. One of the biggest debates in comparative political economy at the time was over whether it was the power of the ideas, structures, or material interests that best explained the victory of neo-liberalism.

By the end of this decade neo-liberalism, as a coherent ideological package at least, is in retreat. Rather than move even further to the right, conservative parties in Europe at least, are scrambling toward the middle.[1] In Sweden, the "New" Moderate Party declared itself to be the best defender of social democratic principles and even the "New Labor Party" of Sweden. In Japan, a new government that has just been elected promised to expand social benefits and child-care allowances and improve public services. Finally, and perhaps most importantly, American voters elected a progressive African American as their president and sent him to Washington along with the strongest Democratic majority in Congress seen in the past 40 years. At this moment it is too early to say exactly how much of the promised change will actually be legislated, but it is no doubt significant that one of Obama's first acts as President was to pass a massive "American Recovery and Investment Act," which directly increased public spending by over $550 billion.[2] In short, government is back.

Josef Akerman, whom the *Economist* describes as the "*über*-capitalist and chief of Deutsche Bank," summed up the sentiments of many capitalists in 2008 when he said, "I no longer believe in the market's self-healing power" (Economist 2008a).

WHY GLOBALIZATION DID NOT KILL THE WELFARE STATE

The fear of globalization was an effective tool used by the Right to change public policy around the world. We have all heard the arguments dozens of times: If we don't cut taxes, create a more "investment friendly" environment, jobs will leave the country for more favorable climates. Globalization, we were warned, "may lead to capital flight from high to low tax countries in such large amounts that it deprives a nation of its tax base and, as a consequence, its welfare system" (Schjelderup 1993: 377).

---

[1] See, for example, "The Final Triumph" (*The Economist*, Bagehot, May 10, 2008, p. 42.), This article focuses on the rise of the Conservative Party in Britain. Here they explain New Labor's hegemony by showing that the Conservative revival is due in part to their move to the Left. "Eleven years of New Labour has made compassion compulsory," they note.

[2] The American Recovery and Investment Act of 2009 also gave Americans approximately $250 billion in tax cuts.

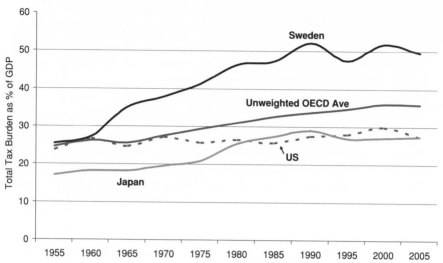

FIGURE 5.1. What Race to the Bottom? *Source:* 1955–1960: OECD. 1981. *Long-Term Trends in Tax Revenues of OECD Member Countries 1955–1980.* Paris: OECD, pp. 11, Table 1; 1965–2005: OECD. 2008. *Revenue Statistics 1965–2007.* Paris: OECD Publication, pp. 94–96, Table 3.

These fears were not unreasonable. After all, in the new global economy everything is more mobile. Many people, including this author, assumed that this fact would fundamentally change the underlying dynamics supporting the modern welfare state (McKenzie and Lee 1991; Steinmo 1994a, 1993). The welfare state, in the end, is the product of a basic compromise between capital and labor. And with the increasing availability of the "exit option" for capital, globalization would change the balance of power upon which this compromise had been struck.

But something funny happened on the way into the twenty-first century: Governments did not roll back taxes (or for that matter public spending) in the era of "globalization," as Figure 5.1 shows. The average tax burden in the OECD, for example, grew from 29.4 percent of GDP in 1975 to 37.6 percent in 2006. In twenty-two of twenty-seven countries in the OECD tax burdens grew in the 1990s. Indeed, only five OECD countries actually cut taxes in the decade in which "globalization" took off. It is worth noting also here, that the virtually universal response to the latest recession has been a massive expansion of government spending – though tax increases have been slow to follow.

Surprisingly few studies have directly examined the effects of social spending or tax burdens on economic performance. Those that did generally found

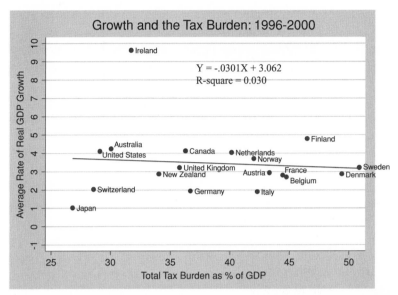

FIGURE 5.2. Impact of Total Tax Burden on Change in GDP, 1990s. *Source:* Total Tax Burden: OECD. 2008. *Revenue Statistics of OECD Member Countries.* Vol. 2008 release 01. [available at: http://www.sourceoecd.org]: Real GDP Growth Rates: IMF. World Economic Outlook Databases. [available at: http://www.imf.org].

mixed results or no significant correlations (Katz et al. 1983; Lindert 2004).[3] Statistical examinations of taxes and economic growth find no, or very weak, correlations between government size or tax levels and economic performance. Figure 5.2 offers a sample picture. *Even in the late 1990s* there was no statistically significant relationship between tax burdens and economic growth (i.e., heavily taxed countries grow no more slowly than low tax countries). It is also interesting to note that countries that *increased* their tax burdens, *even in the 1990s*, did not grow more slowly than countries whose tax burdens remained stable or that were slightly cut back.[4]

[3] Some studies (Cameron 1982; Landau 1983; Grier and Tullock 1989; Barro 1990) show that countries with large governments tend to grow more slowly than countries with smaller governments. On the contrary, Hansson and Henrekson (1994) and Korpi (1985), find no relationship between government expenditures and economic growth. Rabushka and Bartlett (1985) find a positive correlation between total tax burden and GDP growth in a sample of LDC's. Finally, in a much debated article Ram (1986) using Summers-Heston data from 115 countries finds a strong positive relationship between increased government consumption and economic growth.

[4] These figures shown here are clearly very blunt. They do not demonstrate that there is no relationship between taxes and economic performance. They simply demonstrate that a very simple relationship does not exist. This is an important point because it is often (indeed generally) argued or assumed that a *simple* relationship should exist. The fact that it does

The absence of a statistically significant relationship between taxation or public spending and economic performance does not of course mean that there is no relationship. Similarly, demonstrating that there was no wholesale rollback in taxes or spending does not suggest that rich capitalist democracies did not change much in the past 10 or 20 years. Quite the contrary, as we have seen, there have been very significant changes in recent years. But rather than seeing these changes as in absolutist or essentialist terms (e.g., "The End of Redistribution," or "Where Corporative Rule the World," or even "The World is Flat") we should instead view these changes as yet another iteration of a continuous *adaptive process*.

In the previous chapters we have seen how Sweden, Japan, and the United States have each adapted and evolved along with and within the international political economy, which, in turn, was the product of the growth and development of national capitalist systems. To be sure the United States was by far the most important actor in this regard. However, not even the United States controlled or directed the evolution of modern capitalism. Capitalism itself should be seen as an adaptive system, the evolution of which is the product of the complex interaction of its sub-system parts and is thus an emergent process (Kauffman, 2008, pp. 150–58).

There can be no gainsaying that the increased economic competition (which was partly due to the liberalization of trade and partly the result of massive technological change) imposed new and increased pressures on all three countries studied here. But as we saw, economic competition for capital and/or labor was far from the only challenge pressuring political and economic elites in these countries. Indeed, in many ways the changing demographic futures facing these countries and the growing disaffection with public services posed equal, if not more intense, pressures.

To be sure the narratives told here would be simpler if I were to focus solely on economic competition and, say, corporate tax policy. I have done this kind of analysis in the past and learned a great deal from it. But if we want to get purchase on the larger questions of how different countries are changing and/or why they are not traveling along the predicted patterns so logically laid out by pundits and economists, then we are forced to accept complexity. What we see from this vantage is not only a multivariate problem in which attitudes toward government, demographic shifts and economic competition interact and intersect with one another, but also that the structure and weighting of each of these factors varies over time and across these three countries in important ways.

not forces us to look more closely into the structure of the tax system, the structure of the welfare system, and the underlying political economy.

In Sweden, for example, demographic change, economic competitiveness, and trust in public institutions are hugely important challenges. But up to this point, at least, Sweden appears to be dealing with these challenges remarkably effectively. There is no doubt that the Swedish elite have made good choices: Building a universal welfare state; bringing women into the workforce; increasing already generous spending on education and research; and generally pursuing policies that maintain high levels of income equality and thereby economic opportunity. However it is too simple to argue that these outcomes are purely a matter of smart choices. Sweden has benefited from significant advantages as well. Some of these, as we saw in Chapter 2, were matters of timing, geography, and good fortune. Equally, the choices available in the 1990s were the result of other choices made (often by other individuals) in decades past. Indeed, the menu of choices available to Swedish political elites was remarkably different from the menus available to either Japanese or American elites – even while each of these countries faced a broadly similar set of challenges at the end of the twentieth century.

Of course, I have not even mentioned the political institutions in which Swedish elites had to operate. I have made much of the importance of institutional structure both in this book and in my previous writing. But in this analysis I emphasize the *context* in which institutions function, operate and structure political choices. This should not be interpreted to imply that institutions do not matter. Any reading of the previous chapters will show that institutions are central to the analysis. *I mean to highlight here that institutionalists need to move beyond static institutional analyses and the first step in this direction requires embedding institutions into their broader historical and evolutionary context.*

The United State also faces significant challenges from international competition, demographic change, and declining public confidence. At the same time, the United States has different advantages. America is the richest and most powerful country in the world, both because of its enormous resource endowment and because of its highly flexible, dynamic and innovative economic system. Perhaps the resource advantage that the United States has benefited from over the past century will be less important as ownership and investment in commodities is "globalized," but the risk taking, entrepreneurial culture that has evolved on American soil will almost certainly continue to yield rewards, at least to those who are able to take advantage of them.

The demographic challenge in America is less about an ageing society than it is a problem of an increasingly divided and unequal society. As we have seen, inequality has long been intertwined with issues of race and ethnicity in this country (Liberman, 2002; King, 2004). However, the choice to target benefits and use the tax system as a mechanism of social and economic distribution has had, and will continue to have, important implications for the United State as it enters the twenty-first century.

The good will and obvious intelligence of Barack Obama and his advisors are very unlikely to overcome the hard fact that America has become an extraordinarily unequal society or that Americans increasingly distrust their public institutions. Once again, political institutions are central to this analysis. As we have seen, however, the institutions themselves have evolved over time. Although FDR could once overcome the centrifugal forces of American politics, he governed over a far less fragmented polity than does the current president. Indeed, given the behavior and the incentives facing America's political leaders in recent years, Americans' skepticism and distrust is, in my view, justified (Hibbing and Theiss-Morse 2001).

Japan's challenges, while broadly similar, appear even more intractable. Many now point to the current economic crisis in Japan arguing that the collapse of the export markets is the key problem. The analysis presented here suggests instead that these economic problems are the tip of the iceberg. The Japanese economic model was based on a system of deference to authority and the widespread confidence that those in power would use their authority for the long-term interest of the whole. By the end of the first decade of the 2000s, however, these beliefs were shattered both by the neo-liberal policies of successive governments and by the growing realization that the society was not prepared for the rapid aging of Japanese society. Although the economic institutions driving the Japanese economy were highly modern, Japanese attitudes toward gender and foreigners were still quite traditional. The result has been a mismatch between social values and economic and demographic imperitives that present this country with challenges far more severe than the collapse of property values or export markets. The new government in Japan, much like their American counterparts, has promised "change." In the Japanese case there appears to be a growing understanding that the paucity of social welfare programs contributes to the increasing insecurity in society and, thus, is at the core of Japan's malaise. However, given the high levels of distrust of public authority and the massive budget deficits in Japan, it is very difficult to imagine how this country will be able to pay for the public social welfare institutions that can help them transition toward a system that retains social responsibility while concomitantly offers more individual liberty and economic flexibility.

In sum, although it is true that there are broadly similar challenges facing these advanced capitalist democracies, when you look closer at the cases it becomes clear that the structure and nature of these challenges is quite different indeed. As Vivian Schmidt has convincingly shown in her book, *The Futures of European Capitalism*, "although all European countries' political economic practices have changed considerably in consequence of their liberalizing political-economic policies, this has not led to a convergence toward market capitalism, as most of the globalization literature assumes." But as she also notes, "[n]either has it resulted in a binary division of capitalism into market capitalism or managed capitalism, with the concomitant demise of state capitalism, as much of the literature on the varieties of capitalism seems to imply" (Schmidt 2002: 306).

If we see political economies as complex adaptive systems rather than equilibrium solutions, one should expect quite different responses to an environmental change like "globalization." First, one would expect that different systems would adapt differently. Second, one would expect parts of each system to experience dramatic changes and others to be virtually unaffected – at least in the short run. Finally, one would expect the unexpected. No one writing about globalization in the 1990s could have predicted the collapse of the financial markets in the first decade of the new century, any more than one could have predicted that a radical fundamentalist clique would fly passenger airplanes into the World Trade Center. However, if the *sin qua non* of your version of science is predictability, you may have a problem.

Researching this book I've learned a great deal about modern welfare states and how they are adapting to the new international political economy in which they live. I've discovered that capitalist democracies are resilient and I've learned that social welfare policies are not necessarily bad for the economy, – even in a globalized world. But, perhaps more importantly, I've come to understand that the very predictions I and others made about globalization's implications were based on a faulty model of politics. The *reason* people expected all states to react in similar ways to a common environmental factor was that we implicitly viewed politics in mechanistic terms. We expected all states to behave in similar ways because we implicitly assumed that the welfare state was some kind of a static equilibrium which globalization had upset. This line of logic led us to conclude that the context had changed and a new (lower) equilibrium would be formed.[5]

---

[5] This analysis agrees with Massey, Sanchez, and Behrman, whose survey of the implications of neo-liberalism in developing countries suggests that: "No magic formula for economic development applies to all nations at all times and all places. Rather, a plethora of potential formulas can only be determined on a case-by-case basis using trial, error, experimentation,

There can be no doubt that liberal ideas influenced policy makers in all three countries studied here. However, liberal policy ideas have had very different implications when translated into different contexts. Allow me to illustrate this point with an example drawn from the evolution of tax policy. As I note in this book and elsewhere, there was once a broad consensus among elites across the democratic world that taxation *should* be used to redistribute income and wealth in society. By the late 1990s, however, these ideas had largely been abandoned. Why? Because the context in which these policy ideas were developed had itself changed. First, because economic growth had pushed more and more taxpayers into ever higher tax brackets and, thereby, incentivized them to find ever more clever means of avoiding taxes. Second, the increasing openness of the world economy and ease of moving money around the world gave high tax earners the means to send their money where national tax authorities could not capture them. Swedish Minister of Finance, Kjell Olof Feldt, put the dilemma he faced quite well in the mid-1980s when he said that, "the Social Democratic Party has to recognize that high taxes will reduce efficiency and stimulate inflation, slow down economic growth and ultimately, undermine social equity" (Lohr 1987: 44).

We saw in the previous chapters, however, that these basic ideas were implemented in quite different ways in each of the countries we studied. Thus, while marginal tax rates, for example, were cut substantially in all three countries, the overall redistributive consequences of these cuts were hugely different – depending on the broader structure of the social welfare system and political economy in each case.

WELFARE STATE AS INSURANCE

Before we leave our discussion of globalization and the welfare state, I would like to add a final point on the *advantages* of public spending. As Professor Hans Werner-Sinn pointed out some time ago, most economic analyses on the welfare state focus only on the negative or disincentive effects of welfare state spending and taxes. He notes, for example, that in the 1994 book, *Turning Sweden Around*, by Sweden's most famous economist Assar Lindbeck and his colleagues, none of the allocative effects of state spending

and evaluation" (Massey et al. 2006). Although, at this point, this may seem even obvious, as their impressive work and that of many others has shown, it is important to remember that there was indeed a "consensus" that a singular model could and should be used to help the developing world draw itself out of poverty (Williamson 1993).

is even mentioned. Indeed, Lindbeck's widely read and important analysis (in Scandinavia, at least) does not even include the redistribution of income as one of the "basic responsibilities of the state" (Lindbeck et al. 1994: cf 14–16). Sinn reminds us, however:

> Economists have learned so much about the Laffer curve, Leviathan, and a myriad of disincentive effects brought about by government intervention that they have lost sight of the allocative advantages of the welfare state... From an allocative point of view, the main advantage of the welfare state is the insurance or risk reducing function of redistributive taxation. To finance commonly accessible public goods and public transfers, governments take more taxes from the rich than from the poor, thus reducing the variance in lifetime incomes... Every insurance contract involves a redistribution of resources from the lucky to the unlucky, and most redistributive measures of the state can be interpreted as insurance if the time span between judging and taking these measures is sufficiently long. Redistributive taxation and insurance are two sides of the same coin. (Sinn 1994: 1)

This is a very important point. No thoughtful analyst seriously believes we should live without the insurance functions that redistributive welfare states provide. The key issue modern states are facing today is whether the economic *disadvantages* of the welfare state and redistributive taxation outweigh the *advantages*. But there can be no doubt that the welfare state has many economic advantages. The massive economic crisis of 2008–10 appears to be bringing many people to similar conclusions. Countries with larger social welfare budgets appear to be suffering less than their more liberal counterparts, precisely because they have been purchasing social *insurance* for decades.[6]

The current economic crisis offers substantial evidence of Anton Jemerijck's insightful argument that, although "The Scandinavian welfare states are undoubtedly expensive in terms of revenue requirements... Nonetheless, they are demonstrably better adapted to the exigencies of post-industrial change – in large part due to their service intensive, women and child 'friendly' public policy profiles" (Hemerijck 2002: 184).

Different welfare states can be more or less welfare-enhancing, *depending on the particular state*. Thinking of the welfare state as a large insurance company can help illustrate this point. Consider the following: How much life insurance should an individual buy? The answer to this question depends

---

[6] It strikes me, as the height of irony, that the United States and the United Kingdom, which have smaller welfare states, are begging their European counterparts to increase public spending in order to stimulate the world economy. This seems analogous to a young person who purchased a new car instead of health insurance and then asks his friends (who did buy insurance instead of a car) to pay for his medical bills after an accident.

on a number of factors such as the individual's family status, whether they are the major or sole income earner in that family, their age, health, the nature of their job, tolerance for risk, etc. It would be absurd to suggest that all individuals should have the same level of life insurance coverage. Clearly, it would be *economically inefficient* for all individuals to have the same insurance coverage.

Polities, like individuals, are quite different from each other. Even societies as similar as Japan, Sweden, and the United States are different along many of the same dimensions as individuals: They vary by age structures, job/employment structures, family patterns, tolerance for risk, etc. Since polities or societies are different, it would be economically inefficient for all welfare states to be the same. If globalization created political pressures to homogenize or "converge," it would, in effect, bring about an economically inefficient outcome.

The interesting quest for every country is to find the appropriate balance between a tax/welfare state that balances the insurance function advantages against the inefficiencies, economic costs and bureaucratization that are part of modern government. Again, we should be skeptical of those who promote a "one size fits all" argument. Arguing that a smaller welfare state is necessarily more efficient is akin to arguing that a small company is necessarily more efficient than a large company. Certainly, there are advantages to smaller size (i.e., closer communication between segments of the company, less bureaucratic waste, potentially greater market flexibility and adaptability, etc.), but it is equally clear that there are gains to be had from larger size.

The key is how the institutions are structured. It is possible that small companies can be run inefficiently. It is equally clear that a large company can be managed efficiently. Is there an "optimal size" for any company? Obviously not. If not, why should it be the case that there is an "optimal size" for every welfare state?

DO WE NEED AN EVOLUTIONARY THEORY OF POLITICS?

Recently I was asked if we "need" to use concepts of evolution or evolutionary theory to understand politics? "If we take 'evolution' out your analysis, can't we explain the phenomenon you are interested in anyway? In other words, do we need to borrow ideas and concepts from another discipline to help us understand politics and history?" he asked. "Couldn't your book be read as a straightforward historical account of the development of three political economies without the evolutionary language and concepts?" Interesting questions. But I think we should first ask ourselves the question: *Do*

Institutions Evolve? If human social institutions do "evolve," then it rather makes sense to me to think about the evolutionary processes as evolutionary processes. It also seems logical that we might learn something from scientists who have studied evolution in other domains. As many students of history have done in the past, I have borrowed concepts from evolutionary biology (e.g., allopatry, symbiosis, and exaptation) in this book to help illustrate particular processes. However, I do not believe that institutional evolution is identical to biological evolution. Evolutionary theory is ***not*** simply a theory in biology. Evolutionary theory has been developed in the study of language, technology, innovation, zoology, computer science, artificial intelligence, anthropology, psychology, and many other scientific domains. Moreover, political scientists use the term "evolution" constantly when they describe political and historical change.[7]

One political scientist who has taken an evolutionary turn is Ian Lustick. In a recent exchange, I posed the question to him directly: What is the "value added" of an evolutionary perspective? His response was, in part, as follows:

Consider as a quick way to respond to the "value added" critique, the likely and historically recorded responses of Ptolemaic astronomers to Kepler and Galileo. "Why bother thinking of the universe as revolving around the sun and not the earth? We can account very nicely for all our observations and predict, with our training and skills and our elliptical cycles and epicycles and epi-epicylces, just when there will be eclipses and when planets will appear in various places."

Indeed there is no theory that ever was advanced, no matter how much more powerful it was than those preceding it, which could match the "story-telling" ability of existing (poor) theories in the hands of advanced practitioners. Consequently, for colleagues to pursue evolutionary lines of thinking will require of them ambitions much greater, in terms of generalization, systematic comparison, and depth of insight, than are likely to animate those among them experiencing professional success with available techniques.

To this I add that if we believe that institutions evolve, *why wouldn't we* try to think more systematically about the evolutionary processes at work, and why would we eschew ideas and understandings of the mechanisms of evolution developed in other domains? The appropriate question is, once again, *do* institutions evolve? Are political and economic institutions complex adaptive systems? Or are they better understood as fixed or mechanical

---

[7] As we noted in Chapter 1, terms such as co-evolution, punctuated equilibrium, adaptation, and increasing returns have become part of the regular repertoire of historical institutionalism. This is because we see similar processes at work in many evolutionary substrates.

"structures," as we also sometimes refer to them? If institutions are mechanical, physical, or architectural structures, then it would be fair to say that they do not evolve, and evolutionary theories do not apply. Clearly, structures can change. A building can be built by conscious human design and can stand (at equilibrium) until outside forces (i.e., weather, termites, etc.) erode its foundations and/or its roof. The equilibrium would be broken and the building would change, perhaps eventually into a pile of rubble. Such a process is certainly one of change and even transformation, but it is *not* evolution. If we think/believe that human social institutions are more like buildings or structures, which are fixed and stable (at equilibrium) unless a designer consciously changes them, then evolutionary theory and concepts are probably of little use and should be only referred to as a vague metaphor meaning simply "change."

If, on the other hand, we think human social institutions are better understood as complex systems, which like language or technology, adapt within an ever-changing context and change along or according to dynamics that are outside or beyond the particular agents that create them, then these changes can be thought of as evolutionary. Complex systems evolve. Houses do not. Buildings have architects. Complex systems are emergent and have no single designer.

IDEAS, AGENTS, AND INSTITUTIONAL CHANGE

The most interesting and important argument against thinking about human institutions in evolutionary terms lies deeper, within a fundamental ontology regarding human agency. For some, human beings are unique in the living world by virtue of the fact that we are sentient beings. Humans, in this view, have unique capacities to plan, calculate, and *choose*. Evolution is an unplanned process and therefore, this argument holds, evolutionary theory cannot apply to human institutions. Mutations, for example, are random: It is the environment that selects which mutation will be successfully reproduced, not the gene, the organism, or even the population. In the case of human institutions, however, it is actors who calculate, strategize, plan, and eventually choose. Consequently, this argument suggests, human institutional change is fundamentally different from biological or linguistic evolution.

This is an important argument. It gets to the heart of the differences between institutional evolution and biological evolution, but it does not lead to the conclusion that human social institutions don't evolve.

One of Charles Darwin's key insights was that the enormous variation witnessed in the natural world was at the core of the evolutionary process. Though he did not understand the sources of this variation at the time, he correctly understood that some creatures could be slightly different from their parents and, in *some* cases, this might give this individual a competitive advantage in its environment. *If* the conditions were just right and *if* this trait could be passed on to other individuals in the population (in this case, through inheritance), *then* evolutionary change could occur. Over time, this pattern could be repeated and entire populations could evolve. He called this "descent with modification." I believe that human social history can also been seen through this lens.

Humans are at root social creatures and institutions are simply the rules that govern social life among social creatures.[8] They are in a sense the "genes" of society.[9] The key question is *how* do they evolve? Understanding the implications and sources of institutional variation is the key here. I submit that the most important source of the evolution of human social institutions is human creativity. Humans, like all creatures, are forever in a struggle to improve their lives in a sometimes highly competitive environment. We build institutions to increase our chances of success in this competition. The most important way societies can improve their competitive success is through innovating and adapting the social rules that govern our social lives – the institutions.

The human brain has evolved an enormous capacity to innovate or create, to communicate and to copy successful strategies learned from others (Boyd and Richerson 2005b; Cosmides and Tooby 1997; Dunbar 1996). This fact has two distinct implications for institutional evolution. First, when rules governing behavior appear to have beneficial consequences, humans are able to copy or modify these rules to other contexts (this can be within a society or population, or even sometime from one population to another). Second, just as in the case of biological inheritance, copying rules from one context

---

[8] The idea that man was once in a state of nature, in which he was alone, is clearly out of step with the fossil record. Well before homo sapiens came to dominate their eco-systems, their predecessors were social animals. Humans *later* in evolutionary history developed the capacity to rationalize and calculate their individual self-interest (see Richerson and Boyd 2000). Fredrich von Hayek, makes a remarkably similar argument, though he draws rather different conclusions from it (Hayek and Shenfield 1983).

[9] Note that humans are far from the only creatures that have constructed social institutions. Indeed, without social rules (institutions) social life would be impossible. Humans, clearly, have the most complicated and sophisticated social institutions. But only in this sense are they unique.

to another is an highly imperfect process (Lewontin 2000). In some cases the new modification may prove to enhance the efficiency of the rule adopted, in many other cases it will not.

Social systems are sets of complex rules. The very act of participating in complex societies requires significant cognition and agency. This is because rules are never 100 percent consistent or applicable in all real world situations. Therefore, even a straightforward interpretation of social rules requires some degree of human creativity. As Streeck points out, "the conditions under which social rules are supposed to apply are inevitably unique and varying in time, due to the fact that the world is more complex than the principles we have devised to make it predictable." Consequently, "[t]his forces actors to apply rules creatively, actualizing and modifying them in the process. Moreover, social actors are far from being norm-following machines; in fact they command a defining capacity to re-interpret or evade rules that are supposed to apply to them" (Streeck 2010b: 7). "Both creative modification and cunning circumvention are a permanent source of disturbance – and, from the perspective of the institution – of random variation from below, resulting in the reproduction of social institutions through their enactment being always and inevitably *imperfect*" (ibid.). Once again, imperfect reproduction is the key to evolutionary change for much evolutionary change (Lewontin 2000).

Seen in this light, we can understand human agency as a means of generating variation. But the point is not simply that humans generate random variation because of some kinds of misinterpretations. Instead, human creativity can also create *intentional variation*. Humans are remarkably good problem solvers. Human beings are clearly the most innovative and creative creatures on this planet. If we think of human social institutions as systems of rules, similar to genetic rules that govern cell behavior, then human agency (i.e., creativity, innovation) can be seen as being something akin to mutations. Which ideas or innovations – just like which mutations – emerge and are successfully reproduced has at least as much to do with the environment as with the ideas itself.

We saw several examples of this in the previous chapters. The foundation of American political institutions provides the most obvious case: Clearly, neither the idea that citizens should be able to choose their governors, nor the idea that individuals should have more freedom from government were invented by America's Founding Fathers. But as Tocqueville and many others have noted, these notions flourished in this new country precisely because of the wealth found in this new continent and because there was no previously ensconced ruling class that could dampen the democratic fervor. This *does not imply* that James Madison, for example, was unimportant. On the contrary, his ability to articulate and translate these general ideas into specific institutions and constitutional principles mattered a great deal. But it is quite useless to argue over whether the ideas, the agents, or context "caused" the outcome: The evolution of American liberal democracy was an emergent process in which these, and many more, "variables" interacted and intertwined to create a unique outcome (DiZerega 1989). What we can say is that neither the ideas, the institutions, nor the agents are, or were, "independent" of the process in any meaningful sense.

Another obvious example of the complex role of agency in institutional evolution is found in the development of Sweden's particular constitutional system and the subsequent foundation it laid for the kind of compromise-laden political economy that eventually evolved. As we saw in Chapter 2, Sweden's much admired corporatist system was the product of specific choices and particular agents bringing forward innovative institutional solutions to the country's political and economic challenges. But in this case, as in many others, the fact that institutions are the product of human choice does not imply that those individuals get what they hoped for. In the Swedish case, early in the twentieth century the conservative ruling elite hoped to protect their interests by instituting their famous "conservative guarantee,"[10] protecting themselves with at least a share of power as the working class mobilized and organized. These elites were surely correct in their assessment of the ineluctible growth of a working class in a rapidly industrializing nation. However, they miscalculated. The eventual effect of these new electoral rules was to usher in a political system that effectively created a "Social Democratic Guarantee" that lasted over 50 years.

Another interesting and important case of the power of human agency and the role of creative ideas in shaping institutional evolution was seen in the development of Sweden's famous "solidaristic" wage policy. This was one of a package of wage negotiation institutions that were introduced by the Social Democrats in early 1950s that led to a constant upgrading of workers' skills at the same time that it pushed capital into the hands of Sweden's most effective capitalists. The labor union economists, Gösta Rehn and Rudolf Meidner, after whom the system was named, were obviously important agents as they formulated these remarkable economic institutions. But once again, it would be absurd to argue that these individuals

---

[10] This was a set of electoral rules, most importantly, the move to a proportional representation electoral system for the lower house of the Riksdag and a sequential electoral system for the upper house.

caused this system. Indeed, they were not even the first to argue for a wage bargaining system that would both hold back wages at the national level and support the lowest paid at the same time. Instead, many individuals were involved in thinking through these policies and the wage bargaining system that eventually emerged (Heclo and Madsen: 115).[11] In short, there is no doubt that these agents and their ideas were hugely important in shaping the course of their country's history. However, it is equally obvious that these individuals and their ideas were themselves products of their time and embedded within their own institutional and historical context.

A final example of agency and its sometimes unintended consequences illustrates the complexity of this issue: As we saw in Chapter 3, Japan's economic policy choices in the 1990s reminds us that, although man makes his own history, it does not always turn out the way he hoped it might. Faced with the economic crisis evoked by the property and stock market crashes at the beginning of the 1990s, Japanese elites *chose* to pursue a neo-liberal agenda: They cut taxes on the rich, scaled back lifetime employment security, and generally promoted policies favoring risk taking and individual initiative. In the context of the economic crisis and the apparent hegemony of neo-liberal ideas around the world, these policies made eminent sense. The promoters of these ideas and institutions did not appreciate, however, the extent to which these policies might undermine social solidarity and the deference to leadership which had been foundation stones of the Japanese political economy. In short, many of the extraordinary difficulties facing the new Japanese government today are directly the result of policy *choices* made by previous governments.

THE NATION AS AN EVOLUTIONARY UNIT?

Modern evolutionary theory has moved beyond the old debates over whether the gene, the organism or the population is "really" the unit of evolutionary change. Although there are still scholars who hold onto particular emphases (mostly derived from their disciplinary background), the consensus view today is that there are multiple levels of evolutionary change and selection (Mayr 1991; Wilson 1979, 2002). I submit that political science should take this view as well. Institutions evolve at many levels, and equally clearly, there are multiple mechanisms operating at different levels. In this analysis

---

[11] Swenson demonstrates that economists working for the employer federation were equally important for defining the eventual outcome (Swenson 2002: 124–26; See also Blyth, 2002: 119–22).

I have emphasized the nation or the nation state. But I do not mean to privilege this level of analysis. Clearly, focusing on the evolution of very specific institutions at the micro level (as Elinor Ostrom does brilliantly) offers another level of complementary analysis (Ostrom and Basurto 2009).

The focus in this book, however, has been the nation state. I treat these three nations as complex adaptive systems within which there are many sub-systems. These systems, still, have integrity as conceptual units. As Peter Hall has argued,

> Conceptions of national interest are rooted in and moved by real-world events... What this means is that, to understand how governments form preferences over policies, we need to employ something like the eventful sociology William H. Sewell (1996) proposes. We have to trace the process through which critical events or experiences shift perceptions of the problems a nation or its government faces and of the available solutions for those problems. The implication is that policy is driven only partly by material forces and the institutional structures developed to come with them. Its route also depends on the sequence of events a nation experiences and the grand narratives devised to explain what it should do in the face of such events. (Hall 2005: 15)

This is very clearly true for the countries I study in this book. One cannot understand what Japan, Sweden or any other country does without appreciating its self-understanding or its own self-conception. An example of this is found in the comparison of how different nations rebuilt their political economies after World War II. Quite simply, one cannot begin to explain post-war social and economic policy without understanding differing national *interpretations* of the war itself. A comparison of Germany and Japan after World War II is particularly illustrative: Both countries were defeated after starting wars of aggression, but the *interpretation* of the war and the defeats were quite different in these two countries. Both countries, moreover, had democratic institutions imposed by the allies, but the ways in which these institutions were adapted and changed to "fit" local circumstances had more to do with each nation's understanding of what went wrong before and during the war as it did with the structure of these institutions themselves. Both countries began these wars as massively successful military industrial complexes. Both countries engaged in brutal wars of expansion and empire. Both countries practiced genocide.

Germany's post-war leadership came to accept that their country had been responsible for a Holocaust and believed that it was the failure of their democratic institutions, as well as the economic collapse of the 1930s, that allowed the country to be led astray by Adolf Hitler. In short, their *interpretation* was that Germany had erred in a moral sense because of the failure of their democratic institutions and the weakness of their civil society. Consequently, it was important to rebuild both democracy and social institutions so that they could never return to the horrible days of war and holocaust.

Japan, on the other hand, did not embrace defeat in this way. The Japanese interpretation of their defeat was that they lost a war against a stronger and more powerful adversary. Their misdeeds were swept under the carpet, the emperor retained his status as a demi-god, and although the military was cut back, the bureaucratic elite quickly returned to power. Democratic institutions were imposed by the Americans, but the idea of popular rule was not fully embraced. The problem for Japan was not how to atone for their sins, but rather, how to rebuild a strong and powerful nation without a strong military (Samuels 1994).

In the German case, great efforts were put into creating social institutions and public insurance to improve the life of citizens. Democracy and a good life would prevent the return of a Hitler. In Japan, at least in the first decades after the war, the emphasis was in building an even stronger export oriented economy. Strong economic performance, for the Japanese, would allow Japan to return to its rightful position as one of the great powers in the world. If this took sacrifices on the parts of business and consumers, these sacrifices would be worth it.

Grand narratives developed after World War II in Sweden and America also helped forge a national identity that shaped policy making in the decades that followed. Swedes saw themselves as the moral victors in World War II. Having quite narrowly escaped the attractions of fascism before the war (Berman 1998), Sweden emerged both economically strong and socially "just."[12] Thus, Sweden had a torch to carry after the war. One cannot fully understand the subsequent developments of the Swedish Social Democratic model without some appreciation of how this understanding of itself as a moral and just nation lit the path for many subsequent choices in post-war history. An outsider might well ask how Swedes "put up with" their high taxes, knowing that many people cheat the system. The answer, in part, is simply that the Swedes think of themselves as being better than that. I have been told by many Swedes, "We are the kind of people who help even those who are not willing to help themselves" (Edlund 1999b; Svallfors 1996,

---

[12] I will eschew the temptations to grill Sweden for its role as an arms trader to the world during the war (to say nothing of the transport of troops across their country in the German attack and occupation of Norway) simply because it is the country's *interpretation* of events which is important here. And Sweden's self-perception was of itself as having taken the moral high ground *and* having succeeded.

1997). As we saw in Chapter 2, Swedish economists and many political elites pressed hard to have Sweden take a more neo-liberal turn in the late 1980s and 1990s and many steps were taken in this direction. However, even the Conservatives and Liberals who pushed hard for these changes never argued (and I believe never really believed) that Sweden should follow America's path. Why? Because Sweden is better than that.

Lastly, America's perception of itself as the "Land of Freedom" is important for understanding the policy choices America has made over the past 50 years. As I have argued elsewhere, America's perception of itself as the country of both "equal opportunity" and "individual freedom" has long been in conflict (Steinmo and Kopstein 2007; McClosky and Zahler 1984).[13] There can be no gainsaying, however, that the dominant narrative Americans came to believe after the war was that the free market had defeated the strong state. Notwithstanding the wartime planning and government coordination of the economy,[14] the interpretation was that "freedom" defeated "dictatorship." This powerful rhetoric became an immensely important tool in the hands of those who fought government expansion into the economy and society *and* has become an enormously important feature of the "grand narrative" that *is* a part of America's perception of itself (Blyth 2002; Lipset 1996).

The reader may note that I have published several articles which specifically argue that the United States is *not* distinctive simply because of its "political culture" (Steinmo 1994b, 1995). My point here is not to backtrack on these arguments, which essentially argue that "culture" is too often a vacuous concept and that we need to understand how institutions shape choices and ultimately preferences. Instead, we need to more explicitly acknowledge the role of beliefs and perceptions, if we hope to gain an understanding of the larger structures and evolutionary changes in historical events. Beliefs, preferences and ideas about the way in which the world works evolve over time, just as the political institutions in which they are formed also evolve. Preferences are not "given:" They are learned. They are learned in the context of the real world in which people grow up *and* in the context of how they are taught to interpret that world. Rational choice scholars have also come to accept this basic point. As Ira Katznelson and Barry Weingast note,

---

[13] I suggest that it was far from obvious during the Roosevelt administration, for example, that America would become the most unequal country in the modern world by the end of the century. America's perception of itself, after all, was as the most equal country in the world and had consequently pioneered egalitarian policies like offering new immigrants free land and free public education (Hirshland and Steinmo 2003).

[14] Not to speak of the massive resources (both natural and human) available in this country (see Steinmo 2006).

"rational choice scholars have become far more empirical, conditional, and situational in deploying preferences...No longer simply imputed by the theorist-observer, here the interactive play of the game itself in part induces actor preferences. Context and situations matter deeply" (Katznelson and Weingast 2005: 8).

But purely structuralist accounts, whether rational choice or historical institutionalist, discount the role and importance of ideas and beliefs, at least in their formal analysis. Although structuralists may be willing to acknowledge that ideas matter, in point of fact they are brought in through the back door.[15] This is partly because, as we have seen, beliefs/ideas/preferences change. Moreover, ideas are not tidy bits of information that can be easily captured, described and categorized. Instead, they are often incoherent and contradictory. They still matter because they, just like institutions, frame what policy makers can do and provide incentives to move in some directions over others. A political leader would be no more successful in the United States announcing that the health care crisis could be solved through a government takeover of the industry than would the Swedish counterpart win votes by declaring that everyone should be responsible for their own health insurance in Sweden.

My goal, then, has been to offer historical narratives that weave together the evolution of political institutions and political ideas in these different countries. I do not take an essentialist or primal view of beliefs and preferences. They evolve out of experience. Similarly, I do not take a fundamentalist approach to institutions. They are constructed by people who believe things. Even when institutions are imposed from abroad, as in Japan, they are adjusted, manipulated, and used in accordance with the preferences and beliefs of the actors that work with them. Moreover, institutions change (evolve) as they are the subjects of political struggles. The most intense political fights are specifically over the structure of institutions, not just because institutions can structure subsequent strategies, but also because they can affect ideas about what goals ought to be pursued.

A central weakness of many institutionalist accounts is that they are in fact static equilibrium analyses (Nelson and Winter 2002; Thelen 2003). Given a particular set of institutions (and preferences) the analyst conducts an algebraic computation. There are three parts in this equation: (A) preferences (B) institutions (C) decisions (outcomes).

A standard account then is: $A \times B = C$. Thus, if we know A and B, we can predict C. If we know A and C, we can induce B, and so on. But

---

[15] See, (Schmidt 2002), for an excellent example of the attempt to bring institutionalist and ideational approaches together.

this algebra only works (at least in simple form) if these variables remain constant. What if A changes with experience? Worse yet, what if A changes in *unpredictable*[16] ways? Surely, we can model short detailed events and, perhaps, we can characterize much about political behavior. But if we want to understand how and why a country follows certain paths and not others, why a people chooses certain types of outcomes and not others, and most importantly, why things change over time, we cannot limit ourselves to static equilibrium analysis.

As Katznelson and Weingast suggest, we need to "consider how institutions that result from historical causes themselves induce the formation of preferences, and how it is that these preferences then recursively enter into the larger dynamics of historical development and change. Sometimes preferences are exogenous to institutions; at other times, they are the products of the process by which institutions endogenize preferences" (Katznelson and Weingast 2005: 15).

INSTITUTIONS AND EVOLUTION

If we take evolution seriously and say that political economies *evolve* (not just randomly change) then we are saying that there are mechanisms for generating variation, selecting and reproducing the successful variations (Dennett 1995). The idea that market-based economies evolve seems easy to accept: Market based economic systems have come to dominate the modern world precisely because they have more mechanisms for generating variation, selecting successful variations, and for reproducing successful variations than any other systems of economic organization we know of today (Beinhocker 2006; Nelson 2007; Nelson and Winter 2002). Indeed, it seems rather clear that the evolutionary capacity of market based economies explains why these systems are generally able to out compete other forms of economic organization, including family based economies, tribal non-trading economies, feudal economies, and totalitarian state directed economies. But there are many kinds or versions of market based political economies, even within the general category of democratic capitalism. I submit that some of these systems have different evolutionary capacities.

Clearly, all three countries in this study are market based economies. None, however, is a "free market:" All three countries regulate their markets

---

[16] I use the term unpredictable not to suggest complete randomness (i.e., no causation), but rather as it is understood in chaos theory. With human institutions we also should understand creativity as a source of randomness and unpredictability. See (Kingdon 2003) for a very insightful discussion on this point.

in innumerable ways. The United States version of market economics appears to be particularly good at generating innovation and variation. The Swedish system is accomplished at selecting successful variations. Finally, the Japanese system appears to be proficient in reproduction but is less well designed for generating variation.

In political systems the same basic evolutionary logic applies. If we are to say political systems EVOLVE, they must have mechanisms for variation, selection and reproduction. I believe that it is possible to say that modern democratic systems offer their citizens competitive advantages over one party regimes, hereditary rulers, or military dictatorships, for example. This is because these regimes offer their populations comparatively efficient means for generating variation (through freedom of press, speech, etc.), selection (through electoral competition and voting) and reproduction (through the rule of law and permanent bureaucracies). In short, they have greater capacities for evolutionary change than do other regime types. This should neither be taken to imply that modern democracies have some higher moral order or value in a teleological sense. (They may or may not. That is not the point here.) Nor should this argument be taken to suggest that these systems are evolutionarily stable and/or that they have advantages over all other potential systems. Finally, it is extremely important to remember that within the broad category of "democracy," there is huge variation in the particular mechanisms of variation, selection and reproduction. Indeed, these particularities have been the central focus of this book. Furthermore, an evolutionary approach would lead one to *expect* that attributes that offer advantages in one historical context may have little utility or may even be disadvantageous in another context. A system that fragments political authority may offer significant advantages in a context where there appears to be virtually limitless resources, but not be particularly efficient in an era when resources are limited and cooperation is called for.

DIVERGENCE IN A GLOBALIZING WORLD

I began researching this book, trying to understand why we didn't see convergence as a race to the bottom at the end of the twentieth century. As I learned more and more about these countries, I learned that not only did they react or adapt to "globalization" in different ways, but in fact because these systems are so different, the main challenges confronting these countries early in the twenty-first century are themselves quite different. To be sure, increasing economic competition is an issue for each of these countries, but in all three cases competition reveals a different set of issues.

Sweden, for example, enters the new millennium a very strong and remarkably adaptable competitor. Although many would have predicted that high taxes and its large welfare state would weigh the system down and make it impossible for Sweden to succeed in the globalized world, we find just the opposite. Taxes are indeed very high, but remarkably to some, the government does not take this money and burn it in trash barrels behind the Prime Minister's office. Instead, Sweden's high taxes are used rather effectively to fund insurance, reinvestment, infrastructure, education, and social welfare. Once again, social welfare has a positive connotation in Sweden. Perhaps, the most interesting fact about the modern Swedish social welfare state is that it has embraced so many of neo-liberal ideas about competition and flexibility. Today social programs and even education may be provided by state institutions, or may not be. In a remarkable number of arenas, the "customer" gets to decide (Kumlin 2002b). From the government's point of view, the key issue is not *who* provides the services but *how good* the social welfare services are.

Sweden does face significant challenges, both today and in the immediate horizon. The most obvious is that Sweden is no longer an ethnically homogeneous society and this growing diversity does present this country with difficulties. As we saw in Chapter 2, Sweden was able to construct its extensive and universal welfare state, in part, because it was a relatively homogeneous society. When the recipient of social benefits had a great deal in common with the tax payer, that voter could be more easily convinced that the insurance might one day be paid back.

What if the recipient of social welfare payment looks less and less like the payer? What if a growing number of people accept child payments and maternity leave and have larger and larger families in order to keep women out of the labor market? What if people take advantage of school choice or vouchers to put their children in schools that emphasize religious fundamentalist values rather than secular humanist ones? What happens when the society's commitment to equality and individual freedom conflicts with a sub-population's commitment to the traditional family structure and/or beliefs that women should be subservient to men?

The honest answer to these questions is that we don't know. To be sure, the universalist character of the Swedish welfare state gives this system an advantage when dealing with many of these issues, precisely because this system encourages women to enter the workforce and offers significant opportunities for low income or less educated citizens (whatever the national or cultural origins) to upgrade skills and effectively become more integrated and socialized into Swedish society. However, in no modern society are these easy issues to overcome. Perhaps as the second and third generation immigrants grow up they will become better integrated and better acculturated. What it means to be a Swede does appear to be evolving as the identity of the immigrant communities diffuses and become less coherent. Perhaps, in this sense, Sweden will follow a pattern more like nineteenth or twentieth century America. Moreover, social trust remains high and this county's commitment to social equality is likely to continue to be a key lubricant for an adaptable society.

Japan, in contrast, faces huge problems adapting in the twenty-first century. Ironically, having too heavy a tax burden or too large a welfare state is not among them. Indeed, it is perfectly clear that Japan needs to significantly grow both. The fact that the Japanese government is incapable of balancing its budget, or building a reasonable public social welfare system, is symptomatic of Japan's challenges. In policy terms, of course, the crushing debt will only get worse as this society ages – and it is aging quickly. But precisely because they have not built a successful welfare state or established the social welfare services that could facilitate female career employment, women choose to marry late and have fewer and fewer children. At the same time, the Japanese refuse to open their borders to immigrants who could both provide a workforce to support the aging Japanese and, at least potentially, provide the children who could help repopulate the Japanese islands.

These policy solutions are obvious to all who look at them. The underlying question is why they continue to be so difficult to introduce in Japan. Certainly, part of the answer to this question is found in Japan's unique political institutions. But even as Japan has changed its electoral rules in the direction of a more cogent parliamentary democracy with stronger cabinets (Estevez-Abe 2008), it continues to grapple with the underlying conflicts between the traditional hierarchical social norms, on the one side, and the need for greater individual flexibility and equity, on the other. In Sweden and the United States, social norms and ideas about class, gender and, eventually even race, have co-evolved along with the increasingly liberal and egalitarian political and economic institutions. To be sure, social norms and attitudes have also changed and evolved in Japan as well. Class structure is far less rigid than it was in the pre-war period, but attitudes toward hierarchy, seniority, gender, race and authority appear to be ill suited for a rapidly changing, indeed "globalizing," world.

Women are no longer expected to walk behind their husbands in Osaka and Tokyo, but they are expected to end their careers when they have children and to care for their husband's parents as they get older. Women are not, moreover, expected to sit at the boardroom table. This gender-based discrimination is a problem for three reasons: (1) it deprives Japan of a significant workforce; (2) it contributes to the inflexibility of Japan's labor market and economy; and (3) it gives women no incentive to have more children.[17]

Some of Japan's fiscal and demographic problems could also be addressed by allowing increased immigration. Here again, what is obvious from a liberal economic point of view appears virtually impossible because of prevailing social values. Japanese have traditionally seen themselves as an ethnically pure nation. For centuries, the Japanese have cherished their cultural and ethnic homogeneity. Many Japanese believe that opening their doors to large numbers of immigrants would force Japan to change the social foundations of this traditional society.

Perhaps one could argue that it is pure racism that motivates the fear of foreigners in Japan. Certainly racism plays a role here – as it does in all countries, including Sweden. But this problem is made far more intractable both because of Japan's underdeveloped social welfare institutions and because it has such strong corporate units. The strong sense of team identity in Japanese firms has unquestionably contributed to their productive success. Japan has not yet built mechanisms for social inclusion, even while they have introduced policies that have increased interpersonal competition and growing inequality. In this context, one should not be surprised that Japanese workers and citizens are fearful of foreign immigration and that their politicians play to those fears.

At this moment of history (mid 2009), it is easy to point to Japan's extreme economic difficulties (i.e., GDP decline of more than 6 percent, budget deficit increase of 12 percent of GDP, loss of export markets, etc.) as evidence of Japan's problems. In my view, however, to focus solely on the short-term economic crisis misses the point. The more fundamental problem for Japan seems to be that the friction between its political and social institutions make it ever more difficult for Japan to adapt in an increasingly dynamic world. Perhaps the current crisis will prove to be just the kind of ecological challenge that will stimulate new ideas and creative adaptations (Kingdon 2003: 222–26). The analysis here, however, strongly suggests that Japan is unlikely to successfully adapt if it continues to simply import policies from abroad. Its leaders should instead consider *both* how to adapt new ideas

---

[17] In 2009, the government reported that only 13 percent of the country's population (127,6 million people) were below the age of 15. On the other hand, 22.5 percent are over 65 years old.

to the system's strengths and weaknesses, *as well as* consider what kind of country they would like to build.

The remarkable dynamism of America is obvious to anyone who knows this country. As we have seen, the United States was hugely advantaged by its continental size, its enormous natural resources and the massive influx of tens of millions of immigrants from around the world. But these variables alone cannot explain America's success. Instead, just as the founding fathers had hoped, the fragmentation of political power made for a weak national state. Since no one could control the state, the nation thrived. The opportunities available to most citizens helped develop a culture of optimism in which individual initiative and the creative spirit were rewarded, admired and reinforced.

As the Americans expanded across the continent, and eventually the world, they became ever more confident in their belief that freedom was the source of their success and that strong government was inherently evil. Thus as the task of governing grew more complex, instead of building stronger government with which to manage these challenges, the United States further divided and subdivided public power. In the end, they crippled the state.

In the context of an expanding nation with a continent (and then a world) to exploit America's weak state proved remarkably successful. Ironically, the liberalization of the world economy that the United States so confidently promoted may now work to undermine the geographic and resource advantages that once benefited this country so greatly. Certainly the dynamism and creativity of the American people and their economic system will continue to offer competitive advantages for this country. But as the fruits of this system are distributed ever more unequally, one is left to wonder how the foundational principles of equality and opportunity can continue to thrive.

In his classic text, *Private Power and American Democracy*, Grant McConnell argued that dividing public authority does not eliminate power (McConnell 1966). Instead, he argued, it simply offers the well organized more opportunities to target benefits on their constituents. Indeed, as we have seen repeatedly in this book, the increasing fragmentation of political power in America has not built walls between public and private power as might have been hoped. It has instead made these institutions easier to manipulate by increasingly narrow and selfish interests. Faction fights faction while the public becomes ever more alienated.

As America enters the second decade of the new millennium, a new and rather remarkable President holds the reigns of power. Only a few months before the election in November 2008, most analysts (including this one) would confidently predict that America could not possibly be ready for an

African American president. Of course, we were once again wrong, just as we had been wrong in our predictions of globalization's inevitable implications for the social welfare state.

This election should remind us that even while politics is complex, new leaders with new ideas can emerge onto the political agenda and change the path of history. In short, we should remember the fundamental importance of both contingency and human creative agency in the account offered here. It is surely possible that this or some future leader will be able to introduce the kinds of institutional and policy changes that could rebuild American's faith and trust in their democracy. If so, this president could help set the country toward a new evolutionary path.

Let's hope he, or she, does.

Works Cited

Åberg, Rune. 1989. "Distributive mechanisms of the welfare state – a formal analysis and an empirical application." *European Sociological Review* 5: 188–214.

Åsard, Erik. 1984. *Industrial and economic democracy in Sweden: From consensus to confrontation.* Paper read at ECPR, 12th Joint Session, 13–18 April, at Salzburg, Austria.

Adema, Willem, and Maxime Ladaique. 2005. "Net Social Expenditure, 2005 Edition: More Comprehensive Measures of Social Support." In *OECD Social Employment and Migration Working Papers, No. 29.* Paris: OECD Publishing.

Agell, Jonas, Lennart Berg, and Per-Anders Edin. 1995. "Tax reform, consumption and asset structure." In *Tax reform evaluation report 16.* Stockholm: National Institute of Economic Research.

Agell, Jonas, Peter Englund, and Jan Södersten. 1996. "Tax reform of the century – the Swedish experiment." *National Tax Journal* 49 (4): 643–64.

Ahmadjian, Christine. 2002. *lecture,* March 7, 2002, at Hitotsubashi University, Tokyo Japan.

Akaishi, Takatsugu, and Sven Steinmo. 2003. *"Why are corporate taxes so high in Japan?".* Nagasaki and Boulder: University of Nagasaki, University of Colorado.

––––––. 2006. "Consumption Taxes and the Welfare State in Sweden and Japan " In *The Ambivalent Consumer: Questioning Consumption in East Asia and the West,* ed. S. Garon and P. Maclachlan. Ithaca: Cornell University Press.

Alford, John. 2001. "We're all in this together: The decline of trust in govenrment, 1958–1996." In *What is it about government that Americans dislike?,* ed. J. HIbbing and E. Theiss-Morse. New York: Cambridge University Press.

Andersson, Jenny. 2007. "Socializing capital, capitalizing the social: Contemporary Social Democracy and the knowledge economy." In *Center for European Studies Working Paper Series.* Cambridge.

Andrews, David. 1994. "Capital mobility and state autonomy." *International Studies Quarterly* 38: 193–218.

Arthur, Brian. 1994. *Increasing Returns and Path Dependency in the Economy.* Ann Arbor: University of Michigan Press.

Atack, Jeremy, and Peter Passell. 1994. *A New View of American History*, 2nd Edition. New York: W.W. Nortn Co.

Axelrod, Robert M. 1984. *The evolution of cooperation*. New York: Basic Books.

———. 1997. *The complexity of cooperation agent-based models of competition and collaboration*. Princeton: Princeton University Press.

Axelrod, Robert M., and Michael D. Cohen. 2000. *Harnessing complexity: organizational implications of a scientific frontier*. New York: Basic Books.

Bäckström, Urban. 2007. "Financial Crisis: The Swedish Experience." ed. Riksbanken. Stockholm: Swedish Central Bank.

Bank of Japan. *Kokusai Hikaku Tokei [International Comparative Statistics]*.

Bartels, Larry. 2007. "*Unequal democracy: The political economy of the new guilded age.*" Princeton.

Beinhocker, Eric D. 2006. *The origin of wealth: evolution, complexity, and the radical remaking of economics*. Boston, Mass.: Harvard Business School Press.

Bennett, Stephen Earl. 2001. "Were the Halcyon days really golden? An analysis of Americans' attitudes abouty the political system, 1945–1965." In *What is it about government that Americans dislike?*, ed. J. HIbbing and E. Theiss-Morse. New York: Cambridge University Press.

Belfrage, C. (2008) "*The Neoliberal Restructuring of the Welfare State: Pension System Reform in Sweden, A Critical Case Study,*" Ph.D. thesis, Department of Political Science and International Studies, University of Birmingham.

Bennhold, Katrin. 2009. "Europe's safety net getting a fresh look." *International Herald Tribune*, Wednesday, January 28, 2009, 1, 20.

Bergh, Andreas. 2006. "Is the Swedish welfare state a free lunch?" *Econ Journal Watch* 3 (2): 210–35.

Bergh, Andreas. 2008. "Explaining the Survival of the Swedish Welfare State: Maintaining Political Support Through Incremental Change." *Financial Theory and Practice* 32 (2): 233–54.

Berman, Sheri. 1998. *The social democratic moment: ideas and politics in the making of interwar Europe*. Cambridge, MA: Harvard University Press.

Björklund, Anders. 2006. "Does family policy affect fertility?" *Journal of Population Economics* 19 (3): 3–23.

Blyth, Mark. 2002. *Great transformations: Economic ideas and institutional change in the twentieth century*. New York: Cambridge University Press.

———. 2006. "Great punctuations: Prediction, randomness, and the evolution of comparative political researach." *American Political Science Review* 100 (4): 493–8.

———. 2007. "One Ring to Rind Them All: American Power and Neoliberal Capitalism." In *Growing Apart? America and Europe in the 21st Century*, ed. J. Kopstein and S. Steinmo. New York: Cambridge University Press.

Borg, Anders. 2008. "*Re-Establishing the Swedish Model.*" Stockholm Sweden: Ministry of Finance.

Borrus, Michael, James Millstein, John Zysman, and United States Congress Joint Economic Committee. 1982. *U.S.-Japanese competition in the semiconductor industry: a study in international trade and technological development*. Berkeley: Institute of International Studies University of California Berkeley.

Boulding, Kenneth. 1981. *Ecodynamics: A new Theory of Societal Evolution*. Beverly Hills: Sage.

Boyd, Robert, and Peter Richerson. 2005a. "Solving the Puzzle of Human Cooperation." In *Evolution and Culture*, ed. S. Levinson. Cambridge: MIT Press.

Boyd, Robert, and Peter J. Richerson. 2005b. *The origin and evolution of cultures*. New York: Oxford University Press.

Boyd, Robert, and Jeremy Richersson. 2000. Institutional Evolution in the Holocene: The Rise of Complex Societies. Paper read at British Academy/Novartis Foundation meeting on The Origin of Human Social Institutions, at London.

Brandolini, Andrea, and Timothy Smeeding. 2006. "Patterns of economic inequality in western democracies: Some facts on levels and trends." *PS Political Science and Politics* XXXX (1): 21–6.

Brooks, David. 2005. "Fear and Rejection." *New York Times*, June 2, 2005.

Brooks, Stephen. 2000. *Understanding the Recent Change in the Structure of Global Production (Chapter 4)*. Ph.D., Political Science, Yale University, Princeton.

Bruenker, John. 1985. *The income tax and the Progressive era*. New York: Carland Publishing Inc.

Bruszt, Laszlo, and Gerald McDermott. 2008. "Transnational Integration Regimes as Development Programs." Florence.

Campbell, John. 1992. *How policies change: The Japanese government and aging society*. Princeton: Princeton University Press.

_____. 2004. *Institutional change and globalization*. Princeton: Princeton University Press.

Carrapico, Francisco. 2009. "The symbiotic phenomenon in evolutive context." In *Unity of Science: Essays in honour of Otto Neurath*, ed. O. Pombo, J. M. Torres and J. Symon. New York: Springer.

Castles, Francis. 1978. *The social democratic image of society*. London: Routledge Keegan and Paul.

_____. 2004. *The future of the welfare state: Crisis, myths and crisis realities*. Oxford: Oxford University Press.

Centeno, Miguel Angel. 2002. *Blood and debt: war and the nation-state in Latin America*. University Park: Pennsylvania State University Press.

Childs, Marquis. 1974. *Sweden: the middle way*. New Haven: Yale University Press.

Clearinghouse on International Developments in Child, Youth and Family Policies, Columbia University. *Table 1 Maternity, Paternity, and Parental Leaves in the OECD Countries 1998–2002* [cited. Available from http: //www.childpolicyintl .org/issuebrief/issuebrief5table1.pdf.

Conway, Paul, Véronique Janod, and Guiseppe Nicoletti. 2005. "Product Market Regulation in OECD Countries: 1998 to 2003." In *OECD Economics Department Working Papers, No. 419*. Paris: OECD.

Cosmides, Leda, and John Tooby. 2007. *Evolutionary Psychology: A primer*. University of California, Santa Barbara 1997 [cited 2007].

Countryman, Edward. 1985. *The American Revolution*. New York: Hill and Wang.

Cowie, Roger. 1993. "Using Tax Incentives to Improve American Competitiveness." *American Business Law Journal* 31/3 (November 1993): 435–7, 9, 41, 43, 45.

Curtis, Gerald. 1999. *The logic of Japanese politics: Leaders, institutions and teh limits of change.* New York: Columbia University Press.

Dahl, Robert Alan. 1967. *Pluralist democracy in the United States: conflict and consent.* Chicago: Rand McNally.

David, Paul A., and Gavin Wright. 1997. "Increasing Returns and the Genesis of American Resource Abundance." *Industrial and Corporate Change* 6 (2: March 1997): 203–45.

Davidsson, Johan. 2007. *New risks, not so new welfare.* unpublished paper, SPS, European University Institute, Florence.

_____. 2008. "*Work without welfare.*" European Universty Institue.

Dawkins, Richard. 1976. *The selfish gene.* New York: Oxford University Press.

_____. 2009. *Afterward: The selfish gene: Thirty years on.* LSE 2006 [cited 2009]. Available from http://www.edge.org/3rd_culture/selfish06/selfish06_index.html.

Dept. of Economic Statistics. 2004. *Statistics Sweden.* Stockholm.

Deeg, Richard. 2005. "Change from Within: German and Italian Finance in the 1990s." In *Beyond Continuity,* ed. W. Streeck and K. Thelen. Oxford: Oxford University Press.

Democratic, Party of Japan. 2009. "Basic Policies." In *Party Platform.* Tokyo: DPJ.

Dennett, Daniel C. 1995. *Darwin's Dangerous Idea.* New York: Simon and Schuster.

Derthick, Martha. 1979. *Making policy for social security.* Washington, DC: The Brookings Institution.

DeWit, Andrew. 1998. *Trench Warfare on the Tax Fields: Fiscal Sociology and Japan's Centralized Tax State.* PhD. Dissertation, Political Science, University of British Columbia, Vancouver.

_____. 2002. "Dry rot: The corruption of general subsidies in Japan." *Journal of the Asia Pacific Economy* 7 (3): 355–78.

_____. 2009. ""*Change*" Comes to Japan." Tokyo: Rikkyo University.

DeWit, Andrew, and Sven Steinmo. 2002. "Policy vs. Rhetoric: The Political Economy of Taxation and Redistribution in Japan" (with Andrew DeWitt) vol. 5, no. 2." *Social Science Japan Journal* 5 (2).

Die Bundesreigerung (German Federal Government). 2003. *Pensions* [Article]. Die bundesreigerung, 3/25/03 2003 [cited 6/23/03 2003]. Available from http://eng.bundesregierung.de/frameset/index.jsp.

DiZerega, Gus. 1989. "Democracy as a Spontaneous Order." *Critical Review* (Spring 1989): 206–40.

Dobbin, Frank. 2002. "Is America becoming more exceptional?" In *Restructuring the Welfare State-Political Institutions and Policy Change-,* ed. B. Rothstein and S. Steinmo. New York: Palgrave Macmillan.

Dodd, Lawrence. 1981. "Congress, the Constitution and the Crisis of Legitimacy." In *Congress reconsidered,* ed. L. C. Dodd and B. I. Oppenheimer. Washington, DC: CQ Press.

Dodd, Lawrence C., and L. Schott Richard. 1979. *Congress and the administrative state.* New York: John Wiley and Sons.

Downs, Anthony. 1960. "Why government's budget is too small in a democracy." *World Politics* 12: 541–63.

Drucker, Peter F. 1986. "The changed world economy." *Foreign Affairs* 64 (4): 768–91.

Dudziak, Mary L. 2000. *Cold War civil rights: race and the image of American democracy*. Princeton: Princeton University Press.

Dunbar, Robin. 1996. *Grooming, Gossip and the Evolution of Language*. Cambridge: Harvard University Press.

Economist. 2000. "Have factory will travel." *Economist*, 65–6.

———. 2001a. "A magician in Japan." April 28, 2001.

———. 2001b. "Is government disappearing?" *Economist*, September 27, 2001.

———. 2004. "What goes up must come down." *The Economist (web edition)*, July 15, 2004.

———. 2006. "Reinfeldt explained." *The Economist*, September 21, 2006.

———. 2007. "Sweden's Government: One year on." *Economist*.

———. 2008a. "Fixing finance." *Economist*, April 5, 2008, 13–4.

———. 2008b. "The Swedish Model." *Economist*, July 12, 2008.

Edin, P.-A., and P. Fredriksson (2000): "LINDA Longitudinal Individual Data for Sweden," Working paper 19, Department of Economics, Uppsala University."

Edlund, Jonas. 1999a. *Citizens and taxation: Sweden in comparative perspective*. Umeå: Umea University Press.

———. 1999b. "Trust in government and welfare regimes: attitudes to redistribution and financial cheating in the USA and Norway." *European Journal of Political Research* 35: 341–70.

Ehrlich, Paul. 2000. *Human Natures: Genes, cultures, and the human prospect*. New York: Penguin.

Eisenstadt, Samuel. 2006. "Multiple modernities in the framework of a comparative evolutionary perspective." In *Understanding change: Models, methodologies and metaphors*, ed. A. Wimmer and R. Kossler. New York: Palgrave McMillan.

Elvander, Nils. 1972. *Svensk skattepolitik 1945–1970 [Swedish tax politics 1945–1970]*. Stockholm: Raben and Sjögren.

———. 1988. *Den svenska modellen*. Stockholm: Liber Forlag.

Energy Information Administration. 1998. "*International Energy Annual.*" ed. D. O. Energy. Washington DC: Department of Energy.

Esping-Anderson, Gosta. 2002. "Toward a good society, once again?" In *Why we need a new welfare state*, ed. G. Esping-Andersen. Oxford: Oxford University Press.

Estevez-Abe, Margarita. 2002. "Negotiating Welfare Reforms: Actors and Institutions in the Japanese Welfare State." In *Restructuring the Welfare State-Political Institutions and Policy Change-*, ed. B. Rothstein and S. Steinmo. New York: Palgrave Macmillan.

———. 2008. *Welfare and capitalism in postwar Japan*. New York: Cambridge University Press.

Edvinsson, Rodney. 2005. *Growth Accumulation Crisis*. Stockholm: Almquist and Wicksell.

Fackler, Martin. 2008. "A campaign for change, or mere kabuki?" *The International Herald Tribune*, September 17, 2008, 8.

Feldt, Kjell-Olof. 1991. *Alla Dessa Dagar (All Those Days)*. Stockholm: Norstedts.

Finance, Ministry of. 2000. "National Report on Economic Reform: Product and Capital Markets." Stockholm: Ministry of Finance.

Finansdepartementet. 2002. "*Sweden's Economy.*" Stockholm: Ministry of Finance, Sweden.

Fiorina, Morris. 1995. "Rational Choice and the New (?) Institutionalism." *Polity* XXXVIII (1 (Fall)): 107–15.

Ford, Richard Thompson. 2008. "Play the race card at your own peril." *Washington Post*, Sunday, February 17, 2008, B 01.

Forster, Michael, and Marco Mira d'Ercole. 2005. "Income dirstibution and poverty in OECD countries in teh second half of the 1990's." In *OECD Social, Employment and Migration Working Papers*, ed. OECD. Paris: Organization for Economic Cooperation and Development.

Förster, Michael, and Marco Mira d'Ercole. 2005. "Income Distribution and Poverty in OECD Countries in the Second Half of the 1990s." In *OECD Social, Employment and Migration Working Papers*. Paris: OECD.

Frankfort-Nachmias, Chava, and David Nachmias. 2008. *Research methods in the social sciences.* 7th ed. New York: Worth Publishers.

Friedman, Joel, Richard Kogan, and Denis Kadochnikov. 2003. *Administration Tax Cut Proposals Would Cost $2.7 Trillion Through 2013.* Vol. 2009. Washington, DC: Center on Budget and Policy Priorities.

Fritz, Martin, and Birgit Karlsson. 2003. "Dependence and National Supply: Sweden's economic relations with Nazi Germany." In *Sweden's relations with Nazism, Nazi Gemany and the Holocaust*, ed. S. Ekman and K. Åmark. Stockholm: Almqvist and Wiksell.

Fujii, Rina. 2003. "Breaking the Bank." *Harvard International Review* 25 (2): 1–2.

Fukukawa, Shinji. 1999. "Japan's challenge for economic revitalization." In *Columbia Business School Distinguished Lecture Series.* CJEB Occasional Paper no. 44. New York: Columbia Business School.

Futuyma, Douglas J., and Montgomery Slatkin. 1983. *Coevolution.* Sunderland, MA: Sinauer Associates.

Garon, Sheldon. 1997. *Molding Japanese minds: The state in everyday life.* Princeton: Princeton University Press.

———. 2006a. "Japan's post-war 'consumer revolution,' or striking a 'balance' between consumption and saving." In *Consuming Cultures, Global Perspectives: Historical Trajectories, Transnational Exchanges*, ed. J. Brewer and F. Trentmann. Oxford: Berg Press.

———. 2006b. "The Transnational Promotion of Saving in Asia: 'Asian Values' or 'The Japanese Model'?" In *The Ambivalent Consumer: Questioning Consumption in East Asia and the West*, ed. S. Garon and P. Maclachlan. Ithaca: Cornell University Press.

Garon, Sheldon, and Mike Mochizuki. 1993. "Negotiating social contracts." In *Postwar Japan as history*, ed. A. Gordon. Berkeley: University of Carifornia Press.

Gerring, Josh. 1998. *Party Ideologies in America: 1828–1996.* Cambridge, MA: Cambridge University Press.

Gershenkron, Alexander. 1962. *Economic backwardness in historical perspective.* Cambridge, MA: Harvard University Press.

Gill, Tom. 2001. "Homelessness: a Slowly Dawning Recognition." *Social Sciences Japan* (21): 17–20.

Gintis, Herbert. 2000. *Game theory evolving: A problem-centered introduction to modeling strategic behavior*. Princeton: Princeton University Press.

Goldsteen, R. L., K. Goldsteen, J. H. Swan, and W. Clemena. 2001. "Harry and Louise and health care reform: Romancing public opinion." *Journal of Health Politics Policy and Law* 26 (6): 1325–52.

Gould, Stephen Jay. 1989. *Wonderful life: The Burgess Shale and the nature of history*. New York: Norton.

———. 2002. *The structure of evolutionary theory*. Cambridge, MA: Belknap Press of Harvard University Press.

Greif, Avner, and David Laitin. 2004. "A theory of endogenous institutional change." *American Political Science Review* 98 (4): 633–52.

Grieder, William. 1981. "The education of David Stockman." *Atlantic Monthly*: 5.

Hacker, Jacob. 2005. "Policy Drift: The hidden politics of the US Welfare State." In *Beyond Continuity*, ed. W. Streeck and K. Thelen. Oxford: Oxford University Press.

Hacker, Jacob S. 2002. *The Divided Welfare State*. Cambridge, UK: Cambridge University Press.

Hadenius, Axel. 1966. *Facklig organizationsutveckling: En studie av lansorganisationen i Sverige (Labor organization development: A study of the LO in Sweden)*. Lund: Gleerup.

———. 1985. "Citizens strike a balance: Discontent with taxes, content with spending." *Journal of Public Policy* 5 (3): 349–63.

———. 1986. *A crisis of the welfare state? Opinions about taxes and public expenditure in Sweden*. Stockholm: MiniMedia AB.

Hadenius, Stig, Bjèorn Molin, and Hans Wieslander. 1967. *Sverige efter 1900, en modern politisk historia*. Stockholm: Bokfèorlaget Aldus/Bonniers.

Hall, Peter. 1989. *The Political Power of Economic Ideas*. Princeton: Princeton University Press.

———. 2003. "Aligning Ontology and Methodology in Comparative Research." In *Comparative historical analysis in the social sciences*, ed. J. Mahoney and D. Rueschmeyer. Cambridge: Cambridge University Press.

———. 2005. "Preference formation as a political process: The case of monetary union in Europe." In *Preferences and Situations*, ed. I. Katznelson and B. Weingast. New York: Cambridge University Press.

———. 2008. "Historical Institutionalism in rational choice and sociological perspectives." In *Explaining Institutional Change: Ambiguity, Agency, and Power in Historical Institutionalism*, ed. J. Mahoney and K. Thelen: forthcoming.

Hall, Peter, and David Soskice. 2001. "An Introduction to Varieties of Capitalism." In *Varieties of Capitalism*, ed. P. Hall and D. Soskice. Oxford: Oxford University Press.

Hancock, Donald. 1972. *Sweden: the politics of post-industrial change*. Hindsale, IL: The Dryden Press.

Hartz, Louis. 1983. *The liberal tradition in America: an interpretation of American political thought since the Revolution*. San Diego: Harcourt Brace Jovanovich.

Hattam, Victoria Charlotte. 1993. *Labor visions and state power: the origins of business unionism in the United States*. Princeton: Princeton University Press.

Hayek, Freidrich A. 2007. *The Road to Serfdom*. Edited by W. W. B. III. The Definative Edition, 2007 ed. Chicago: University of Chicago Press.

Hayek, Friedrich A. von, and Arthur A. Shenfield. 1983. *Knowledge, evolution and society*. London: Adam Smith Institute.

Heckscher, Eli F., and Gunner Heckscher. 1954. *An economic history of Sweden*. Cambridge: Harvard University Press.

Heller, Richard. 2001. "The new face of Swedish socialism." *Forbes*, March 19, 2001.

Hemerijck, Anton. 2002. "The self-transformation of the European social model(s)." In *Why we need a new welfare state*, ed. G. Esping-Andersen. Oxford: Oxford University Press.

Hibbing, John R., and Elizabeth Theiss-Morse. 2001. *What is it about government that Americans dislike?* Cambridge; New York: Cambridge University Press.

Hieda, Takeshi. 2010. *The Comparative Political Economy of Long-Term Care, Department of Politics and Social Science*, European University Institute, Florence.

Hirshland, Matt, and Sven Steinmo. 2003. "Correcting the record: The Federal government and American education." *Education Policy* 17 (3): 343–64.

Hiwatari, N. 1989. *Organized Markets and the restrained state: Instituions for industrial policy, incomes coodination, and political quiescence in postwar Japan*. Ph.D., Political Science, University of California, Berkeley, California.

———. 1991. *Sengo Nihon no Shijyo to Seiji (The market and Politics in Postwar Japan)*. Tokyo: Tokyo Daigaku Shuppan-kai (University of Tokyo Press).

Hodgson, Geoffrey. 2002. "Darwinism in economics: From analogy to ontology." *Journal of Evolutionary Economics* 12: 259–73.

Hoffman, Mathew, and John Riley. 1999. "*The Science of Political Science: Linearity or Complexity in Designing Social Inquiry.*" St. Louis: Washington University.

Hofstadter, Richard, ed. 1963. *The progressive movement 1900–1915*. Englewood Cliffs, NJ: Prentice-Hall, Inc.

Holland, John. 1992. "Complex Adaptive Systems." *Daedelus* 121 (winter): 17–30.

Holmberg, Sören, and Lennart Weibull. 2008. "Swedish Trends 1986–2007." In *SOM-Institutet*. Gothenberg: University of Gothenberg.

Hopkin, Jonathan, and Mark Blyth. 2006. "*Equality versus efficiency? Structural reform, inequality, and economic performance in Western Europe.*" London and Baltimore.

Horioka, Charles Yuki. 2006. "Are Japanese Unique? An Analysis of Consumption and Savings Behavior in Japan." In *The Ambivalent Consumer: Questioning Consumption in East Asia and the West*, ed. S. Garon and P. Maclachlan. Ithaca: Cornell University Press.

Howard, Christopher. 1997. *The hidden welfare state*. Princeton, NJ: Princeton University Press.

———. 2003. "Is the American welfare state unusually small?" *PS Political Science and Politics* XXXVI (3): 411–6.

———. 2007. *The welfare state nobody knows*. Princeton: Princeton University Press.

Huh, Chan, and Sun Bea Kim. 1994. "How bad is Japan's 'Bad Loan' Problem?" *Federal Reserve Board of San Francisco Economic Review* 94 (2): 1.

Huntington, Samuel. 1982. "American ideals versus American institutions." *Political Science Quarterly*.

Hurst, Cameron, and Fred Notehelfer. 2009. "Japan: History." In *Encyclopedia Britannica*: Encyclopedia Britannica.

Ibison, David. 2008. "Voucher plan aims to rejuvenate care of Sweden's elderly." *Financial Times*, Friday May 16, 2008, 2.

Ikegami, Eiko. 1995. *The taming of the samurai: Honorific individualism and the making of modern Japan*. Cambridge, MA: Harvard University Press.

Immergut, Ellen. 1992a. *Health Politics: Interests and Institutions in Western Europe*. New York: Cambridge University Press.

———. 1992b. "The rules of the game: The logic of health policy-making in France, Switzerland, and Sweden." In *Historical institutionalism in comparative politics: State, society, and economy*, ed. S. Steinmo, K. Thelen and F. Longstreth. New York: Cambridge University Press.

Inglehart, Ronald. 1997. *Modernization and postmodernization: Cultural, economic, and political change in 43 societies*. Princeton: Princeton University Press.

———. 2003. *Human values and social change: Findings from the values surveys*. Leiden; Boston: Brill.

International Labour Office. Bureau of, Statistics. 2009. "LABORSTA Labor Statistics Database [electronic databse]." International Labour Office, Bureau of Statistics.

Ishi, Hiromitsu. 1992. "The conflict between efficency and equity; of tax administration." *Hitotsubashi Journal of Economics* 33 (2): 129–47.

Ishi, Hiromitsu. 1990. "Taxation and public debt in a growing economy: The Japanese experience." *Hitotsubashi Journal of Economics* 31 (1): 1–22.

———. 2002. "*Thinking the Unthinkable: A tax rise of a sustainable future in Japan*." London: Royal Institute of International Affairs.

Israel, Joachim. 1978. "Swedish socialism and big business." *Acta Sociologica* 21 (4): 341–53.

Ito, Mitsutoshi. 1988. "Daikigyo Roshirengo no Keisei (Formation of the Big Business and Labor Coalition)." *Leviathan* 2.

Ito, Takatoshi, and Tokuo Iwaisako. 1995. "Explaining Asset Bubbles in Japan." In *NBER Working Paper, no. 5358*. Washington, DC: National Bureau of Economic Research.

Itoh, Hiroshi. 1973. *Japanese Politics-An Inside View: Readings from Japan*: Cornell University Press.

Jackson, Gregory. 2003. "Corporate Governance in Germany and Japan: Liberalization Pressures and Responses during the 1990s." In *The end of diversity?: Prospects for German and Japanese capitalism*, ed. K. Yamamura and W. Streeck. Ithaca: Cornell University Press.

Jervis, Robert. 1997. *System Effects*. Princeton: Princeton University Press.

Jinno, Naohiko, Taro Miyamoto and Eisaku Ide (2009). *Towards a Decentralized, Smart State*, Research report prepared for Japan National Governors' Association. Tokyo, Japan. June, 2009. (Translated by Andrew DeWit). http://www.pref.iwate.jp/~hpo151/pdf/chihoubunken.pdf

Johnson, Chalmers. 1995. *Japan: Who governs? The rise of the developmental state*. New York: Norton.

Johnson, Chalmers A. 1982. *MITI and the Japanese miracle: the growth of industrial policy, 1925–1975*. Stanford, CA: Stanford University Press.

Jones, Carolyn. 1990. Taxes to beat the axis: a comparison of American and British income tax publicity during World War II. Paper read at The Tenth International Economic Congress, August, at Leuven, Belgium.

Jonung, Lars. 1999. *Med backspegeln som kompass: om stabiliseringspolitiken som läroprocess: rapport till ESO – Expertgruppen för studier i offentlig ekonomi. [With the rearview mirror as a compass: on stabilization policy as a learning process: report to the ESO expert group for the study of the official economy].* Stockholm: Fakta info direkt.

Jordan, Jason. 2006a. "Mothers, Wives, and Workers: Explaining Gendered Dimensions of the Welfare State." *Comparative Political Studies* 39 (9): 1109–32.

———. 2006b. *Who is in? Who is out? Inclusion and exclusion in western welfare states.* PhD Thesis. Political Science, University of Colorado, Boulder. Boulder, Colorado.

Kasa, Kazatoshi. 1999. "Economic Aspects of Public Works in Japan." *Social Science Japan* (17): 15–9.

Kashiwazaki, Chikako, and Tsuneo Akaha. 2006. "Japanese Immigration Policy: Responding to Conflicting Pressures." In *Migration Immigration Source.* Washington, DC: Migration Policy Institute.

Kasza, Gregory. 2006. One World of Welfare. Japan's welfare policies in comparative perspective. Ithaca: Cornell University Press.

Katz, Claudio, Vincent Mahler, and Michael Franz. 1983. "The impact of taxes on growth and distribution in capitalist countries: a cross – national study." *American Political Science Review* 77 (4): 871–86.

Katz, Richard. 2003. *Japanese pheonix: The long road to economic revival.* Armonk, NY: M. E. Sharpe.

———. 2008. "A Nordic Mirror: Why Structural Reform Has Proceeded Faster in Scandinavia than Japan." *Center on Japanese Economy and Business, Columbia Business School.* Working Paper series (265): 91.

Katznelson, Ira, and Barry Weingast. 2005. "Intersections between historical and rational choice institutionalism." In *Preferences and Situations*, ed. I. Katznelson and B. Weingast. New York: Cambridge University Press.

Kawakami, Naotaka. 2003. "What does the consumption tax mean to Japanese society and U.S. society?" In *Working Paper Series.* New York: Center on Japanese Economy and Business, Columbia Business School.

Keidanren (Japan Business Federation). 2004. "*Survey on Corporate Welfare Expenditures for FY 2001.*" Tokyo: Keidanren.

Kerr, Peter. 2002. "Saved from extinction: Evolutionary Theorising, Politics and the State." *British Journal of Politics and International Relations* 4 (2): 330–58.

King, Anthony. 1973a. "Ideas, Institutions and Policies of Governments: A comparative analysis, part I and II." *British Journal of Political Science* 3 (4): 291–313.

———. 1973b. "Ideas, Institutions and the Policies of Governments: A comparative analysis, part III." *British Journal of Political Science* 3 (4): 409–23.

King, Desmond S. 1995a. *Actively seeking work?: The politics of unemployment and welfare policy in the United States and Great Britain.* Chicago: University of Chicago Press.

———. 1995b. *Separate and unequal: Black Americans and the US federal government.* Oxford: Oxford University Press.

_____. 2000. *Making Americans: Immigration, Race and the Origins of the Diverse Democracy.* Cambridge: Cambridge University Press.

King, Desmond S., and Rogers M. Smith. 2005. "Racial Orders in American Political Development." *The American Political Science Review* 99 (1): 75–92.

King, Ronald. 1984. "Tax expenditures and systematic public policy: An essay on the political economy of the Federal Reserve Code." *Public Budgeting and Finance*: 14–31.

Kingdon, John W. 2003. *Agendas, alternatives, and public policies.* 2nd ed. New York: Longman.

Knight, Jack, and Itai Sened. 1995. *Explaining social institutions.* Ann Arbor: University of Michigan Press.

Koblik, Steven. 1975. *Sweden's development from poverty to affluence, 1750–1970.* English ed. Minneapolis: University of Minnesota Press.

Kolko, Gabriel. 1967. *The triumph of conservatism: a re-interpretation of American history, 1900–1916.* Chicago: Quadrangle Books.

Korpi, Walter. 2006. "Power Resources and Employer-Centered Approaches in Explanations of Welfare States and Varieties of Capitalism: Protagaonists, Consenters, and Antagonists." *World Politics* 58 (2): 167–206.

Korpi, Walter, and Michael Shalev. 1979. "Strikes, industrial relations and class conflict in capitalist societies." *British Journal of Sociology* 30 (2): 164–87.

Krantz, Olle, and Lennart Schön. 2007. *Swedish Historical National Accounts 1800–2000.* Vol. 41. Stockolm: Almqvist and Wicksell.

Krugman, Paul. 2004. *Japan's trap*, May 1998 1998 [cited July 16 2004]. Available from http: //web.mit.edu/krugman/www/japtrap.html.

Kume, Ikuo. 1998a. *Disparaged Success-Labor Politics in Postwar Japan-.* Ithaca and London: Cornell University Press.

_____. 1998b. *Nihon-gata Roshi Kankei no Seiko-Sengo Wakai no Seiji Keizaigaku-(Labor Politics in Postwar Japan).* Tokyo: Yuhikaku.

Kumlin, Steffan. 2002a. "Institutions – Experience – Preferences: Welfare state design affects political trust and ideology." In *Re-Structuring the Welfare State: Institutional Legacies and Policy Change*, ed. B. Rothstein and S. Steinmo. New York: Palgrave.

_____. 2002b. *The personal and the political: How personal wlefare state experiences affect political trust and ideology.* Gothenburg: University of Gothenburg.

Kumlin, Steffan, and Bo Rothstein. 2010. "Questioning the New Liberal Dilemma: Immigrants, Social Networks and Institutional Fairness." *Comparative Politics* forthcoming.

LaPorte, Todd. 1975. "Organized social complexity: an explanation of a concept." In *Organized social complexity: Challenges to politics and policy*, ed. T. LaPorte. Princeton: Princeton University Press.

Lash, S. 1985. "The end of neo-corporatism? The breakdown of centralized bargaining in Sweden." *British Journal of Industrial Relations* (23): 215–39.

Laurin, Urban. 1986. *Pa Heder och Samvete (Upon my honour).* Stockholm: Norstedts.

Lee, Taeku. 2002. *Mobilizing Public Opinion: Black insurgency and racial attitudes in the civil rights era.* Chicago: University of Chicago Press.

Leonhardt, David. 2008. "In the U.S., that was the boom that wasn't." *International Herald Tribune*, April 10, 2008, 15.

Leuchtenburg, William. 1963. *Franklin Roosevelt and the New Deal*. New York: Harper Torchbooks.

Levi, Margaret. 1988. *Of rule and revenue*. Berkeley: University of California Press.

Lewin, Tamar. 2006. "Boys are no match for girls in completing high school." *New York Times*, April 19, 2006.

Lewis, Orion, and Sven Steinmo. 2008. "Do Institutions Evolve?" Paper presented at the *American Political Science Association Annual Meeting*. September 2, 2008. Washington DC.

———. 2010. "Taking evolution seriously in Political Science." *Theory and Biosciences*.

Lewontin, Richard. 2000. *The triple helix: Gene, organism and environment*. Cambridge: Harvard University Press.

Lieberman, Robert. 2002. "Political institutions and the politics of race in the development of the modern welfare state." In *Restructuring the Welfare State-Political Institutions and Policy Change*, ed. B. Rothstein and S. Steinmo. New York: Palgrave Macmillan.

Lijphart, Arendt. 1971. "Comparative politics and the comparative method." *American Political Science Review* 65 (3): 682–93.

Limerick, Patricia Nelson. 1987. *The legacy of conquest: The unbroken past of the American West*. 1st ed. New York: Norton.

Lindbeck, Assar. 1997. *The Swedish experiment*. Stockholm: Studieförbundet Näringsliv och samhälle.

Lindbeck, Assar, P. Molander, T. Persson, A. Sandmo, B. Swedenborg, and N. Thygesen. 1994. *Turning Sweden Around*. Cambridge and London: MIT Press.

Lindblom, Charles. 1973. *Politics and markets*. New York: Basic Books.

Lindert, Peter H. 2004. *Growing public: Social spending and economic growth since the eighteenth century*. Cambridge, UK; New York: Cambridge University Press.

Lindquist, L. L. 1980. *The hare and the tortoise: Clean air policies in the United States and Sweden*. Ann Arbor: University of Michigan Press.

Lindvert, Jessica. 2002. *Feminism som politik (Feminism as Public Policy)* Umeå: Borea Bokforlag.

———. 2008. "The political logics of accountability: From 'doing the right thing' to doing the thing right'." In *Organized Transnational Accountability*, ed. C. Garsten and M. Bostrom. London: Edward Elgar.

Lipset, Seymour Martin. 1996. *American exceptionalism: A double edges sword*. New York: W. W. Norton.

Lodin, Sven-Olof. 1982. *Skatter i kris [Taxes in crisis]*. Lund: Norstedt and Sons.

Lohr, Steve. 1987. "SWEDEN: Home of tax reform, arms scandals and a strong defense." *New York Times*, 6 September.

Lopez-Claros, Augusto. 2005. "*Global Competitiveness Report 2005–2006.*" Davos, Switzerland: World Economic Forum.

Lundqvist, Torbjorn. 2006. "Competition policy and the Swedish model." In *Institute for Future Studies Working Papers*. Stockholm.

Lustick, Ian. 2005. "Daniel Dennett, Comparative Politics, and the Dangerous Idea of Evolution." *Comparative Politics Newsletter*, Summer 2005, 19–23.

Luxembourg Income Study. 1998. *"Wave IV."* Luxembourg: LIS, http://www
.lisproject.org/

Magnusson, Lars. 2000. *An economic history of Sweden.* Stockholm: Routledge.

Mahoney, James. 2000. "Path Dependence in Historical Sociology." *Theory and Society* 29: 507–48.

Margulis, Lynn. 1998. *Symbiotic Planet: A new look at evolution.* New York: Basic Books.

Margulis, Lynn, and Dorian Sagan. 1993. "Microbial Microcosm." In *In Context: A Quarterly Journal of Sustainable Culture*, no. 34. *available at:* http://www.context
.org/ICLIB/IC34/TOC34.htm

Marmor, Theodore R., and Jan S. Marmor. 1973. *The politics of Medicare.* Rev. American ed. Chicago: Aldine.

Massey, Douglas, Magaly Sanchez, and Jere Behrman. 2006. "Of myths and mar- DꞐ
kets." *The Annals of the American Academy of Political and Social Science.* 606; 8.

Maynard Smith, John. 1982. *Evolution and the theory of games.* Cambridge; New York: Cambridge University Press.

Mayr, Ernst. 1982. *The growth of biological thought: Diversity, evolution, and inheritance.* Cambridge, MA: Belknap Press.

———. 1988. *Toward a new philosophy of biology: Observations of an evolutionist.* Cambridge, MA: Belknap Press of Harvard University Press.

———. 1991. *One long argument: Charles Darwin and the genesis of modern evolutionary thought.* Cambridge, MA: Harvard University Press.

———. 1992. "The idea of teleology." *Journal of the History of Ideas* 53 (1): 117–35.

———. 2001. *What evolution is.* New York: Basic Books.

———. 2004. *What makes biology unique? Considerations on the autonomy of a scientific discipline.* Cambridge, UK; New York: Cambridge University Press.

McCarty, Nolan, Keith Poole, and Howard Rosenthal. 2006. *Polarized America: The dance of ideology and unequal riches.* Cambridge: MIT Press.

McClosky, Herbert, and John Zahler. 1984. *The American ethos.* Cambridge, MA: Harvard University Press.

McConnell, Grant. 1966. *Private power & American democracy.* [1st] ed. New York,: Knopf.

McCormack, Gavan. 1996. *The emptiness of Japanese affluence.* London: M.E. Sharpe.

McKenzie, Richard B. 1989. "Capital flight: the hidden power of technology to shrink big government." *Reason* 20 (10): 22–6.

McKenzie, Richard, and Dwight Lee. 1991. *Quicksilver capital: How the rapid movement of wealth has changed the world.* New York: Free Press.

McKinsey, Global Institute. 2000. *"Why the Japanese economy is not growing."* New York: McKinsey & Co.

Meidner, Rudolf. 1980. "Our concept of the third way: Some remarks on the socio-political tenets of the Swedish labor movement." *Economic and Industrial Democracy* 1 (3): 343–70.

Mendelberg, Tali. 2001. *The race card: Campaign strategy, implicit messages, and the norm of equality.* Princeton: Princeton University Press.

Meyer, Bruce D., and Douglas Holtz-Eakin, eds. 2001. *Making work pay: The earned income tax credit and its impact on America's families.* New York: Russell Sage Foundation.

Milbank, Dana. 2004. "From his 'Great Goals" of 2000, President's achievements mixed." *Washington Post*, September 2, 2004, A 01.

Milly, Deborah. 1999. *Poverty, Equality and Growth: The Politics of Economic Need in Postwar Japan.* Cambridge: Harvard University Asia Center.

Ministry of Finance (Japanese Government). 2003. "*Current Japanese fiscal conditions and issues to be considered.*" Tokyo: Ministry of Finance.

———. 2007. "*Current Japanese Fiscal Conditions and Issues to be Considered.*" Tokyo: Ministry of Finance.

Mitchell, Brian R. 2007. *International historical statistics: Africa, Asia & Oceania 1750–2004.* 3. ed. Basingstoke: Macmillan.

Miura, Mari. 2002. From Welfare Through Work to Lean Work: The Politics of Labor Market Reform in Japan. Ph.D., Political Science Department, University of California, Berkeley, Berkeley.

Moberg, Vilhelm. 1951. *The emigrants: A novel.* New York: Simon and Schuster.

———. 1975. *Utvandrarna.* Stockholm: Bonnier.

Moore, Barrington. 1966. *Social Origins of Dictatorship and Democracy: Lords and Peasant in the Making of the Modern World.* Boston: Beacon Press.

Morishima, Michio. 1982. *Why Has Japan "Succeeded?" Western Technology and the Japanese Ethos*: New York: Cambridge University Press.

Moses, Jonathon. 2000. "Floating fortunes: Scandinavian full employment in the tumultuous 1970s-1980s." In *Globalization, europeanization and the end of Scandinavian social democracy?*, ed. R. Geyer, C. Ingebritsen and J. Moses. London: Macmillan.

Mosk, Carl. 2001. *Japanese Industrial History.* Armok, NY: M. E. Sharpe.

Muramatsu, Michio, and Elis Krauss. 1990. "Dominant Party and Social Coalitions in Japan." In *Uncommon democracies: the one-party dominant regimes*, ed. T. J. Pempel. Ithaca: Cornell University Press.

Myrdal, Gunnar. 1982. "Dags för ett bättre skattesystem [Time for a better tax system]." In *Skatter [Taxes]*, ed. L. Jonung. Malmo: Liberforlag.

NCHEMS, (National Center for Higher Education Management Systems). 2000. "Public high school graduation rates." NCHEMS.

Nelson, Richard. 2007. "Universal Darwinism and evolutionary social science." *Biology and Philosophy* (22): 73–94.

Nelson, Richard, and Sidney Winter. 2002. "Evolutionary theorizing in economics." *Journal of Economic Perspectives* 16 (2): 23–46.

Nivola, Pietro, ed. 1997. *Comparative disadvantages: Social regulations and the global economy.* Washington, DC: The Brookings Institution.

Noble, Gregory. 2005. Stealth Populism: Administrative Reform in Japan. Paper read at The Repositioning of Public Governance: Global Experience and Challenges, November 18–19, 2005, at Taipei.

———. 2006. "Koizumi and neo-liberal economic reform." *Social Science Japan* (34): 6–9.

Norr, Martin, Frank Duffy, and Harry Sterner. 1959. *Taxation in Sweden.* Boston: Little Brown.

Notermans, Ton. 2000. "Europeanization and the crisis of Scandinavian social democracy." In *Globalization, Europeanization and the end of Scandinavian social democracy?*, ed. R. Geyer, C. Ingebritsen and J. Moses. London: Macmillan.

Noto, Nonna. 2004. "Tax expenditures compared with outlays by budget function: Fact sheet." In *CRS Report for Congress*. Washington, DC: Congressional Research Service.

OECD. 1981. *Long-Term Trends in Tax Revenues of OECD Member Countries 1955–1980*. Paris: OECD.

———. 1984. *Tax expenditures: A review of the issues and country practices*. Paris: OECD.

———. 1999. "*Economic Surveys, Sweden*." Paris: OECD Publishing.

———. 2001a. *Revenue Statistics, 1965–1999*. Paris: OECD Publishing.

———. 2001b. *Society at a Glance and Social Expenditure Database*. Paris: OECD Publishing.

———. 2002. *Employment Outlook, July*. Paris: OECD Publishing.

———. 2002b. *Taxing Wages Special Feature Taxing Pensioners 2000–2001*. Paris: Organisation for Economic Co-operation and Development.

———. 2006a. *Revenue Statistics*. Paris: OECD Publishing.

———. 2006b. *Society at a Glance*. Paris: OECD Publishing.

———. 2007a. "*Health Data*." Paris: OECD Publishing.

———. 2007b. "*Population and Labour Force Statistics*." Paris: OECD Publishing.

———. 2007c. "*Source OECD National Accounts Statistics*." Paris: OECD Publishing.

———. 2008. *Revenue Statistics 1965–2007*. Paris: OECD Publishing.

———. 2009. *OECD Factbook 2009: Economic, Environmental and Social Statistics*. Paris: OECD Publishing.

———. various years. *Trends in international migration*. Paris: OECD Publishing.

Ohlsson, Lennart. 1969. *Utrikeshandeln och den ekonomiska tillväxten i Sveriga 1871–1966, (Foreign trade and economic growth in Sweden, 1871–1966)*. Stockholm: Almqvist och Wicksell.

Ohtake, Hideo. 1991. "Hatoyoam, Kishi Jidai no Chiisai Seifu Ron (The small state debate of the Hatoyram and Kishi years)." *Nenpou Seijigaku*.

Olessen, Jeppe. 2010. *Privitizing Health Care in Sweden, Britain and Denmark, Social and Political Science*, PhD dissertation, Social and Political Sciences. European University Institute, Florence, Italy.

Olson, Mancur. 1982. *The rise and decline of nations*. New Haven: Yale University Press.

Onishi, Norimitsu. 2007. "Starving man's diary prompts new look at Japan's welfare system." *International Herald Tribune*, October 11, 2007.

Ostrom, Elinor, and Xavier Basurto. 2009. The evolution of institutions: Toward a new methodology. Paper read at *Do Institutions Evolve?*, May 8–9, 2009, at European University Institute.

Palme, Joakim. 2003. *How is the Swedish model faring?* [WEB page]. SWEDEN.SE, June 12, 2003 2003a [cited June 12, 2003 2003]. Available from http: //www.sweden.se/templates/PrinterFriendlyArticle.asp?id=2891.

———. 2003. *The 'Great' Swedish Pension Reform* [Article]. Swedish Institute, 3/24/03 2003b [cited 6/20/03 2003]. Available from http: //www.sweden.se/templates/Article___5524.asp.

Palme, Joakim, Åke Bergmark, Olof Bäckman, Filipe Estrada, Johan Fritzell, Olle Lundberg, Ola Sjöberg, Lena Sommestad, and Marta Szebehely. 2003. "A Welfare Balance Sheet for the 1990s." *Scandanavian Journal of Public Health* 60 (supplement): 1–125.

Paster, Thomas. 2008. *The voice of business in the evolution of the German welfare state*. PhD, Social and Political sciences, European University Institute, Florence, Italy.

Patterson, James. 1967. *Congressional conservativism and the New Deal*. Lexington: University of Kentucky Press.

Pempel, T. J. 1974. "The bureaucratization of policymaking in Japan." *American Journal of Political Science* 18: 647–64.

———. 1978. "Japanese foreigh economic policy: The domestic bases for international behavior." In *Between power and plenty: foreign economic policies of advanced industrial states*, ed. P. J. Katzenstein. Madison: University of Wisconsin Press.

———. 1982a. *Policy and politics in Japan: Creative Conservatism*. Philadelphia: Temple University Press.

———. 1982b. *Politics and Policy in Japan: Creative Conservatism*. Philadelphia: Temple University Press.

———. 1989. "Japan's creative conservatism: Continuity under challenge." In *The comparative history of public policy*, ed. F. Castles. Cambridge: Polity Press.

———. 1990. *Uncommon democracies: the one-party dominant regimes*. Ithaca: Cornell University Press.

Pempel, T. J., and Keiishi Tsunewaka. 1979. "Japan: Corporatism without labor? The Japanese anomoly." In *Trends toward corporatist intermediation*, ed. P. Schmitter and G. Lehmbruch. Beverly Hills: Sage.

Pennisi, Elizabeth. 2005. "How did cooperative behavior evolve?" *Science* 309: 93.

Pfarr, Susan. 2000. "Official's misconduct and public distrust: Japan and the trilateral democracies." In *Disaffected Democracies*, ed. S. Pfarr and R. Putnam. Princeton: Princeton University Press.

Pierson, Paul. 2000. "Increasing Returns, Path Dependence and the Study of Politics." *American Political Science Review* 94 (2): 251–68.

———. 2001a. "Coping with austerity: Welfare state restructuring in affluent democracies." In *The New Politics of the Welfare State*, ed. P. Pierson. New York: Oxford University Press.

———. 2004. *Politics in time: History, institutions, and social analysis*. Princeton: Princeton University Press.

———, ed. 2001b. *The New Politics of the Welfare State*. New York: Oxford University Press.

Pierson, Paul, and Theda Skocpol. 2007. *The transformation of American politics: Activist government and the rise of conservatism*. Princeton: Princeton University Press.

Piketty, T., and E. Saez. 2007. "Income and wage inequality in the United States, 1913 – 2002." In *Top incomes over the 20th century*, ed. T. Atkinson and T. Peketty. London: Oxford University Press.

Polsby, Nelson. 1968. "The institutionalization of the House of Representatives." *American Political Science Review* 62 (1).

Polsby, Nelson W. 1964. *Congress and the Presidency*. Englewood Cliffs, NJ: Prentice-Hall.

Pontusson, Jonas. 1986. *Labor reformism and the politics of capital formation in Sweden*. Ph.D. dissertation, Deptartment of Political Science, UC Berkeley, Berkeley, CA.

———. 1992. *The limits of social democracy: Investment politics in Sweden*. Ithaca: Cornell University Press.

———. 2000. "Labor market institutions and wage distribution." In *Unions, Employers and Central Banks: Macro-Economic Coordination and Institutionals Change in Social Market Economies*, ed. T. Iversen, J. Pontusson and D. Soskice. New York: Cambridge University Press.

———. 2005. *Inequality and prosperity: Social Europe vs. liberal America*. Ithaca: Cornell University Press.

Pontusson, Jonas, and Peter Swenson. 1996. "Labor markets, production strategies, and wage bargaining institutions: The Swedish employer offensive in comparative perspective." *Comparative Political Studies* 29 (2): 223–50.

Popper, Karl R., and William Warren Bartley. 1982. *The open universe: An argument for indeterminism*. Totowa, NJ: Rowman and Littlefield.

Porter, Michael, and Hirotaka Takeuchi. 1999. "Fixing what really ails Japan." *Foreign Affairs* 78 (3): 66–81.

Potter, David. 1954. *A People of Plenty: Economic Abundance and the American Character*. Chicago: Chicago University Press.

Przeworski, Adam, and Henry Teune. 1970. *The logic of comparative social inquiry*. New York: Wiley-Interscience.

Ramseyer, J. Mark, and Frances McCall Rosenbluth. 1993. *Japan's political marketplace*. Cambridge, MA: Harvard University Press.

Reed, Steven R. 1993. *Making common sense of Japan*. Pittsburgh: University of Pittsburgh Press.

———. 2003. *Japanese Electoral Politics: Creating a New Party System*. London: Routledge.

Reich, Robert B. 1992. *The work of nations: Preparing ourselves for 21st century capitalism*. 1st Vintage Book ed. New York: Vintage Books.

Republican National Party. 1994. *Contract with America*. Vol. 2006. Washington, DC: Republican National Party.

Rhodes, Martin. 1995. "Subversive Liberalism: Market integration, globalization and European welfare states, *European Journal of Public Policy*, vol. 2, no. 3: 384–406.

Richerson, Peter, and Robert Boyd. 2000. "Institutional evolution in the holocene: The rise of complex societies." In *British Academy/Novartis Foundation meeting on The Origins of Human Social Institutions*. Unpublished manuscript, London, http://tuvalu.santafe.edu/~bowles/Holocene.pdf.

Richerson, Peter J., and Robert Boyd. 2005. *Not by genes alone: How culture transformed human evolution*. Chicago: University of Chicago Press.

Ridley, Mark. 2003. *The cooperative gene: How Mendel's demon explains the evolution of complex beings*. New York: Harper Collins.

Roberts, Adam. 2003a. "Krybbe to Grav (Cradle to Grave)." *Economist*, June 12, 2003.

————. 2003b. "Mix and Match." *Economist*, June 12, 2003.

Rodriguez, Enrique. 1980. *Offentlig inkomstexpansion: En analys av drivkrafterna bakom de offentliga inkomsternas utveckling i Sverige under 1900-talet [Public revenue growth: An analysis of the forces behind the expansion of public revenues in Sweden in the 1900s]*. Uppsala: CWK Gleerup.

Roper Organization. 1994. "A polling review of the great debate: The public decides on health care." *The Public Perspective* 5 (6): 28.

Rothstein, Bo. 1992. "Labor market institutions and working class strength." In *Structuring Politics: Historical institutionalism in comparative politics*, ed. S. Steinmo, K. Thelen and F. Longstreth. New York: Cambridge University Press.

————. 1998. *Just Institutions Matter: The Moral and Political Logic of the Universal Welfare State*. New York: Cambridge University Press.

————. 2000. *"Trust, Social Dilemmas, and Collective Memories."* Gothenburg, Sweden: Department of Political Science.

————. 2005. *Social Traps and the Problem of Trust*. New York: Cambridge University Press.

Rothstein, Bo, and Jonas Bergström. 1999. *Korporatismens Fall: och den svenska modellens kris [Corporatism's Fall: and the Swedish model's crisis]*. Stockholm: SNS Forlag.

Roubini, Noureil. 1996. Japan's economic crisis. Paper read at Business Practice and Entrepreneurial Spirit in Japan and the United States, November 12, 1996, at Tokyo.

Ruggie, Mary. 1984. *The state and working women*. Princeton: Princeton University Press.

Ruin, Olof. 1981. "Sweden in the 1970's: police-making (sic) becomes more difficult." In *Policy styles in Western Europe*, ed. J. Richardson. London: George Allen and Unwin.

Rustow, Dankwart. 1955. *The politics of compromise*. Princeton: Princeton University Press.

Sainsbury, Diane. 1996. *Gender, Equality, and Welfare States*. Cambridge and New York: Cambridge University Press.

Saito, Mitsuo. 2000. *The Japanese Economy*. Vol. 1. London: World Scientific Publishing.

Samuels, Richard J. 1994. *Rich nation, strong Army: National security and the technological transformation of Japan*. Ithaca: Cornell University Press.

Sandholtz, Wayne, and Berkeley Roundtable on the International Economy. 1992. *The Highest stakes: The economic foundations of the next security system*. New York: Oxford University Press.

Sapp, Jan. 2003. *Genesis: The evolution of biology*. Oxford: Oxford University Press.

Savage, James. 2002. "The origins of budgetary preferences: The Dodge Line and the balanced budget norm in Japan." *Administration and Society* 34 (3): 261–84.

Sawyer, R. Keith. 2005. *Social Emergence: Societis as complex systems*. New York: Cambridge University Press.

Scharpf, Fritz. 2000. "The viability of advanced welfare states in the international economy: Vulnerabilties and options." *Journal of European Public Policy* 7 (2): 190–228.

Scheiner, Ethan. 2005. "Pipelines of pork: Japanese politics and a model of local opposition party failure." *Comparative Political Studies* 38 (7): 799–823.

Schickler, Eric. 2001. *Disjointed pluralism: Institutional innovation and the development of the U.S. Congress*. Princeton: Princeton University Press.

Schjelderup, Guttrom. 1993. "Optimal taxation, capital mobility and tax evasion." *Scandinavian Journal of Economics* 95 (3): 377–86.

Schmidt, Vivien Ann. 2002. *The futures of European capitalism*. Oxford; New York: Oxford University Press.

Scholz, John Karl, and Kara Levine. 2000. "The Evolution of Income Support Policy in Recent Decades." In *The Past and Future of Poverty in the United States*. Institute for Research on Poverty at the University of Wisconsin-Madison.

Schumpeter, Joseph Alois. 1947. *Capitalism, Socialism, and Democracy*. 2d ed. New York; London: Harper & Brothers.

Schwartz, Herman. 1993. "Small States in Big Trouble: State Reorganization in Australia, Denmark, New Zealand and Sweden in the 1980s." *World Politics* 46: 527–55.

Schwartz, Nelson. 2009. "At Davos, Crisis Culls the Guest List." *International Herald Tribune*, January 25, 2009, 1, 11.

Shalev, Michael, and Korpi Walter. 1980. "Working class mobilization and American exceptionalism." *Economic and industrial democracy* 1.

Shinkawa, Toshimitsu. 2000. "Failed reform and policy changes." In *Power Shuffles and Policy Processes*, ed. O. Hideo. Tokyo: Japan Center for International Exchange.

——. 2004a. "The Japanese familial welfare state mix at a crossroads." In *Public and Private Social Policy: Health and Pension Systems in a New Era*, ed. D. Beland and B. Gran. Hampshire, UK: Palgrave.

——. 2004b. "The politics of pension reform in Japan: Institutional legacies, credit-claiming and blame avoidance." In *Aging and Pension Reform Around the World*, ed. G. Bonoli and T. Shinkawa. Cheltenham: Elgar.

——. 2007a. "Democratization and social policy development in Japan." In *Democracy and Social Policy*, ed. Y. Bangura. New York: Palgrave.

——. 2007b. "Public and private policy change: Pension reform in four countries." *Policy Studies Journal* 35 (3): 349–71.

Shonfield, Andrew. 1965. *Modern capitalism: The changing balance between public and private power*. Oxford: Oxford University Press.

Sieff, Martin. 2001. "Analysis: Koizumi primary win shakes Japan." *United Press International*, April 23, 2001, Monday.

Sinn, Hans-Werner. 1994. *"A theory of the welfare state."* Cambridge, MA: National Bureau of Economic Research.

Skocpol, Theda. 2007. "Government activism and the reorganization of American civic democracy." In *The transformation of American politics: Activist government and the rise of conservatism*, ed. P. Pierson and T. Skocpol. Princeton: Princeton University Press.

Skocpol, Theda, and John Ikenberry. 1983. "The political formation of the American welfare state in historical and comparative perspective." *Comparative Social Research* 6: 87–148.

Skowronek, Stephen. 1982. *Building a new American state: The expansion of national administrative capacities 1877–1920.* Cambridge: Cambridge University Press.

Slemrod, Joel. 1995. "Professional Opinions About Tax Policy: 1994 and 1934." *National Tax Journal* 48 (1): 121–47.

Smith, Roger. 1993. "Beyond Tocqueville, Myrdal and Hartz: The Multiple Traditions in America." *American Political Science Review* 87 (3): 549–66.

Smitka, Michael. 1998. *Japanese prewar growth: Lessons for development theory?* New York: Garland.

Snyder, Thomas D., Sally A. Dillow, and Charlene M. Hoffman. 2008. *Digest of Education Statistics 2007 (NCES 2008–022).* Washington, DC: National Center for Education Statistics, Institute of Education Sciences, U.S. Department of Education.

Socialdepartementet Ministry of Health and Social Affairs/ Riksfoersaekringsverket (RFV) National Social Insurance Board. 2003. *The National Swedish Pension System.* Ministry of Health and Social Affairs, Swedish Government 2003 [cited 6/26/03 2003]. Available from http: //social.regeringen.se/pressinfo/pdf/pensioner/alderspensioneno306_en.pdf.

Södersten, Jan. 1987. The taxation of income from capital in Sweden. Paper read at *The Conference on Capital and Income Taxation*, 11 November, at Harvard University.

SOU. 1977. *Beskattning av Företag (Taxation of companies).* Stockholm: SOU.

Spencer, Herbert, and J. D. Y. Peel. 1972. *Herbert Spencer on social evolution. Selected writings.* Chicago: University of Chicago Press.

Statistics Bureau, Ministry of Internal Affairs and Communications. 2000. *Japan Statistical Yearbook.* Tokyo: Japan Statistical Association.

Stein, Herbert. 1969. *The fiscal revolution in America.* Chicago: University of Chicago Press.

Steinmo, Sven. 1984. The carrot and the stick: taxation as a tool of economic policy. Paper read at The Workshop on the Politics of Taxation, European Consortium of Political Research, 13–19 April, at Salzburg, Austria.

———. 1986. "So what's wrong with tax expenditures: A re-evaluation based on Swedish experience." *Journal of Public Budgeting and Finance.*

———. 1988. "Social democracy vs. socialism: Goal adaptation in social democratic Sweden." *Politics and Society* 16 (4): 403–46.

———. 1993. *Taxation and democracy: Swedish, British and American approaches to financing the modern state.* New Haven: Yale University Press.

———. 1994a. "An end to redistribution? Tax reform and the globalization of the world economy." *Challenge* Nov/Dec.: 1–9.

———. 1994b. "Rethinking American exceptionalism: Culture or institutions?" In *Dynamics of American politics: approaches and interpretations,* ed. C. Jillson and L. Dodd. Boulder: Westview Press.

———. 1995. "Why is Government So Small in America?" *Governance* 8 (3): 303–34.

———. 2003. "Bucking the trend: Swedish social democracy in a global economy." *New Political Economy* 8 (1): 31–48.

———. 2006. *In the Land of Milk and Honey: A Short History of America and the People it Created:* unpublished manuscript in progress.

_____. 2008. "What is historical institutionalism?" in *Approaches in the Social Sciences*, ed. D. D. Porta and M. Keating. Cambridge: Cambridge University Press.

Steinmo, Sven, and Jeffrey Kopstein. 2007. "Growing Apart? America and Europe in the 21st Century." In *Growing Apart? America and Europe in the 21st Century*, ed. J. Kopstein and S. Steinmo. New York: Cambridge University Press.

Sterelny, Kim. 2001. *Dawkins vs. Gould: Survival of the fittest*. Cambridge, UK: Icon Books.

Stiglitz, Joseph. 2006. "A Progressive Response to Globalization." In *The Nation*.

Stockman, David. 1986. "The triumph of politics." *Newsweek*, 21 April, 44, 50.

Stråth, Bo. 1996. *The organisation of labour markets: Modernity, culture, and governance in Germany, Sweden, Britain, and Japan*. London; New York: Routledge.

Streeck, Wolfgang. 2009. *Re-forming capitalism: Institutional change in the German political economy*. New York: Oxford University Press.

_____. 2010a. "Epilogue. Institutions in History: Bringing Capitalism Back In." In *Handbook of Comparative Institutional Analysis, Oxford: Oxford University Press, 2010*, ed. J. Campbell, C. Crouch, P. H. Kristensen, G. Morgan, O. K. Pedersen and R. Whitley. Oxford: Oxford University Press.

_____. 2010b. "Institutions in History: Bringing Capitalism back In." In *Handbook of Comparative Institutionals Analysis*, ed. J. Campbell, C. Crouch, P. H. Kristensen, G. Morgan, O. K. Pedersen and R. Whitley. Oxford: Oxford University Press.

Streeck, Wolfgang, and Kathleen Thelen. 2005. "Introduction: Institutional change in advanced political economies." In *Beyond Continuity*, ed. W. Streeck and K. Thelen. Oxford: Oxford University Press.

Svallfors, Stefan. 1989. *Vem älskar välfärdsstaten? Attityder, organiserade intressen och svensk välfärdspolitik [Who loves the welfare state? Attitudes, organized interests and Swedish welfare policy*. Lund: Arkiv.

_____. 1996. *Välfärdsstatens moraliska ekonomi: Välfärdsopinionen i 90-talets Sverige*. Umeå: Borea.

_____. 1997. The Middle Class and Welfare State Retrenchment: Attitudes Toward Swedish Welfare Policies. Paper read at Third Conference of the European Sociological Association, at University of Essex, August 27–30, 1997.

Svallfors, Stefan. 1998. "*Mellan risk och tilltro: Opinionsstödet för en kollektiv välfärdspolitik*." Umeå: Department of Sociology, Umeå University.

_____. 2003. "Välfärdsstatens legitimitet: Åsiketer om Svensk Välfärdpolitik I komparativ belysning," (Welfare state's legitimacy: Perspectives on Swedish welfare policy in comparative perspective." In *Sjukskrivning – Försäkring eller försörjning? Rapport från forskarseminariet i Umeå 2003*. Stockholm: Försäkringskasseförbundet.

Swedish Tax Agency. 2008. "*Income self assessment and taxes in Sweden*." Stockholm: Svenske skatteverket.

Swenson, Peter. 1989. *Fair shares: Unions, pay, and politics in Sweden and West Germany*. Ithaca: Cornell University Press.

_____. 1991. "Labor and the limits of the welfare state." *Comparative Politics* 23 (4): 379–99.

Swenson, Peter A. 2002. *Capitalists against markets: the making of labor markets and welfare states in the United States and Sweden*. Oxford; New York: Oxford University Press.

Sydow, Björn von. 1989. *Vagen till enkammar riksdagen: Demokratisk forfat-tningspolitik i Sverige 1944–1968*. Stockholm: Tidens forlag.

Sydow, Björn von, and Riksbankens jubileumsfond. 1997. *Parlamentarismen i Sverige: utveckling och utformning till 1945*. Hedemora: Gidlund i samarbete med Riksbankens jubileumsfond.

Tabuchi, Hiroko. 2009. "Opposition Woo's Japanese Voters with Costly Vows." *New York Times*, August 3, 2009.

Tachibanaki, Toshiaki. 1996. Public policies and the Japanese economy: Savings, investments, unemployment and inequality. Edited by M. Falkus and N. Niino. New York: St. Martin's Press.

———. 2000. "Japan was not a welfare state, But...." In *From Austerity to Afflu-ence*, ed. R. Griffiths and T. Tachibanaki. London: Macmillan.

———. 2005. *Confronting Income Inequality in Japan: A Comparative Analysis of Causes, Consequences and Reform*. Cambridge, MA: MIT Press.

Tanzi, Vito. 2002. "Globalization and the Future of Social Protection." *The Scottish Journal of Political Economy* 49 (1): 116–27.

Tanzi, Vito, and Ludger Schuknecht. 2000. *Public spending in the 20th century: a global perspective*. Cambridge, UK; New York: Cambridge University Press.

Teles, Steve, and Daniel A. Kenney. 2006. "Spreading the Word: The Diffusion of American Conservatism in Europe and Beyond." In *Growing Apart: America, Canada and Europe in the 21st Century*, ed. J. Kopstein and S. Steinmo: under review.

Teles, Steven. 1996. *Who's welfare? AFDC and elite politics*. Lawrence: University of Kansas Press.

Thelen, Kathleen. 1993. "West European labor in transition: Sweden and Germany compared." *World Politics* 46 (1): 23–49.

———. 1999. "Historical Institutionalism in Comparative Politics." *Annual Review of Political Science* (2): 369–404.

———. 2003. "How institutions evolve: Insights from comparative historical anal-ysis." In *Comparative Historical Analysis in the Social Sciences*, ed. J. Mahoney and D. Rueschemeyer. New York: Cambridge University Press.

———. 2004. *How institutions evolve: The political economy of skills in Ger-many, Britain, the United States and Japan*. New York: Cambridge University Press.

Thelen, Kathleen, and Sven Steinmo. 1992. "Historical institutionalism and compar-ative politics." In *Structuring Politics: Historical institutionalism in comparative politics*, ed. S. Steinmo, K. Thelen and F. Longstreth. New York: Cambridge University Press.

Thomma, Steven. 1994. "Tuesday's big loser: President Clinton." *Boulder Daily Camera*, November 9, 1994, 8a.

Thurow, Lester C. 1980. *The zero-sum society: distribution and the possibilities for economic change*. New York: Basic Books.

———. 1985. *The zero-sum solution: Building a world-class American economy*. New York: Simon and Schuster.

———. 1992. *Head to head: The coming economic battle among Japan, Europe, and America*. New York: Morrow.

Tingsten, Herbert. 1973. *The Swedish social democrats: Their ideological development*. Totowa, NJ: Bedrinster Press.

U.S. Census Bureau. 2000. *Statistical Abstract of the United States*. Washington, DC: Government Printing Office.

U.S. Immigration and Naturalization Service. various years. *Statistical Yearbook of the Immigration and Naturalization Service*. Washington, DC: U.S. Immigration and Naturalization Service.

U.S. Census Bureau. 2007. "Income, Poverty and Health Insurance Coverage in the United States: 2006." Washington, DC: U.S. Government Printing Office.

Veblen, Thorstein. 1898. "Why is economics not an evolutionary science?" *Quarterly Journal of Economics* (12): 373–93.

Verba, Sidney. 1987. *Elites and the idea of equality: A comparison of Japan, Sweden, and the United States*. Cambridge, MA: Harvard University Press.

Verney, Douglas. 1957. *Parliamentary Reform in Sweden, 1866–1921*. Oxford: Oxford University Press.

Vogel, David. 1986. *National styles of regulation: Environmental policy in Great Britain and the United States*. Ithaca: Cornell University Press.

———. 1995. *Trading up: Consumer and environmental regulation in a global economy*. Cambridge, MA: Harvard University Press.

———. 1996. *Kindred strangers: The uneasy relationship between politics and business in America*. Princeton, NJ: Princeton University Press.

Vogel, Ezra. 1979. *Japan as number one*. Cambridge: Harvard University Press.

Vogel, Steven. 2006. *Japan remodeled: How government and industry are reforming Japanese capitalism*. Ithaca: Cornell University Press.

Washington Monthly. 2003. *The Mendacity Index*. Vol. 2009. Washington, DC: Washington Monthly.

Watts, Jon, and Sven Steinmo. 1995. "It's the Institutions, Stupid! Why Comprehensive National Health Care Insurance Always Fails in America." *Journal of Health Politics, Policy and Law* 20 (2): 329–72.

Weir, Margaret. 1989. "Ideas and politics: The acceptance of Keynesianism in Britain and the United States." In *The political power of economic ideas: Keynesianism across nations*, ed. P. A. Hall. Princeton: Princeton University Press.

Weir, Margaret, and Theda Skocpol. 1985. "State structures and possibilities for 'Keynsian' responses to the Great Depression in Sweden, Britain and the United States." In *Bringing the state back in*, ed. P. Evans, D. Rueschemeyer and T. Skocpol. Cambridge: Cambridge University Press.

Wettergren, Anders. 2000. "En traditionell socialdemokrat [a traditional social democrat]." *Götenburgs-Posten*, May 30, 2000, 2.

Williamson, John. 1993. "Democracy and the "Washington Consensus"." *World Development* 21 (8): 1329–36.

Wilson, David Sloan. 1979. *The natural selection of populations and communities*. Menlo Park, CA: Benjamin/Cummings Pub. Co.

———. 2002. *Darwin's cathedral: evolution, religion, and the nature of society*. Chicago: University of Chicago Press.

Wimmer, Andreas. 2006. "Models, methodologies, and metaphors on the move." In *Understanding change: models, methodologies, and metaphors*, ed. A. Wimmer and R. Kossler. Houndmills, Basingstoke, Hampshire, U.K.; New York: Palgrave Macmillan.

Witte, John. 1983. "The distribution of federal tax expenditures." *Policy Studies Journal* 12: 131–46.

———. 1985. *The politics and development of the federal income tax.* Madison: University of Wisconsin Press.

Wolferen, Karel van. 1990. *The enigma of Japanese power.* New York: Vintage Books.

Wolff, Edward D. 2004. "Changes in Household Wealth in the 1980s and 1990s in the U.S." In *Economics Working Paper.* Annandale-on-Hudson, NY: The Levy Economics Institute.

World Bank. 2005. "Correspondence on Income Distribution Data." In *Human Development Index.* Washington, DC: World Bank.

World Bank. 1984. *World tables: From the data files of the World Bank.* 3rd ed. Baltimore: Johns Hopkins University Press.

———. 2000. *World Development Indicators, 2000.* Washington, DC: World Bank.

———. 2007. *World development indicators (CD-ROM).* Washington DC: World Bank.

———. 2005a. "Correspondence on Income Distribution Data." In *Human Development Index.* Washington, DC: World Bank.

———. 2005b. *World development indicators.* CD-ROM ed. Washington, DC: World Bank.

———. 2007. *World development indicators (CD-ROM).* Washington, DC: World Bank.

———. April, 2005. "*Correspondence on income distribution data.*" Washington, DC: World Bank.

World Economic Forum. 2004. "Global Competitiveness Index."

Yamamura, Kozo, and Wolfgang Streeck. 2003. *The end of diversity?: Prospects for German and Japanese capitalism.* Ithaca: Cornell University Press.

Yoshikawa, Hiroshi. 1997. *Kodo Seicho-Nihon wo kaeta 6000 nichi – (High Economic Growth-6000 Days that made Japan Changed-).* Tokyo: Yomiuri Shinbunsha.

Young, H. Peyton. 1998. *Individual Strategy and Social Structure: An evolutionary theory of institutions.* Princeton, NJ: Princeton University Press.

Zimmer, Carl. 2001. *Evolution: The triumph of an idea.* New York: Harper Collins.

Zuckerman, Alan S. 1997. "Reformulating Explanatory Standards and Advancing Theory in Comparative Politics." In *Comparative Politics,* ed. M. I. Lichbach, & Zuckerman, Alan S., eds.,. Cambridge: Cambridge University Press.

Zysman, John. 1977. *Political strategies for industrial order: State, market, and industry in France.* Berkeley: University of California Press.

———. 1983. *Governments, markets, and growth: Financial systems and the politics of industrial change.* Ithaca: Cornell University Press.

Index